Celibacy

Means of
Control *or*
Mandate of
the Heart?

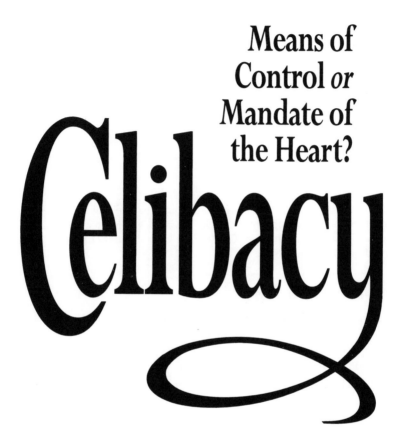

Celibacy

Michael H. Crosby

AVE MARIA PRESS   Notre Dame, Indiana 46556

© 1996 by Ave Maria Press, Inc.

Cover and text design by Elizabeth J. French
Printed and bound in the United States of America.

Library of Congress Cataloging-in-Publication Data

Crosby, Michael, 1940-
   Celibacy: means of control or mandate of the heart / by Michael H. Crosby.
     p. cm.
   Includes bibliographical references.
   ISBN 0-87793-569-6 (pbk.)
   1. Celibacy—Catholic Church. 2. Spiritual life—Catholic Church.
3. Catholic Church—Clergy. 4. Catholic Church—Doctrines.
5. Intimacy (Psychology)—Religious aspects—Christianity.
6. Crosby, Michael, 1940- . I. Title.
BV4390.C76 1996
248.4'7—dc20   95-45295
                                                                CIP

Acknowledgments

Writing acknowledgments for a book like this is not easy. Because of the sensitivity of the subject, I probably consulted more people about its contents than I did with any of my other books.

Those whom I consulted will remain anonymous. There are two main reasons people seek anonymity: because of humility or because of fear. I have no reason to question the humility of any of these people; yet I do not want to test their fear, since they hold positions of ministry in the institutional church. These people know who they are and have already been thanked; I only wish the climate in our church were different that I might be able to thank them publicly.

Given the topic of this book, I also do not always mention people's names in relating various incidents. Sometimes I have changed things around just enough to avoid revealing their identities. In most cases, except for public matters, when I use people's real names, I have received their permission. When I use fictitious names, it is either because they have asked this to be done to protect their need or desire for anonymity, or because I did not seek their permission. The latter represents times when I make reference to an incident involving them believing their identity will remain unknown or because I suspected I would not receive their permission.

When I was in seminary I had an editor whom I have always used as a benchmark, against whom I have evaluated my subsequent editors. Bob Hamma at Ave Maria Press has met and surpassed this criteria. I am deeply indebted to him for his expertise, his insights, and his patience. In all of this we both were highly supported by Frank Cunningham, publisher at Ave Maria.

As I conclude my acknowledgments, I'd like to remember those men I've known in my order and elsewhere who have resigned from active ministry. Now that they have left, their innumerable gifts and talents, once expressed in church-related ministries, are being shared elsewhere. Our loss in the Roman Church is other people's gain. With their leaving, our friendships have been tested and our relationships changed, but I have fond memories of our shared past and greater hopes for what the future promise. I hold these men and those they love in my heart and prayer, and I thank them for their continued care for me.

—Michael H. Crosby, O.F.M. Cap.
August 7, 1995

Contents

Introduction

I have always been a virgin, but I have not always been a celibate. The more I know about the two notions, the more I believe they can differ greatly, especially as far as men are concerned. And that's the perspective from which I write this book.

To me, virginity is a biological condition: a virgin is simply one who has not had genital intercourse. Celibacy, while having a biological dimension involving abstinence from genital intercourse, represents something more. That "something more" about celibacy involves a stance that goes far beyond a dictionary definition as a "state of not being married," or "abstention from sexual intercourse," or even "abstention by vow from marriage."[1]

Above all, celibacy represents an attitude. Celibacy characterizes the way people choose to live as virgins. Or, even if some may no longer be virgins in the biological sense, their chosen celibacy represents a way of fidelity they choose to live. We will see that, while celibacy involves the embrace of a divinely offered gift inviting one to freely choose a life-commitment of abstention from genital intimacy, it also finds expression in an alternate type of intimacy with God and others.

When I was in Catholic grade school, the calendar of saints had a special category for virgins. Noticeably, the category was only filled with women. Women were either martyrs or virgins. Unmarried men were something else, usually confessors or doctors.[2] Did the creators of the calendar have some conventional (or ecclesiastical) wisdom about the differences between men and women vis-à-vis virginity and celibacy that we don't have today?

Identifying virginity with women is not limited to the old liturgical calendar. Dictionaries do the same. The first three examples Webster's uses to define virginity identify it with women.[3] Funk and Wagnall's defines a virgin as "a person, especially a woman, who has had no sexual intercourse with the opposite sex."[4]

The emphasis on women and virginity reminds me of a conversation I had years ago with a man named "John." John was gay and a member of a religious community. He came before the Justice and Peace Committee of the Milwaukee Priest's Senate, which I chaired, and introduced a resolution asking the senate to deal with homophobia among priests. Needless to say, this caused the anxiety level to rise to great intensity by the time the resolution moved from the committee level to the floor of the senate. To my knowledge, homophobia was the only justice issue until that time that had to be addressed in executive session!

John had some troubling views on homosexuality. He endorsed same sex intercourse among seminarians, priests, and members of religious orders. When I asked him how he could justify this position, his response seemed to make explicit the first definition of a virgin. "I'm a virgin," he explained, "because I have never had sex with a woman."

"John," I retorted, "the fact that you're gay and I'm not gives you no more right than me to act out genitally. The vow is the vow." John disagreed.[5]

With such confusion surrounding the definition of virginity, I feel it necessary to nuance my opening statement: I am a virgin who has never had any form of genital sex with anyone, male or female. However, even with this nuance, it still does not mean I have always been celibate. In my opinion and in my experience of virginity and celibacy, the two remain very different.

My argument for this book does not arise from my unhappiness as a celibate. It is based on the deeper conviction that the present dispensation of celibacy has resulted from historical factors that will not be repeated in the foreseeable future. It rests on the way I have experienced celibacy in my own life and from listening to many others' experience as well, including conversations in the internal forum (i.e., confession). Above all, my argument finds its main justification in a deeper source than sociology, in the words of Jesus in Matthew's gospel: "There will be few who can truly accept it."

I am convinced that when celibacy is no longer imposed, only a few, and especially only a few males, will make themselves celibate. In the future few will accept this pattern of life because we will have appropriated in a healthier way the understanding of Matthew's Jesus and those first disciples of what we call celibacy. Jesus' statement will be the norm: it will be a rare exception when people "make themselves" eunuchs. Their truly free decision will have little or nothing to do with the tradition, law, or practice of past centuries. It will not be connected to ministry or to orders. Neither will it be a "fall-back" position because one has found no other life alternatives. Rather it will result from a free choice arising from one's understanding of the force of God's reign in one's life and how that presence can be expressed wholeheartedly in the world. This will occur when we truly ground celibacy in the theology of "gift" and "charism" which, by their own definitions, imply behaviors free of outside coercion, conditions, and/or control. Only then will celibacy reflect a truly authentic way of life for some of the people of God. In my mind, this future cannot come too soon.

The End of the Age of Innocence

The present climate in the church, which has been created by the rule of mandatory celibacy, and the dilemma it poses for many celibates, was brought home with great force to me by the film *The Age of Innocence.* Released in 1993, the film is Martin Scorsese's adaptation of Edith Wharton's novel. It is a satire on the culture and customs, the manners and morals, of an inbred, elite circle of New Yorkers.

Scorsese has made a name with such violent films as *Raging Bull, Goodfellas,* and *Taxi Driver.* One might wonder how he would move from such explicitly violent films to this story of upper-class New York in the 1870s. I soon discovered Scorsese was remaining true to the genre of violence; only now it would have a different social location and institutionalized expression.

Like so many of Wharton's novels, *The Age of Innocence* addresses the limited choices which people face when forces over which they have no real power make super-human demands and impositions on them. This tension between convention and conformity on the one hand and resistance and rebellion on the other is dramatized in the main characters of the story.

The setting is New York City's upper echelon of the 1870s. The book depicts the culture of the times, how the social arbiters ruled within it, how people tried to live up to other people's rules and the effect the resulting struggle to conform had on their lives. With Edith Wharton, love never conquers all. Instead, society's moral conventions (which are imposed on people who never have fully embraced them) conquer all.

After viewing the film with my long-time priest-friend Joe, I commented to him, "That film is the story of my life. Newland Archer is me." When Joe insisted that he did not understand what I was saying, I realized how different his experience of celibacy is from mine. Nevertheless, Joe's reaction led me to question my own. So I decided to read as many reviews of the film as I could.[6]

I didn't need to go further than Jack Kroll's review of the film in *Newsweek*. Kroll quotes a number of the stars of the film, including Michelle Pfeiffer. Her comments convinced me that I was correct in viewing the movie as a critique of a kind of sexual repression similar to that which I had experienced in the clerical culture of our church. She said, "Marty [Scorsese] considers this his most violent movie."[7] Unlike the violence of hoods and boxers with raised voices, in *The Age of Innocence* no voices are raised, no hands are clenched, and only dinner parties are featured. Any rage is sanitized in an institutionalized form.

The Story

As the film opens, Scorsese's camera pans to reveal the main actors in their box seats. We see Newland Archer (Daniel Day-Lewis), a rich young lawyer and head of one of the city's most distinguished families. He sits in his box with a white gardenia placed ever so correctly in the buttonhole of his opera jacket.

Mr. Archer will soon be engaged to the plain and proper daughter of another powerful family, May Welland (Winona Ryder). She belongs to the Mingott family which is presided over by her grandmother (Miriam Margolyes). May's grandmother is so overweight that she must remain on the first floor of her house. Here she receives her relatives and the social arbiters who come for her valued insights on the issues of the day.

The first hint of dysfunction in the family appears with the arrival in the Welland's box of the Countess Ellen Olenska (Michelle Pfeiffer). She is the cousin of May, and another granddaughter. Against the wishes of the Family (which Edith Wharton always capitalized when it went beyond the Mingott's to the social arbiters), she had married someone outside her class. Her husband, a Polish Count, also proved to be a philanderer and debaucher. She has just left him and returned to New York where she now hopes to be reinstated into the Family.

Ellen's appearance in the Mingott box seems to indicate that the grandmother and the rest of her family are willing to take her back (on its terms, we will see). However, the Family will not be so forgiving. At the conclusion of the opera, upon meeting Newland, Ellen's first words to him recall an earlier day of their shared childhood, with its greater spontaneity and freedom: "You kissed me once behind a door." Until the end of the film viewers wonder if they will ever get behind another door where they might find real happiness, away from the world in which they were constrained to be born and bred.

As the story unfolds, the Mingott and Archer families do all they can to get Ellen into society's good graces. Despite their efforts, she hits a stone wall of resistance when she announces she intends to divorce the Count. In that era, in that Family, no respectable woman divorced her husband. Nobody denies that Ellen's marriage to the Count has been unhealthy, however promises made cannot be broken; commitments must be honored.

Newland Archer is chosen to persuade Ellen to abandon her divorce plans. "Our legislation favors divorce," Newland explains, "but our customs don't." The charade must continue, the masks must be worn, and social respectability must prevail if the code of honor is to continue to be the glue that holds this world together. Politeness and courtesy are its hallmarks. These must be preserved regardless of the human cost.

At one of the early dinner parties, Newland Archer and the Countess Olenska are guests. In that era, among such people, the custom was that a woman would sit modestly exchanging pleasantries with whomever would come to her place. Instead, spying Newland, Ellen leaves her place. To the collective dismay of everyone, she walks toward him and seats herself beside him. Here is a woman applying to herself the same freedoms and rights granted to men. Adding insult to this social injury she has inflicted by breaching the code of etiquette, she says to Newland Archer as the party is ending: "Tomorrow, then, after five—I shall expect you." While Newland is stunned (and fascinated) by her unilateral action, society is shocked by her shamelessness.

In the process of trying to convince Ellen not to divorce, Newland begins to discover how he has been trapped in a world of convention and correctness. He also realizes he is in love with her. As the others gradually become aware that the two may be in love, it is decided that their relationship must be ended. No scene describes the time and the date of their decision. Everyone understands what must be done to protect the code. All must work together for the good of the system, to preserve its values.

By now something about Ellen begins to intrigue Newland even more. That "something" lies beyond her beauty, wit, and spontaneity. It is her honesty. At one point she plaintively asks

Newland: "Does no one want to know the truth here, Mr. Archer? The real loneliness is living among this kind of people who only ask one to pretend." At another meeting, after he tells her that "everyone" in New York wanted to help her, she responds, "I know. But on the condition that they don't hear anything unpleasant."

Such integrity on the part of Ellen fascinates Newland. Yet he is torn between his promise to May and the expectations of his culture on the one hand, and his personal feelings and attraction to Ellen on the other. The Countess seems to represent what Newland has desired but never received: freedom from his restrictive social world and the experience of unconventional love. Yet he is a victim of promises made, without inner freedom, to satisfy that culture's expectations. He is torn between the two.

On the way home from one of his efforts to be a family emissary to Ellen, Newland passes a flower shop. There he sees some bright yellow roses, full of life. Breaking convention, he sends them to Ellen. To May he presents dainty and pedestrian virginal white lilies of the valley. Suddenly remorseful that he is falling deeply in love with Ellen, Newland rushes to Florida where May and her family are spending winter. He begs her to advance their marriage date. May, aware of his feelings for Ellen, tells him she wants him to feel free to break his promise (even as we know he is no longer free because society will no longer let him be free). As for Ellen, because May has been faithful to her, she must reciprocate. She supports his decision to follow through with the marriage.

Once married, it takes only as long as the honeymoon for Newland to realize how mistaken he was in deciding to marry the woman who already had wedded herself to society's mores. "There's no point in liberating someone who doesn't realize she is not free," he notes. But May is not the only prisoner of privilege. Newland himself has become bound by his bond. As Anthony Lake notes:

> With the wife, the wealth, and the wardrobe, his path of contentment is laid down, as if on rails, from here to the grave. However nicely cushioned, it is a kind of doom, and it fortifies the central grievance of the story: that such a society demands everything you have, provides everything you need, and means nothing at all.[8]

Within Newland's ticket-to-nowhere marriage, he gradually becomes obsessed with Ellen. She personifies the deep longing for freedom from convention and release from cultural codes he feels he has lost forever. Given the awareness of their mutual love, Ellen decides she will not return to Europe so that they can be close. However, with the cultural patterns also demanding obedience rather than love, she warns him that if he "lifts a finger" she will return to the Count. So, while they continue to meet clandestinely, the two never so much as kiss each other on the lips.

Another time, when the Countess comes to New York to visit her sick grandmother Mingott, Newland tracks her down at Pennsylvania Station in Jersey City. Once by themselves, enclosed within the confines of a horse-drawn carriage, the two share a torrid and erotic love scene. Yet, there is only one piece of clothing removed—a glove. Boxed into the carriage, Newland reaches for one of her gloved hands. With passion building in him, Newland leaves his seat and kneels down in the carriage at the knees of Ellen. Then gently he takes her right hand. One by one he carefully opens the buttons of her glove. Then finally, he peels back the glove from her hand as she quietly watches. Once her hand is exposed to his eyes, he raises it to his face, and fiercely rubs it against his cheek. In response to this wordless display of his passion, the Countess simply asks: "Is it your idea, then, that I should live with you as your mistress?"

Surprised, and somewhat taken aback by her response, Newland begs: "I want somehow to get away with you into a world where words like that—categories like that—won't exist, where we shall simply be two human beings who love each other, and nothing else on earth will matter!" Ellen sighs and asks, "Oh my dear—where is that country? Have you ever been there? I know so many who have tried to find it and, believe me, they all got out by mistake at wayside stations—at places like Bologna, or Pisa, or Monte Carlo—and it wasn't at all different from the old world they'd left, but only rather smaller and dingier and more promiscuous."

Now Newland seems ready to make a move. Having surmised that Newland is about to ask for a separation, May also makes her move. She tells Ellen "confidentially" that she is pregnant, even though she only suspects she may be. This is enough for Ellen to decide to leave Newland and not betray the family that gave her support in her hour of need. She declares she will return to Europe. There she will live apart from the Count. Although it still seems clear to Newland that he will soon be joining her, the newly-married Archers decide to give their first dinner party as a bon voyage for Ellen.

As the sumptuous meal progresses, Newland Archer discovers for the first time that all these socially correct guests eating their canvasback ducks have believed for months that he and the Countess have been lovers. Now the whole family has rallied around his wife to preserve her, her marriage, and their mores. Yet all act genteelly, as though nothing has happened. In the words of Wharton, this was society's way of taking life without bloodshed: "the way of people who dreaded scandal more than disease, who placed decency above courage, and who considered that nothing was more ill-bred than 'scenes,' except for the behavior of those who gave rise to them."

After the meal, when he has helped put Ellen's cloak on her shoulders, she reaches out her hand and says, "Good-bye." He almost shouts in surprised reaction: "But I shall see you soon in Paris!" "Oh," she responds with a resolve in her voice, "if you and May could come."

May has already seen to it that any such plan for Newland, alone or with her, will be nipped in the bud. Once the dinner guests have departed she finds her husband alone, pensively sitting in his study near his fireplace. She begins with small talk about the dinner. And then she reveals to him the real reason for her presence there: she is pregnant. As she tells him she is with child, a log collapses in the fireplace. As though it's an afterthought, she tells Newland that she told Ellen two weeks before that she was sure she was pregnant. Newland now knows why Ellen decided to leave. May's pregnancy scuttles any chance Newland will join Ellen in France. The love affair is over. Newland will remain with May. They will raise three children. Everyone will have abided by the codes. And the system will survive.

The final scene in the film takes place twenty-six years later in Paris. Newland Archer is now fifty-seven years old and a leading citizen of New York. He had been a faithful husband, but now is a widower. May had died years before after contracting infectious pneumonia while nursing one of the children back to health. Their years together had taught him that "it did not so much matter if marriage was a dull duty, as long as it kept the dignity of a duty." In that honor/shame culture, as in all such cultures, the fulfillment of duty represented the ultimate badge of honor.

Newland Archer and his architect son take a trip to Paris. There the son takes his father to visit the Countess who lives alone as a widow. Now there is no law to keep her and Archer apart. He muses that he is "only fifty-seven." Even though it may be too late for "summer dreams," it's not too late for a "quiet harvest of friendship, of comradeship in the blessed hush of her nearness."

On the way to her apartment in the fashionable Hotel des Invalides district, the son tells his father something that his mother had confided to him earlier: she always knew his father had given up the one thing he most wanted in life for her and their family: a life with Ellen. Upon hearing that, all along, May actually did understand his predicament and was concerned about it, Newland Archer was moved deeply. His son's disclosure somehow made him feel as if "an iron band" had been lifted from his heart.

Father and son reach the square below the room of the hotel on the Rue de Varenne where Ellen lives. Newland sits at the fountain as his son asks him to join him upstairs with Ellen. Newland asks for time to collect his thoughts. So his son goes to Ellen's quarters while Newland sits and ponders his life and his options. Moments later, a maid of the Countess comes to the window overlooking the square. Gently, but decisively, she closes the shutters of the window that had been open to him. Newland Archer pauses a moment, gets up, and walks away. With this the movie ends.

In commenting on Newland Archer and why he acted the way he did, Martin Scorsese stressed the final sacrifice he made. But why did he make the sacrifice? It wasn't demanded by God. Why then did he make it to a god of the society around him? Why did he sacrifice himself for its ends? "Maybe it's my Catholic viewpoint," Scorsese stated. "Even if God says, 'OK, you don't have to give up anything, I love you anyway,' I still think we have to give up something. God may forgive you, but can you forgive yourself?"[9]

I think the issue isn't that God forgives and that we question whether we can forgive ourselves for not measuring up. The failure to forgive rests in an institution that will not let go of its control despite the costs to others, including its own mission. I got a deeper intimation of where that control, that unforgiving control, in my own ecclesiastical institution lay as I watched one particular scene toward the end of *The Age of Innocence*.

Scorsese creates this in a slow-motion view of a street crowded only with men. All are white. All are dressed in black suits and all wear black derbies. Because of the wind which is buffeting them, they are hanging onto their black hats for dear life. Watching that scene, as I sat in the theater with Joe, I couldn't help but recall visions of black-robed priests and bishops scurrying across the piazza of St. Peter's. I recalled the ordinations where ranks of black-suited clergy welcome the newly ordained into the club by the laying on of their hands. And now the buffeting was beginning in earnest.

While God might not have any rules, the institution does. And whenever its rules have ultimate power, it makes itself god. In the church today we are watching as the rules of those black-dressed clerics are being undermined by the inconsistencies within their own rules. The shutters are being closed against the buffeting winds that are breathing and crying for change. As all this continues, one huge question remains: how many more Newland Archers will be sacrificed at the altar of tradition and conformity before they finally walk away to who knows where? Newland Archer had been formed by his society. It controlled him and had become all-controlling. As Scorsese describes its impact on him and his part in it: "For Newland to have changed his life would have destroyed part of a culture."[10]

Why I Decided to Write This Book

We have witnessed a generation where many who were once committed to celibacy have left the institutional ministry. We have had our eyes opened to see how many who did stay have changed the way they practice or don't practice a truly celibate life. In the process, part of the celibate culture of Catholicism has been destroyed. I believe this is not because of selfishness as some allege, but because of the work of the Holy Spirit who is breathing mightily for this change.

Although the idea had been building in me for years, my decision to write this book arose during the first week of June 1993. I attended a chapter of my province at St. Lawrence Seminary, Mount Calvary, Wisconsin. All perpetually-professed members of the province were expected to be there. As we assembled, a press barrage of allegations of pedophilia, sexual abuse, and other sexual improprieties involving at least five Capuchin friars from our province was in full swing. The day the chapter opened, *Time* ran an article in its "religion" section entitled: "The Secrets of St. Lawrence." Its subtitle charged: "A Capuchin School Provides Catholicism's Latest Sex-Abuse Scandal." The article listed things that had supposedly occurred at the very seminary where we assembled. Some charges pertained to two of the very brothers who sat with us in that room. The provincial who had to respond to these allegations was pictured prominently.[11]

Needless to say, this gathering had a different character than all other chapters in the more than one-hundred-twenty-five-year history of our province. We would spend most of our time listening to Ron Smith, a highly-respected former provincial. He talked to us about power and abuse, powerlessness and the need to come under a "higher power," if we were to overcome the addictive forces that could rule over us. His words applied to us as individual celibates and to ourselves as an institution composed of celibates.

As I pondered Ron's words, I had to deal with a whole host of feelings. I also found myself re-examining previous discussions I'd had with other Capuchins, especially after the allegations were made public. I recalled conversations evoked by reading the headlines in *The Milwaukee Journal* during the three days before Christmas 1992 and the subsequent articles that never seemed to stop. These gave detailed, quite lurid allegations of pedophilia and other forms of sexual abuse and impropriety by our brothers at the seminary.

As we first talked about these allegations and the way the papers reported them, I remembered how often I had said, and how many times I heard other Capuchins say, something that now began to trouble me. We had all alluded to our own past "non-celibate actions." Often these confessions were expressed in comments that went something like: "Well, I've done many things that I don't want exposed in a headline in *The Milwaukee Journal*, but at least I've never fooled around with boys." The rationale seemed to be: it wasn't that the former actions were justified; they just weren't as bad as the latter.

The more such statements echoed in me, the more I began to concentrate on the first part of the sentence rather than the last:

"I've done many things that I don't want exposed. . . ." As I continued reflecting on this phrase, it increasingly seemed to suggest a kind of public cleansing. It appeared to represent an admission on the part of all who said it, that we had failed as vowed religious to be the celibates we publicly had promised we would be. In these semi-public conversations, we all seemed to be saying we didn't want public exposure for our noncompliance with a vow we had publicly promised to observe.

These reflections led me to wonder why nobody even feigned shock at what we were telling each other. It just seemed to be acknowledged that we all had failed in being celibate, at least sometime, in some way. Listening to Ron Smith, I wondered if we publicly-professed religious men were having such difficulties, what dilemmas must diocesan priests be facing, knowing that celibacy was a law that Pope John XXIII said could be changed with the flick of a pen?[12]

Why does this craziness around celibacy continue? Because, like the proverbial elephant unacknowledged in a room, the problem just isn't there. As I have heard from more than one (arch)bishop here and abroad: "We don't have that problem in our (arch)diocese." Or, as I heard many times among ourselves. "That's Calvary's problem, not ours."

So, as I sat at Mount Calvary those days, I became increasingly aware of the historical and internal contradictions connected to the present dispensation of mandatory celibacy. These thoughts led me back to the scriptures. In a play on the response the disciples asked Jesus when he discussed marriage, I began to ask (especially for men): "If such is the case, then who can be celibate?" This book will attempt to show that the answer will be "very few."

Then Who Can Be Celibate?

One might wonder why I am writing another book on celibacy in the church when we seem to have been inundated with them in the past, especially by those who have tried to explain how it might be lived well.

Many books and articles have been written on the history of celibacy or its biblical foundations. Others address psycho-social and developmental issues related to its practice. Still others offer highly-detailed academic apologias for it. Conciliar, synodal, papal, and episcopal letters and documents have expounded on its primacy. My purpose here is not to replicate them or to argue with them, one way or another.

There is also a great debate about the value and accuracy of research data. For instance, A. W. Richard Sipe writes that he had hundreds of interviews which led him to conclude a high number of priests are sexually active; he gets challenged on the data (the size and nature of the sample) and the fact that he's got an ax to grind. Andrew Greeley insists that Sipe is wrong because data he supports shows the vast majority of priests find celibacy to offer them no serious personal problem. Furthermore, Greeley indicates that they also are happy; they just "think their fellow priests are not happy, possibly because the agenda of clerical discussion tend to be set by those who are dissatisfied."[13] A six-year study documenting the decline in priestly ordinations, originally sponsored by the U.S. Catholic bishops, had its support suspended when it showed that the "main cause of the clergy drain is celibacy."[14] The methodology and the rationale for a *Los Angeles Times'* poll on the attitudes of the clergy and religious gets challenged by a member of the hierarchy and then the poll showed they are not dissatisfied with their life! Just from these few examples, the reader should see why I am reluctant to argue from "facts" and "data;" it only seems to invite countervailing arguments.

Despite debate about the data, it has become quite clear that huge concerns and contradictions related to the way celibacy is being lived exist in many parts of the Catholic church today. Celibacy might once have been highly regarded, but, for many religious men, and for many more diocesan priests, it just isn't working. Neither is it working in a third group the institutional church says must be celibate: homosexual persons. Furthermore, many people don't believe people in these groups are being celibate. A main reason the present dispensation still obtains is human law.

My purpose in writing this book is to show that, in too many cases, laws are not being observed, not so much because of selfishness or culture's decline, or because of a breakdown of morality or the erosion of sacrifice,[15] or even because of society's promiscuity or consumerism. All too often, celibacy no longer obtains because of the law's own internal contradictions, its lack of grounding in solid scriptural reflection and spirituality, and the absence of a proper support system to support the truly celibate option. This is especially so for men.

People might wonder why I distinguish between the male and female experience of celibacy and why I say it will be the very rare male who will be celibate in the future. Just as their approach to relationships, sexual intimacy, and genital expression[16] is different, so too I believe women approach celibacy differently than men, for psychological and conditioning reasons. Some may think this assumption of mine indicates a sexist or anachronistic bias. While I hope this may not be so, perhaps one little incident related to the choice for celibacy itself might give support to my contention.

As I wrote this book I discussed its contents with a religious priest who is Vicar for Religious for a major diocese in the United States. In the midst of the conversation I had asked him: "What do you do all day?" He talked of various tasks, including working with religious who want to leave their congregations and take private vows of celibacy under the bishop. This also included those who never were in religious life, but who wanted to make a private vow of celibacy. I asked, "Can I offer you my idea as to who will be asking to take private vows of celibacy?" When he said, "Sure," I responded, "I bet they all are women." He said I was correct. Of the significant number of those requesting to make a private vow of celibacy, not one was a man.

I believe we do ourselves a disservice by remaining in denial. Despite myriad data, as well as the deficits, denial continues. So the data is suppressed and researchers are discredited—most often by those whose interests seem to rest in the preservation of the addictive system of celibate, clerical patriarchy.

Because the objective approaches challenging the present form of celibacy in the Roman Catholic church have not worked, I will be using a more subjective approach. I want to share my reflections (which hopefully will be grounded in good scholarship) and to narrate experiences. The "facts" of one's personal experience cannot be argued. I take this approach hoping that this kind of honesty might help us face what I believe is a problem that is much wider than celibacy. As the saying goes: "We are as sick as our secrets." However, once a problem is admitted, denial's control is challenged. For us, ecclesiastically speaking, this can help us work together for changes that may make us more healthy as persons and as an institution.

The framework of this book is limited by my own social location as a white, male, straight, vowed, Roman Catholic priest who is part of an international congregation with a provincial setting in North America. My own "social location" limits my "story." It automatically colors my horizon or viewpoint. Consequently, what I write may not reflect the horizon of people of color, women, homosexuals, non-vowed or lay Catholics. However, enough discussions with people representing these groups indicate to me that my experience and reflections are not isolated to my own social location.

I will begin by probing the possible scriptural basis for celibacy and the historical role of celibacy as a means of control in the church. I will argue that, while this form of control may have worked at one time, it actually is out of control now. Next I will discuss celibacy and the crisis of meaning in the church today which leads us to find substitutes for the very characteristics that would make us healthy celibates. From there I will reflect on the kind of intimacy that will be needed in the future by healthy celibates and how we might begin to view celibacy as a form of fasting which does not concentrate on what we fast from, but what we are fasting for, and whom we are fasting with. Then I will share my vision regarding the need for communities of support for celibates and the role of contemplation and compassion for the multitudes.

I hope this book will not be viewed as an effort to dismantle celibacy, but rather as an attempt to undermine the present institutional form of celibacy which hinders its authentic, life-giving expression. In the process I hope to contribute to a healthier, holier, and more honest church, and to support celibates in their efforts to live healthier, holier, and more intimate lives.

1

The Scriptures and Celibacy

I will never forget what happened to me as I walked back and forth in the Dubuque Airport studying Paul's First Letter to the Corinthians. It was in 1986 or 1987 and I was preparing for a class to be offered the next day at the Graduate School of Theology in Berkeley. I was reading chapters six and seven which deal with the end times and include Paul's reflections on virginity. However, before I develop my reflections on how his insights touched upon my own celibacy, I think I better contextualize my remarks with a part of my own story.

I was having a difficult time—biologically, psychologically, and spiritually. I was in my mid-years, the time when people normally reassess their lives, especially their work, sexually-defined roles, and commitments. Given what was happening in myself, I must have been quite "normal." Part of my reason for going to Berkeley involved a reassessment of my celibate commitment. Thus it was in this atmosphere that I read the famous passage from Paul that is one of the two from the New Testament traditionally offered as a scriptural basis for celibacy:

> Now concerning virgins, I have no command of the Lord, but I give my opinion as one who by the Lord's mercy is trustworthy. I think that, in view of the impending crisis, it is well for you to remain as you are. Are you bound to a wife? Do not seek to be free. Are you free from a wife? Do not seek a wife. But if you marry, you do not sin, and if a virgin marries, she does not sin. Yet those who marry will experience distress in this life, and I would spare you that (1 Cor 7:25-28).

This letter was not written to women, but to men. The fact that Paul's letter was addressed to males (men are addressed in the

second person "you," women in the third "they") was not so much
what struck me as I paced back and forth in the Dubuque Airport.
The passage that hit me between the eyes was Paul's opening
words about virgins: "I have no command of the Lord, but I give
my opinion."

"Your *opinion*," I found myself challenging Paul. "I thought my
being a celibate was God's will and now you say that you 'have no
command of the Lord'!" My thoughts and emotions returned to
the night before I went to the seminary. I had attended a going-
away party as we finished our last summer of high school. Mary,
the girl I had been dating and thought I loved, didn't come. I felt
terrible, not only about her absence, but about my future without
her. As the night passed, I got more depressed. At one point I went
to the washroom, closed the door, and began to cry. I remember
vividly what happened next. I stood there in the washroom, crying
and questioning God, "Why are you doing this to me? I don't want
to go there. I want to get married, have sex, help make babies. I
want to have a family. I want to be happy; why can't you let me
alone?" I didn't get an answer.

I entered the seminary because I firmly believed it was God's
will, God's "command," to use Paul's words. And now Paul
declared: "I have no command of the Lord, but I give my opinion."
With that, I felt a rage rise from deep within me. The feeling was
expressed in the words: "I've been duped." All along I thought I
was supposed to be this virgin, this celibate, because it was what
God wanted for me. And now I discover God could care less
whether I remain a virgin or not.

My anger then turned to Paul: "Here you say it's only your
opinion. You say your opinion, 'by the Lord's mercy is trustworthy.'
However, I have reason not to place a great amount of trust in your
opinion related to sex, much less celibacy, for various reasons.
Primary among these is your own main rationale: namely the nearness of 'the impending crisis.'"

The impending crisis which colored Paul's First Letter to the
Corinthians was his conviction that the *parousia*, or the end of the
world, was imminent. Since Jesus was going to return very soon, it
was better, Paul figured, that people stay in their present situation
of life. Although Paul understood why married couples would
have sexual relations (1 Cor 7:2-6), he thought they should act as
though they were not married (1 Cor 7:1, 7, 10).

After my rage dissipated, my next reaction was to realize I could no longer blame my celibate predicament on God or Paul, to say nothing of the poor scholarship from formation directors and others. Instead I offered a challenge to myself: "Well, now that you can't blame God or Paul for being celibate, what are you going to do? You've got to find a reason *within yourself* rather than some external referent if you are going to stay. And if you can't, you'd better deal with the consequences."

Some of the chapters which follow will show how I have tried to struggle with that challenge. However, the purpose of this chapter is to discuss the scriptural warrants and foundations for the celibate life, free of ideology and misconceptions that affected people like me.

What was the understanding of celibacy that colored the Jewish Jesus' remarks (as well as Paul's)? Does the New Testament offer any foundation for the celibate commitment as we now know it? Have the scriptures been misused to perpetuate celibacy as a means of control? How might an answer to these questions help offer a direction for the future expression of celibacy in our church?

The Jewish Environment and Celibacy

In the Old Testament, celibacy receives little or no mention as a value. Although virginity is discussed, its value is connected to being a preparatory step to marriage (Gen 24:16; Jg 19:24). In fact, when it is mentioned, virginity seems more identified with sterility than generativity. It reflects God's curse rather than God's blessing (Gen 30:23, 1 Sam 1:11, Jg 11:37). Its only positive meaning seems to have been connected with ritual purity (see Lev 21:7).

The norm for people was marriage; to marry was a duty. To be a virgin (if you were a woman) was a way of preparing for marriage. To be a permanent virgin without children was an aberration, a devastation undermining one's identity and purpose in life. Barrenness brought shame on the childless person. It was considered a misfortune at the least and divine punishment at the most. Thus Rachel lamented, "Give me children or I shall die!" (Gen 30:1ff).

To be a virgin meant to be less free, to be unfaithful. According to *Dufour's Dictionary of Biblical Theology:*

> More than once the prophets gave the name of virgin to a conquered nation (Is 23:12; 47:1; Jr 46:11), and to Israel in particular (Am 5:2; Is 37:22; Jr 14:17; Lm 1:15; 2:13); this is to bewail the loss of her territorial integrity. Likewise, however, when Israel violates the covenant Jeremiah calls her "the virgin Israel" (Jr 18:13) as a reminder of what her faithfulness should have been. The same title recurs in the context of the restoration when Yahweh and his people shall renew relations of love and faithfulness (Jr 31:4,21).[1]

Given the fact that the marriage of a young man and a virgin symbolized the messianic nuptials of God and Israel, that someone like Jeremiah would be told to renounce marriage (Jer 16:2) had nothing to do with promoting celibacy as a value. Rather it was meant to demonstrate how far Israel had separated itself from its spouse through its infidelity to its covenantal promises. Jeremiah is the only person in the Old Testament expressly reported as celibate, and his celibacy served to signify the community's imminent disaster and devastation because of its rupture of the covenant.

When ordinary people may have been unmarried, such virginity was not identified with vows. What vows were taken, furthermore, were not permanent. In fact, as has been shown in *Vows in the Hebrew Bible and the Ancient Near East*,[2] vows were conditional promises made to God based upon a favorable divine response to one's prayer. Neither was virginity connected to "oaths" which were promises with some kind of curse attached.

Where celibacy was demanded, unlike now, its time frame was only for temporary periods. These related to times men would be in battle or priests would serve at the altar. The Jews' anthropology led them to believe there was something unclean connected to genital intercourse and women's menstruation; thus altar consecration involved abstinence (Ex 19:15; Lev 15:16ff.). The levitical codes demanded that, for cultic purity, priests refrain from genital relations with their wives prior to presiding at religious services (Lev 8:31-36; 22:1-4; 1 Sam 21:4). If they had such, they would become unclean; any resulting sacrifice thereby would be sullied.

According to rabbinic Judaism, every Jewish male was under the obligation to marry. Within the marriage the husband was obliged to have genital relations with his wife in order to propagate the race and restrain immorality. Men were encouraged to marry early, in their late teens or early twenties.[3] Yet despite these cultural codes, virginity and celibacy did seem to find some adherents and advocates. Best known among these were some members of the Qumran community. However, the purpose of their celibacy was legal or ritual purity, celibacy was not seen as having value in itself. Otherwise it involved abstention from association with women prior to battle. In either case, as the Rule of the Community indicates, celibacy was not envisioned as a permanent way of life among any of Qumran's members.

Other writings found in contemporaries of Paul, such as the Gospel of Thomas, the narratives and speeches of several apocryphal Acts of Apostles, especially the Acts of Thomas, and much of the literature and ritual of early Syriac Christianity, all attest to a link between virginity and ritual purity. Those embracing virginity were separated from responsibilities of the "ordinary" people in society. This notion of separation would became one of the principal functions for celibacy in later Christianity. In the second-century *Acts of Paul and Thecla*, much of this way of thinking seemed to be attributed to St. Paul.[4]

The Meaning of 1 Corinthians 7:25-28

Much ink has been spilled attempting to explain the rationale and context of Paul's recommendation for virginity in 1 Corinthians. First, what was happening in the Corinthian community that gave rise to his recommendations? Did he really believe the end of the world was imminent? Were some people advocating celibacy for those who were married? Were others promoting "spiritual marriages?" We never will know the specific situation of the church at Corinth that generated Paul's response.

The brunt of Paul's position on virginity can be found in chapter seven. There he begins by stating his view that remaining a virgin, what we think of as celibacy, is better than marriage (1 Cor 7:1, 7, 8-9, 26). Paul was not talking about being a virgin as "not having sex," or marriage as that which enabled one "to have sex." Rather than viewing virginity from the lens of genital intercourse, Paul considered it more as representing a certain stance in life. Also, in his defense, it is clear that his mere wish cannot be raised to the position of a principle; something advised is not a command. Paul himself makes this clear. Furthermore, even if one has chosen to be celibate and then discovered this choice cannot be kept, one "should enter into a normal married relationship without any scruple."[5] This seems a far cry from the demand for all sorts of papers and dispensations required to remove one from the "choice" today. Finally, Paul's comments were in no way to be connected to any sanctions from the community such as cessation from being able to minister if someone chose not to be celibate any longer.

Though having no command on the matter from the Lord, Paul offers two main reasons for his pro-celibacy sentiment. The first reveals his preoccupation with the apocalyptic, the end-times. In light of the "impending distress," which he viewed to be the imminent parousia and end of the world,[6] it was his opinion that "a person remain as he is" (1 Cor 7:26). Paul's second rationale flowed from assumptions related to the first, namely that people should be totally oriented toward the last days. Therefore, he wrote, "I want you to be free from anxieties" (1 Cor 7:32). While Paul himself seems to have been celibate (1 Cor 7:7-8), any "thorn in his side" notwithstanding,[7] he personally believed a celibate's life was less troubled (1 Cor 7:28), less anxious (1 Cor 7:32), more ordered (1 Cor 7:35), and even happier (1 Cor 7:40).

In a comment on Paul's arguments that has implications for the current form of mandatory celibacy, Jerome Murphy-O'Connor has made clear:

> There can be little doubt that Paul was convinced that his way of life was better than the married state. This made it inevitable that he should counsel others to do likewise (v 8), but he did not fall into the trap of imagining that what was best for him was best for everyone else. He was keenly aware of the danger of transferring a theoretical ideal to a concrete situation, and of the cruelty inherent in trying to create instant perfection by fiat.[8]

That Paul promoted reciprocal sexual relations within marriage as well as the need for monogamy supports the notion that Paul did not link the practice of virginity with ritual purity. He did not link it with a way of separating one group of people (the virgins) from others, as seems to have been the case with some of his contemporaries. For him the main reason for celibacy was to better use the days preceding the end-time and the return of the Lord.

Whether married or virgin, Paul believed that all his listeners should be fully directed, without distraction, toward the imminent *parousía*. According to Peter Ellis, Paul's argument:

> seems to be that celibacy is required for total dedication to the work of the Kingdom, a work so great that it calls for sublimating the good of marriage to the greater good of the work of the Kingdom. Paul supports this argument by his own example (cf. 1 Cor 9:5ff); declares it is a charism (7:7b) that not all enjoy (7:9); exhorts those who can take it to take it (7:1, 7, 8-9, 27-28, 32-35, 37-38, 40); but makes it clear that celibacy is neither essential nor obligatory for any Christian.[9]

Given Paul's effort to find reasons why people should be celibate, one might wonder why he did not point to the value of modeling one's life upon that of Jesus, who seems to have been a virgin and celibate. It certainly is one of the main arguments proffered by those today who seek to impose celibacy on others for ministry in the church. However, despite the fact that many in the hierarchy today make such a connection, Paul did not point to Jesus' celibacy nor did Jesus himself suggest his own celibacy as a motive why others should embrace of it. The only rationale, in all their eyes, was for the sake of the kingdom which was about to come.

The Meaning of Matthew 19:10-12

The context for the Matthean passage concerning Jesus' approach to what we call celibacy occurs as part of a deeper discussion on marriage and divorce: "Some Pharisees came to him, and to test him they asked, 'Is it lawful for a man to divorce his wife for any cause?'" (Mt 19:3). This precipitated Jesus' recollection of the traditional teaching on the divinely-ordered indissolubility of marriage (Mt 19: 4-6). In response they said to him, "Why then did Moses command us to give a certificate of dismissal and to divorce her?" (Mt 19:7). Jesus responded that it was because of the hardness of their hearts that "Moses allowed you to divorce your wives, but from the beginning it was not so. And I say to you, whoever divorces his wife, except for unchastity *(porneía)*, and marries another commits adultery" (Mt 19:9). Surprised by his response, Jesus' disciples say: "If such is the case of a man with his wife, it is better not to marry." Jesus answers, "Not everyone can accept this teaching, but only those to whom it is given"(Mt 19:10-11).

Tomes have been written about *porneía*, the word used in Matthew 19:9 for "unchastity." It's not my purpose here to discuss or debate these opinions or offer my own related to its connection to divorce and what happens to married people after they separate. My intent is to look at how the word relates to people outside of marriage. In any case, it is important to realize that any subsequent discussion about "this teaching" in connection to our understanding today of "celibacy" must be contextualized as a result of the disciples' response to Jesus' teaching on divorce and remarriage. Despite the way in which many in the Catholic tradition have interpreted it,[10] I believe we do a disservice to the text by considering it in itself, apart from its preceding context as a teaching of Jesus.[11]

Building on this teaching, Matthew uses one of his triads to express a literary form of a *mashal* or proverb. In this triad, Jesus names the first two categories of eunuchs: eunuchs born so and made so by human operation (castration). These reflect the common understanding of the term then and now. Surprisingly, for his third possibility, Jesus presents a "totally different" category that comes as a complete surprise.[12] In fact, according to Dupont, "it is clear that the first two are only mentioned in order to better assure the effect of surprise that the third is meant to produce."[13] Jesus adds: "And there are eunuchs who have made themselves eunuchs for the sake of the kingdom of heaven. Let anyone accept this who can" (Mt 19:12).

In his classic text on Matthew 19:10-12, Dom Jacques Dupont offers four interpretations related to what Jesus meant by "this teaching." 1) The text refers to celibacy in itself, not as something for the aggrieved spouse in a marriage; 2) the text was meant for celibacy but was placed here by Matthew to serve as a contrast to marriage; 3) the "common" interpretation which sees celibacy as a particular gift from God; and 4) the teaching on celibacy must be seen in the context of 19:3-9 on marriage and divorce.[14] This fourth position reflects that of scholars like Murphy-O'Connor and Dupont. It represents the position I take here.

Given the fact that marriage was the norm, the issue about one's status as the aggrieved party in a divorce is the context of 19:3-9. Jesus makes it clear that his teaching on the matter is that divorce (except for *porneía*) and remarriage is never allowed. The one who remarries after a divorce "commits adultery" (Mt 19:9). Hearing this teaching, his disciples said to him, "If such is the case of a man with his wife, it is better not to marry" (Mt 19:10). So accustomed to marriage as the normal way to live, the disciples just expected, with their contemporaries, that one could marry after a divorce. When Jesus tells them they cannot remarry after a divorce, they wonder if it would be better for the person not to marry in the first place.

It was their astonished reply that elicited Jesus' "teaching." Thus, again, Jesus' answer refers not so much to celibacy as we know it today, but the status of the aggrieved party in a divorce situation. The context for this passage relates to how married people are asked to live when *porneía* is discovered in their partner and divorce results. As Jerome Murphy-O'Connor makes clear, "this passage has nothing to do with celibacy" in the sense that we now understand it.[15] Thus, to make legislation by appealing to a text that does not undergird the rationale that has given rise to what the legislation specifically demands, calls into question any effective force of the legislation. Furthermore, based on Murphy-O'Connor's insight that "Matthew 19:12 is not concerned with freely-chosen celibacy,"[16] to make it foundational for compulsory celibacy is regrettable.

Even when the aggrieved party does not remarry and remains a eunuch because of the teaching of Jesus, this does not mean that such a eunuch will be celibate. The person just does not get married again. Dupont expresses what I have been saying clearly and concisely: "A eunuch is not necessarily a celibate."[17] This must be remembered as we try to understand how the text might have some application to the purpose and role of celibacy and discipleship in the church today and in the future. In all cases and above all, Jesus' own interpretation will be the norm: "Not everyone can accept this teaching . . ." (Mt 19:11).

With this context as a start, Matthew's Jesus continues by making it very clear that celibacy for the aggrieved party in a marriage is a gift: it is for "only those to whom it is *given*." In applying the text to anyone who would be celibate, what is given ("the divine passive"[18]) first of all, has its origins in the divine donation; it has no source in any institutional mandate. Applied to today's situation of mandated celibacy for some, we can say that what is given, secondly, is not to all who would be priests nor to all those who were created homosexual; it will be for some but probably no more than any other group of people. Just because a human institution has decreed it to be so does not mean God's donation will be so executed; this would put God's gifts under the control of human fiat. From the beginning of 19:11 and from 19:12 it is clear that Jesus' vision of celibacy is totally voluntary; it cannot be compulsory or connected as a package with anything else. Celibacy is its own package and must be seen in that sense only for one reason: "for the sake of the kingdom of heaven" (Mt 19:12).

Secondly, the passage makes it clear that those "some" to whom the gift is given need not even accept it. There is no necessity to receive, much less, embrace the gift, especially if they don't think or feel they can hold on to it: "Let anyone *accept* this who can" (Mt 19:12). The notion of "acceptance" in this text has a connection to the notion of "understanding," but not (as Dupont tries to argue)[19] in the oft-used word for understanding so unique to Matthew. It does not mean "grasp" in an intellectual sense as much as "make room for" in the sense of taking on a concept and making it one's own (Mt 15:17). The "acceptance" implied here goes further to the notion of embracing the offer wholeheartedly, or with "purity of heart."

Matthew 19:12 also makes it clear that any celibacy faithful to the vision of Jesus has no necessary connections to a male priesthood: "let anyone (not *him*, which would be expected if this had some kind of patriarchal reinforcement) accept this." Celibacy can't be based on male superiority over women, on some kind of cultic purity connotations, or on something a community or its leaders demand. Neither does it even seem a demand for those who are divorced for reasons of the partner's "unchastity" (Mt 19:9). Furthermore it cannot be mandated for those whose God-given nature orients them to those of the same sex. Rather it represents a free response to the gift-experience of God's reign made present in the teaching and example of Jesus.[20]

Any celibacy that is of God, originates in God's gift. Any divine donation can only come from God. It cannot be imposed by any institution. This is only natural since God, *who naturally made people not to be celibate* (Gen 2:18-25), would have to give a gift to those who would be celibate. The use of the theological passive (to whom it is given) indicates that it is only from the reign and largesse of God that one has the capacity to be celibate for any reason. Consequently, previously-accepted reasons for being celibate (such as "for the sake of being a priest," or "to minister in the church" or "for the reason that I made you homosexual") are insufficient; celibacy can only exist for the sake of God's reign.

In conclusion, there are three types of eunuchs described in Mt 19:12. The first are those physically deformed "from birth." They cannot have genital intercourse. The second are those who have been castrated through the abuse of other men for the sake of their purposes of control, such as to serve as harem guards and courtiers. This form of eunuch specifically was rejected in Deuteronomy 23:1. Finally there are those who have voluntarily chosen not to be married. These ones have made themselves so, not because they don't need intimacy, not because they have a repulsion toward sex or are genitally attracted only to people of their same sex, and not because they are repulsed by the idea of coupling. They can only have made themselves so "for the sake of the reign of God" (see Mt 8:22; 1 Cor 7:17, 25-30). This notion will be developed at much greater length in chapters seven and eight.

Recent Efforts to Find Alternative Scriptural Grounding for Celibacy

With the traditional arguments based on Matthew 19 and 1 Corinthians 7 undermined on the grounds of strict exegetical interpretation, some have looked elsewhere in the scriptures to find a New Testament basis for celibacy. The search has not been without difficulties. In his dissertation studying the history of the discipline around clerical celibacy, Paul Beaudette argues that celibacy's "strongest scriptural justification" rests in the prescription in the pastoral letters, "that elders and deacons should not be married more than once (1 Tim 3:2, 12; Ti 1:6)."[21] For obvious reasons, it does not seem likely that such a quote would be used by those presently trying to find a scriptural basis for clerical celibacy! Consequently, a rationale must be discovered elsewhere.

In the 1990s, Pope John Paul II offered a relatively new papal justification for such a scriptural grounding. In a 1993 allocution the Pope declared that "more than ever" the "church" is in favor of priestly celibacy. The sub-headline in *L'Osservatore Romano* offered an intimation of the scripture texts he would promote: "In the life of celibacy the Church sees a sign of the priest's special consecration to Christ as one who has left everything to follow him."[22]

In the opening paragraph of his talk, John Paul II highlighted two texts found in all of the synoptic gospels to "help us understand the reason for the church's legislation on priestly celibacy. In fact, the church has considered and still considers that it belongs to the logic of priestly consecration and to the total belonging to Christ resulting from it. . . ."[23] The first text quoted by the pope referred to the fact that, "they left everything and followed him" (Lk 5:11; cf. Mt 4:20, 22; Mk 1:18, 20). The second refers to Peter "who remembered this [celibate] aspect of the apostolic vocation and said to Jesus: 'We have given up *everything* and followed you'" (Mt 19:27; Mk 10:28; cf. Lk 18:28).[24]

Most exegetes have linked the "everything" that is abandoned with possessions, not including wives,[25] as will be seen later in this chapter. Although Luke places Jesus' visit to Peter's house (Lk 4:38-39) *before* Jesus' call to discipleship, both Matthew and Mark have this visit (Mt 8:14-15; Mk 1:29-31) *after* the call to discipleship. This indicates at least two things: Peter (at least in Mark and Matthew) did not leave *everything*. Secondly, after the call to discipleship, we find (again, at least in Matthew and Mark) Peter with a "house" which included his mother-in-law. If his mother-in-law was there, it's likely his wife lived with him there as well. That he would have normal forms of genital intimacy with his wife, as any good Jew would do, seems much more plausible than to find in the texts a notion to support him as a celibate.

While the pope stressed these texts, he seems to have overlooked at least one other text indicating that Peter and some of the other apostles appear to have had normal genital relationships with their wives after the resurrection itself. For instance, in the same text from 1 Corinthians where Paul promotes celibacy, he justifies his role as an apostle with the statement: "This is my defense to those who would examine me. . . . Do we not have the right to be accompanied by a believing wife as do the other apostles and the brothers of the Lord and Cephas?" (1 Cor 9:3, 5). Celibacy in light of the parousia is discussed in chapter seven; marriage and the apostolic ministry is discussed in chapter eleven. It seems both existed side by side in Paul's letter to the Corinthians.

I was in Auburn, California giving a retreat when I read about the Pope's allocution noted above in *The Catholic Herald*, the

Sacramento diocesan paper. Under the headline "Celibacy Rule is Reaffirmed by Pope," the CNS article stated:

> The Catholic Church has become more convinced throughout the centuries that celibacy is valuable for its priests and that it follows Christ's design for the priesthood, Pope John Paul II said.
>
> Priestly celibacy reflects Christ's call to his disciples to leave everything and follow him, the Pope said. "Jesus did not promulgate a law, but proposed an ideal of celibacy for the new priesthood he instituted." The ideal was affirmed with increasing insistence and consistency throughout the church's history, he said.[26]

Incredulous at what I had read, I called the diocesan paper and asked for a copy of the full text. I had been taught that, on the one hand, Jesus never formally founded a "new priesthood" as such. Now our Pope was saying that he had not only founded a "new" priesthood, but a celibate priesthood at that! I could not believe the Pope was quoted correctly because his rationale did not seem to have real grounding in the scriptures. However, when the paper sent me the CNS text by fax, the statement was as quoted.

With such questionable scriptural grounds offered for priestly celibacy, and given the manner in which the texts were used, it is little wonder that the argument to authority and tradition often become the only sources left which can be used to "justify" priestly celibacy. Furthermore, such selective use of a text like this seems to represent some kind of misuse, if not abuse, of the scriptures themselves.

Control and Abusive Relations: The Scriptural Justification

In 1992, the United States Bishops released a document entitled "When I Call for Help: Domestic Violence against Women." The well-reasoned statement limited the bishops' discussion to domestic violence wherein the violence is perpetrated by males on females. The bishops equated violence with abuse and stated that violence in any form is *never* justified. On the contrary, it is sinful and quite possibly criminal.

I read the document while giving a retreat to priests in the diocese of Buffalo. I could not help but think of parallels to situations in our patriarchal church where women suffer violence and abuse in various forms at the hands of males who maintain all ultimate

control. Increasingly, it has become clear to me that domestic violence against women has its ecclesiastical counterpart. This connection is even more to the point if we use the bishops' own
definition of abuse, that is: "any kind of behavior that one person
uses to control another through fear and intimidation."[27] In my
mind "one person" can be an individual in a home; it also can be a
corporate person in the institutional church.

At the heart of the notion of abuse is the issue of control.
Control constitutes the underpinnings and infrastructure of power
in all patriarchal relations. Whether these are in the home or in the
church matters little. Their consequence remains the same. Both
leave their victims battered.

The consequence for those in the church who resist these tac-
tics of control is fear and intimidation. Thus, in one place a diocesan priest who speaks against compulsory celibacy is forced to
recant, in another a speaker not seen to be supportive "of the magisterium" on this issue is dis-invited, in still another, a vocal priest
receives no assignment. It is not surprising, then, that in many
places people fear to speak out lest they lose their positions in the
institution.

In their document, the bishops develop reasoned explanations
that show how domestic abuse can be intergenerational. When
abuse gets passed from generation to generation, it can easily
become first normal, then a norm, and finally normative. These
normative values seem to justify "why men batter," and "why
women stay." Again its parallels in church systems seem self-evi-
dent. The very day of my writing the first draft of this chapter, I
was told of a bishop who fired a friend of mine who was the
Director of Religious Education in "his" diocese. This was done
without any warning, simply because "he did not like her style."
In our family system of Roman Catholicism, she has no recourse.
This battered woman has no place to go for help. Despite this, my
friend not only wants to remain "in the house;" she wants to continue to work in that diocese. In this she seems little different from
so many other battered women: she is "trapped in the abusive relationship" and has "no other means of support."[28]

Canadian writer, Jane Ursel has noted: "The essential condition
for the subordination of women within any patriarchal system is
control of women's access to the means of their livelihood." She explains:

> By making women's access to subsistence contingent on
> entry into particular reproduction relations or by restricting
> their ability to be self-sufficient, women's labour, both pro-
> ductive and reproductive, becomes subject to comprehen-
> sive control. This control is the essence of patriarchy, its
> universal function and effect.[29]

After discussing how men abuse women, the bishops show
how the scriptures have been used by men in normative ways to
justify their abuse. Many of these texts are well-known, such as the
"household" codes found in 1 Peter (2:18-3:7) and some of the
Pauline letters (Col 3:18-4:6; 1 Tim 2:1-8; Ti 2:1-10). Although the
bishops don't explain the deeper ways such texts can be used to
reinforce patriarchal control in the ecclesiastical household, they
do show how the scriptures can be used to justify the abuse that
constitutes the heart of control-defined relationships. Then they
make a powerful declaration:

> As a church, one of the most worrying aspects of the abuse
> practiced against women is the use of biblical texts, taken
> out of context, to support abusive behavior. Counselors
> report that both abused women and their batterers use
> Scripture passages to justify their behavior.[30]

In an even more powerful statement following these words,
the bishops declare: "As bishops, we condemn the use of the Bible
to condone abusive behavior." The bishops have already described
abuse as "any kind of behavior that is used to control," Thus when
the scriptures are interpreted (by the Pope or anyone else in
authority in the church) in a way that others are afraid to show the
limitations of this approach, it seems that the bishops' own charac-
terization of abuse can be applied. Thus Sandra Schneiders has
noted:

> The only people who really need to search the New
> Testament for what it says about women are those who are
> convinced, for non-biblical reasons, that women should be
> restricted in some way in the church, and who must justify
> their sexual discrimination (which they admit is unjust in
> any other context except the ecclesial one) by an appeal to
> scripture.[31]

The bishops then conclude: "Can you imagine Jesus battering his church?"[32] It is unimaginable that Jesus would batter his church, and I would hope that no bishop or priest believes he is part of dynamics that batter women in the church either. However, while the male leaders can't imagine that their attitudes and actions might constitute battering, one needs only to listen to the stories of battered women workers who "stay" in the ecclesiastical family for verification. Like the stories told in counseling centers around the world, their tales all too often reveal a consistent pattern of abuse. It is unimaginable but true: those who say they represent Jesus in such a special way, often *are* battering his church.

Over a decade ago, the leader of a very large congregation of women religious wrote an article entitled: "Women Religious: The Battered Women in the Church." Certain officials in Rome had already undermined her authority because they did not agree with her collegial way of exercising authority. Out of fear, she would not allow her name to be printed, lest she and her congregation receive further repercussions from men in Rome. Fear and intimidation ruled her response.

In asking, "What can we do to help?" the first thing the bishops suggest for pastors and pastoral staff is that they make their parish "a safe place where abused women and men who batter can come for help."[33] Unfortunately, this solution is rather impossible to imagine in the area of ecclesiastical violence manifested in clerical control. Such a recommendation appears to many to be tantamount to asking chickens to find a safe place in the fox's den.[34]

Expanding the Scripture Passages to Their "Fuller Meaning"

The facts, supporting the solid arguments, make it quite clear that Matthew 19:10-12 and 1 Corinthians 7 can no longer serve as an underlying rationale for celibacy, especially *vis-à-vis* the institutional imperative for it. This seems all the more true of the effort to find justification for celibacy in other passages such as those proffered by Pope John Paul II. Despite this, I do not believe we can simply say there are no scriptural grounds for celibacy. While this may be true from a strictly exegetical viewpoint, one can't conclude that just because there is no clear exegetical support for celibacy as we now know it, that there is no basis in the New Testament for celibates in the contemporary church. Furthermore, the fact that these texts often have been misinterpreted for all sorts of reasons—from ideological purposes to poor scholarship—should make us even more desirous of finding in them some healthy rationale for the celibate life now and for the future. To do that we must find a message in these texts which transcends a literal interpretation that will be faithful to the legacy of generations of people who have used these texts to support their way of life.

It is the task of each generation to find in the ever-creative word of God a message which speaks to its experience. The text itself, as God's word, has a power greater than the limited understanding of its original author. In this sense, Sandra Schneiders writes:

> This implies that, when read from the vantage point of twentieth-century faith, standing within the tradition of the believing community, the gospel text will undoubtedly yield more and richer meaning than the author was aware of expressing when he wrote it. This surplus meaning is not arbitrary, nor is every interpretation valid. But the process of validation consists in seeing the continuity of the interpretation with the direction of the author's intention and its coherence with the totality of the New Testament message as embodied in the lived faith of the community, rather than verifying that the interpretation coincides by identity with the explicit intention of the author.[35]

In all scriptural hermeneutical efforts, the key question is: What does it mean? Even though the meaning had one sense at one time, this does not mean a fuller, expanded meaning cannot be understood in later generations of people of faith. Therefore the question we must ask about the use of scripture texts such as 1 Corinthians 7:25-29 and Matthew 19:10-12 (especially the latter) is this: Even though the text does not refer to celibacy as we know it today, can the form we know of today find reinforcement in the text?

Rewording the question in this way moves us from an untenable literal interpretation to a fuller understanding of a text that can make it a source of great nourishment for one's discipleship as a celibate. While this will be attempted in later chapters, I believe we find a tentative answer when we consider the *purpose* that the two texts propose for celibacy. In Matthew it is "for the sake of the kingdom of heaven" (Mt 19:12); in 1 Corinthians it is to be "anxious about the affairs of the Lord, how to please the Lord" (1 Cor

7:32). In both cases the center of one's life revolves around God. Consequently, as we will see in the final chapter, the reign of this God will have to constitute the scriptural grounds for any authentic celibacy.

2

The (Ab)Use of Celibacy by the Institutional Church

The previous chapter indicated that there seems to be no clear basis in the scriptures for celibacy as we know it. It also showed how God's word can be abused by people in power who have a vested interest in maintaining celibacy. This chapter will show how this abuse has served the interest of all goals of abuse: to maintain control through fear and intimidation. It will offer a historical study of clerical celibacy[1] to show that this represents just part of an overall effort used and abused by some in the church, especially its leaders, to impose celibacy as a means of ensuring and maintaining their control. In turn this control has reinforced an institution characterized by patriarchal clericalism.[2]

Pope Paul VI stated in his 1967 encyclical letter *On Priestly Celibacy:* "Priestly celibacy has been guarded by the Church for centuries as a brilliant jewel, and retains its value undiminished even in our time when mentality and structures have undergone such profound change."[3] Despite the pope's words, celibacy's value as something to be mandated continually diminishes. Our current experience of this diminishment invites us to return to the sources to examine why the "brilliant jewel" of compulsory priestly celibacy has lost its luster.

In examining how celibacy has been "guarded by the Church for centuries," we can find four main periods. In each we will find that celibacy's unique and singular value has been promoted for basically the same reason—control. Celibacy was promoted during the fourth century when the papacy was beginning to exercise more control: during the period of the "Gregorian Reform" at the turn of the millennium when the papacy tried to break the back of lay investiture and concentrate power in the hands of the clergy; around the time of Trent when the papacy tried to overcome clerical abuses and concubinage; and during the present post-Vatican II era when the papacy insists on its preservation even as more and more parishes go without the eucharist.

No matter what the period, the process has helped create a church characterized by a celibate culture. This celibate culture has tended to gather every significant element of church life under the control of the clerical group in an hierarchical order. According to Philip Sheldrake:

> Those who belonged within the culture were empowered and those outside disempowered. As in all dominant power groups, the control of membership is crucial. Celibacy, in the limited sense of being unmarried, has long been a condition and proof of membership of a clerical class. It guaranteed, too, that the powers and possessions of clerical culture were not dissipated in a network of external relationships and in provision for heirs.[4]

The following pages examine the four periods to show how this hierarchical control of the clergy and the effort of the clergy to control the people has evolved.

The Rise of Celibacy as a Norm in Isolated Areas

From the time of the Apostles until the fourth century no known celibacy-related restrictions were imposed on the clergy by the institutional church. Rather celibacy was a freely embraced option until that time, especially by the groups known as "virgins" and "widows." (Note that there was no group called "widowers"!) Despite this fact, during this time, seeds of an anti-marriage, or at least an anti-sex attitude, were being sown. Tertullian (ca. 150-230) declared celibacy was better than marriage and that sexual desires and delight, even in marriage, had no place if a marriage was to be considered Christian. Origen, his contemporary (ca. 185-255), believed that only a cessation of sexual activity would bring about life without death. Both Tertullian and Origen blamed women for luring men into sexual indulgence. Inspired by Origen, Jerome (ca. 350-420) considered marriage a necessary evil; sexual intercourse was incompatible with a life of prayer.

With the recognition of the church in the Roman Empire, followed by its establishment, and finally, its institutionalization, a certain clericalization seemed inevitable. Yet the origins of this process arose from somewhat earlier origins in the gradual sacralization of the Christian cult and the ministers responsible for it. As Paul Beaudette explains:

> With the sacralization of the church, first of all, it was the clergy, rather than the martyrs and confessors, who became the bulwark against the *saeculum*, the "fighting line" against the world. Secondly, the church's establishment within the empire and the growth of asceticism meant that sexual continence, far from being one aspect of a "daily martyrdom," rose to prominence as its foremost expression.[5]

One of the most significant forms of this sacralization and cultification was represented by one of the very things that Jesus had rejected (see Mk 7:19): the cultic purity of the Old Testament with its distinctions between what was considered unclean or clean. A foremost champion of the notion of periodic continence for priestly service was Cyprian, who promoted the notion as early as the third century.

There were also various sects that promoted various forms of sex-rejection, like the Marcionites and some Gnostics. The Encratites, for their part, taught that salvation *depended* on sexual continence. While the teachings of these groups were considered extreme, they reflected a growing tendency among some Christians to use a unique form of non-sexual expression to mark their boundaries from wider society. Peter Brown writes: "Lacking the clear ritual boundaries provided in Judaism by circumcision and dietary laws, Christians tended to make their exceptional sexual discipline bear the full burden of expressing the difference between themselves and the pagan world."[6]

The "cultic purity" arguments which were based in Jewish Law began to be raised in more earnest at the Council of Elvira in Spain, in the first quarter of the fourth century. The logic seemed to be as follows: since Jewish priests in the Old Testament were required to abstain from genital intercourse at those times they performed altar service, Christian priests offering the perfect sacrifice at the altar should likewise be called to the perfection of purity. And, the argument went on, there is something unclean and, therefore impure, about genital intercourse. Thus celibacy was necessary for cultic purity for priests. This argument seemed to gain strength as daily mass began to come more in vogue by the end of the fourth century.

Bishops of the Iberian peninsula participated in the Council of Elvira. Tradition holds that the nineteen bishops attending this local council spent the majority of their time discussing whether celibacy was a more perfect state than marriage. The council supposedly passed the first canon to have been enacted in the early church demanding celibacy of bishops, priests, and all who serve at the altar. It stated: "It has seemed good absolutely to forbid the bishops, the priests, and the deacons, i.e., all the clerics in the service of the ministry, to abstain from conjugal relations and not to procreate children: whoever should do so, let him be excluded from the honor of the clergy."[7] The link of celibacy with "the honor of the clergy" also reveals a power/control dimension. Shame was connected with having genital intercourse. Honor could be sought elsewhere than the marriage act. Although priests could remain married, they were not to have intercourse.

Canon 33 related to a demand for celibacy among the clergy. However, a review of all eighty-one canons from Elvira makes it clear that this council recognized that clerical control over the laity was necessary and that celibacy was the most effective means of establishing this control. Especially in those canons dealing with sexual matters, Samuel Laeuchli shows that the legislation served two basic functions: the establishment of social coherence in the church's search for identity, and the creation of a clerical image necessary to strengthen the clergy's control over the faithful.[8]

Between this council and the first truly "ecumenical council" at Nicaea in 325, other local councils included various decrees related to the promotion of a celibate clergy (especially Arles and Ancyra, 314, and Neocaesarea, 314-325). Nicaea considered banning priests from marrying but decided against making such a universal decree. Probably the only memorable thing from Nicaea related to celibacy was the legendary intervention of someone called Paphnutius. Defending a married clergy, he declared: "We are not angels but men." The legend persisted until the Gregorian reforms when the papacy decreed that the story could no longer be discussed.[9]

Fifteen years after Nicaea, another local council at Gangres for-
mulated a decree which declared anathema anyone who affirmed
that people should *not* receive communion during a liturgy celebrated by a married priest.

While conciliar decrees had some effect on the gradual imposition of celibacy, the decrees from the papacy seemed to have
greater power. In fact, this gradual imposition of celibacy upon the
clergy, I have shown elsewhere, became the main way of establishing papal control.[10] In 385, Pope Siricius allegedly decreed that
bishops, priests, and deacons should be celibate, including those
who had wives. A year later, he issued a similar decree, grounding
his rationale in arguments about cultic purity. Priestly celibacy got
linked with the notion that sexual intercourse made one impure
and that, if a priest would be offering the pure sacrifice, he could
not be sexually soiled without tainting the sacrifice: "All priests
who want their daily sacrifices to be pleasing to our God must
remain continually chaste."[11]

In 390, at the regional Council of Carthage, some bishops met
in that North African city and issued a decree which made the
celibacy-cultic purity connection quite clear:

> The rule of continence and chastity had been discussed in a
> previous council. Let it [now] be taught with more empha-
> sis what are the three ranks that, by virtue of their consecra-
> tion, are under the same obligation of chastity, i.e., the
> bishop, the priest, and the deacon, and let them be instruct-
> ed to keep their purity. . . . It pleases us all that bishop,
> priest, and deacon, guardians of purity, abstain from [con-
> jugal intercourse] with their wives, so that those who serve
> at the altar may keep a perfect chastity.[12]

As the document seems to imply, despite such legal decrees,
married clergy still were the norm. However the promotion of
celibacy as a manifestation of ritual purity elevated the priest to a
special position in the community. Donald Gelpi refers to this as
"fourth-century sacerdotalism." By this he means that the clergy
were encouraged "to look upon themselves as a moral and spiritual elite that patterned itself consciously on the levitical priesthood."[13]

Another reason for promoting clerical celibacy in the fourth
century was connected with the recruitment of brothers from the
monasteries to be priests and bishops. While making a distinction

between "secular" and "religious" clergy, from this time on, the form of celibate life of the "religious" clergy gradually came to be applied normatively to the "secular" clergy. In time, the celibacy of the anchorites, the cenobites, and the monks became the ideal for all priests. Still, the married clergy continued to be the pattern for the next centuries. Sometimes this situation was allowed under the guise that even married priests were remaining celibate, as is indicated in the communications of Pope Innocent I (401-417).

Pope St. Leo the Great (440-461) extended the requirement of clerical continence to include subdeacons. During his reign and in the years after, many other local councils in Africa, Spain, Gaul, Italy, Armenia, and Persia reaffirmed celibacy for all the clergy. Although Pope St. Gregory the Great (590-605) strongly affirmed celibacy, the succeeding centuries witnessed the discipline challenged, undermined, and generally disregarded. During this time the Latin church allowed its priests to marry, but told them to practice celibacy within married life. Given the confusion which resulted, plus the virtual impossibility of such a situation, the discipline fell into disrepute.

In face of the collapse, many bishops and popes issued decrees to rectify the situation. Yet, as the bishop of Liege discovered, should he enforce the law of celibacy for his priests, he would have to dismiss his entire clergy.[14] Despite the efforts of various reform synods which insisted on celibacy, a practical kind of "don't ask, don't tell" rule took over. Lip service was given to the decrees, and discretion was asked lest there be public scandal.

In the sixth and seventh centuries, various councils tried to reform clerical corruption and the absolutizing tendencies of the papacy, but their efforts were merely futile. Clerics continued creating new ways to maintain their positions; Roman popes played politics to ensure their own increasing power. An understandable result of this dynamic was the transfer of the locus of control from the laity to the clergy. In fact, as Peter Brown ably articulates, it represented the clergy as a group over and against the laity who supported it:

> What made the history of the Christian Church notably different from that of other religious groups was the constant anxiety of its clergy to define their own position against the principal benefactors of the Christian community. Early Christians came to expect that their leaders should possess

recognizable and perpetual tokens of superiority to the laity: they might be expected to give evidence of a charismatic calling; they were encouraged, if possible, to practice perpetual continence; even when both these criteria were lacking, only they had received due ordination through the "laying on of hands." This, in turn, gave them an exclusive role in the celebration of the Eucharist that was the central rite of the Christian community.[15]

The Gregorian Reforms and Gradual Universalization

The second period of concentrated efforts to impose celibacy came with the election of Popes Leo IX (1049) and Gregory VII (1075). With the development of legislation directed by them and their successors in the late eleventh and early twelfth centuries, "the law of clerical continence was transformed into the law of clerical celibacy."[16]

Leo insisted, as papal policy, that subdeacons take a vow of chastity and that unchaste priests be excommunicated. He encouraged the laity to boycott any Mass offered by a married priest. However, his efforts may have been undermined by the possibility that he himself may not have been chaste. Despite his own alleged aberrations, Leo did surround himself with men dedicated to this reform group promoting celibacy. In fact, Peter Damian (later to be declared a saint) became one of his most ardent defenders.

Peter Damian was from a large, poor family and was a victim of abuse himself. He was rejected by his mother, who refused to nurse him. Ironically, he was saved from dying by a neighboring priest's wife. Peter Damian's childhood experience, no doubt had something to do with his attitude toward sex. He considered the body a mass of putrefaction, worms, dust, and ashes. For him incontinence was the chief clerical vice. Like others before him, he placed the blame for clerical deviations and lapses on women. In one of his oft-quoted sermons, the ideological misogyny is represented:

> You vipers full of madness, parading the ardor of your ungovernable lust, through your lovers you mutilate Christ, who is the head of the clergy. . . . You snatch away the unhappy men from their ministry of the sacred altar, in which they were engaged, that you may strangle them with the slimy glue of your passion. . . .The ancient foe pants to

invade the summit of the church's chastity through you. . . .
You suck the blood of miserable, unwary men, so that you
might inflate into their innermost parts a lethal poison.
They should kill you . . . for is there any hand with sacred
chrism that you shake with fear not to touch, or oil that you
do not defile, or even pages of the gospels and epistles that
you do not use familiarly [in an obscene way]?[17]

Leo was succeeded by a series of short-reigning pontiffs.
Although many of these continued to be influenced by Peter
Damian, they did not achieve any great reforms of the clergy or
changes in the celibacy rules. Paradoxically, their pontificates are
notable for the presence of a countervailing force to the increasing
effort to make the clergy celibate. A representation of this is found
in the person of an Italian bishop, Ulric of Imola, who lived in the
middle of the eleventh century. The main thrust of a "rescript" he
allegedly wrote was to condemn the decrees of Nicholas II regarding clerical continence as unjust and impious, non-canonical and
indiscreet. He argued that one of the main effects of compulsory
celibacy would be to drive the clergy into homosexual relationships. Arguing that celibacy is a gift, he concluded that the imposition of celibacy went against nature:

"Since therefore the good of continence, indeed every good,
is the gift of divine grace alone, capable of being embraced
neither through mandate, nor through one's own free will,
they not only err but indeed they labour in vain, who
attempt to force chastity on these men."[18]

He also scored those who distorted the scriptures seeking to
justify the rule of celibacy as "straining the breast of scripture until
it yielded blood instead of milk." The influence of leaders like
Ulric would be great enough to merit his solemn condemnation at
a council in 1079.

Another one of Leo's chief councilors was Hildebrand, who
would one day succeed him as Pope Gregory VII. When Gregory
ascended the throne of the papacy, the reputation of the priesthood
seemed to have reached rock bottom. The clergy had become effectively secularized and feudalized. Candidates for priesthood were
often chosen more on their loyalty to a human lord than the Lord.
The married clergy considered their offices as hereditary; church
endowments enriched priestly families. This created entire priestly

dynasties of clerical bureaucrats. Married priests and bishops often treated their ecclesiastical offices as family property and converted their sacred dignity into family heirlooms.[19] Increasing demands came from the people to be freed from the evils of such clerical aberrations.

Gregory, in an effort to control this corrupt situation, decreed that no one could become a cleric without having made a vow of celibacy. Furthermore he forbade all the laity to participate in any religious service celebrated by any married clergyman be it subdeacon, deacon, priest, or bishop. As the rationale for his efforts, Gregory revealed Peter Damian's influence on his thinking. He wrote that "one cannot touch both the body of Christ and the body of a whore." With such rhetoric, Barstow writes, "Gregory was escalating the conflict by the vehemence of his language, and was using language politically to discredit the marital relations of licit but restricted unions."[20] He was also creating greater control for himself.

First with Leo, and especially with Gregory, came serious church-wide efforts to reform the abuses of the clergy related to marriage. These abuses revolved around lay investiture and simony. However, a side-effect of eliminating these aberrations was an ever-increasing centralization of clerical and papal control in the church.[21] As in any control-defined situation, fear and intimidation were the rules: Gregory demanded that all in major orders live in clerical households, support each other in "moral purity," and report on any deviant behavior among fellow clergymen.

While the engine that generated what is known as the "Gregorian reforms" came from the papacy, the fuel that offered the energy for the generation can be found in the influence of monasticism which was at the heart of a new kind of feudalism. With "the feudalization of the ministry and the sacerdotalization of monasticism"[22] came what Paul Beaudette calls the "monasticization of ministry." By this he means that "the forms of ministry were reduced to service within the monastic community, and the liturgical priesthood. The great liturgies and the private Mass were centered in the monastery. This monastic ideal was presented as a model to priests."[23] The resulting "monastic model" for the diocesan clergy (stressing the vows of poverty, chastity, and obedience in various forms) prevailed well into the mid-twentieth century. One of the earliest signs of the monastic influence on the diocesan clergy came with the creation of various communities of canons regular throughout Europe in the eleventh and twelfth centuries. These were clerics who lived together under a monastic rule.

In 1119, at the Council of Rheims, Pope Callixtus II, a successor of Gregory, saw to it that married clergy would be expelled from office and excommunicated if they continued to live with their wives. Such decrees continued to offer a rationale for such discipline by linking the priest's cultic role with the need for celibacy. Again, not far below that rationale was the issue of control, be it the pope's control over priests or priests' control over the people. As Barstow writes;

> Gradually the clergy were being more closely controlled by their bishops who were, in turn, more tightly supervised by Rome. The priesthood was being set further apart from the laity, who had begun to insist on a celibate ministry. And, as this happened, the priesthood's power through the sacraments, especially of confession and penance, began to increase.[24]

At the First Lateran Council (1123), the clergy were forbidden to marry. Those clergy already in marriages were ordered to dissolve them. This decision, in the eyes of many, represents the final form of a definitive law making the marriages of priests, deacons, and subdeacons invalid. Although there is some debate about whether the First Lateran Council actually made marriage for priests invalid, in 1135 the Synod of Pisa for the first time declared that marriage was impossible for a cleric in major orders. Pisa's decree was appropriated into the decrees of the Second Lateran Council in 1139.

With these decisions, Rome officially began to honor celibacy as a "more perfect way" than marriage. The link to a greater "purity" in celibacy than marriage again was the rationale. This notion of the vow of celibacy taking precedence over marriage vows was established at the Second Lateran Council of 1139. If the marital act was impure, the logic went, and priests had to offer a pure sacrifice, then priests could not be married and, if they were, they could not have sex. The Second Lateran Council, in passing the first universal law of celibacy dealing with validity, declared that ordination was an impediment to marriage.

Succeeding councils, as well as various published collections of legal decrees, reinforced the demand for clerical celibacy. The apogee of the effort of the decretalists came in 1140 with the publication of "Gratian's Decrees," the forerunner to modern canon law. Canonists succeeding Gratian justified clerical celibacy on the grounds that the vow of celibacy was inherent in the sacrament of orders itself. As happened too often with other such legislation, the issue of control, defined the dynamics of the laws, especially the need of the hierarchy to assert its power over priests and, ultimately over the people. Bernard Cooke makes this point clear:

> At every step of the way, the extension of clerical celibacy and its establishment finally as universal discipline was a matter of legislation and enforcement by means of threat and coercion, rather than by way of convincing through intrinsic argumentation or inspiration. This is not to say that such intrinsic reasons for celibacy did not exist, or that the ideal of celibacy should have convinced patristic and medieval clergy; it is simply to observe that the institutionalization of clerical celibacy came through law and sanction, and was effectively imposed only when church authority became absolutely monarchic (and effectively so) under Gregory VII and a succession of powerful medieval popes.[25]

The reasons why priests would violate their promises of celibacy need not be isolated to the argument that many were unlearned. One need only examine the lives of some of the popes—very learned men—to see the opposite. On the contrary, parish priests could emulate popes like Alexander VI by publicly fathering many children. It is not surprising, then, that in fifteenth-century Burgundy, half of the children born out of wedlock for whom legitimation was asked, were children of priests. In the words of church historian Daniel-Rops: "Rome had set the example of a scandal whose repercussions were felt in the most distant corners of the church."[26] Such aberrations begged for reform.

Trent and Succeeding Centuries

Shortly before the Reformation, which might be considered a reaction to the sacralization and cultification of the priesthood, Josse Clichtove (1472-1543) became well-known for his effort to reform the life and spirituality of the clergy. Since many priests were not involved in pastoral work, he promoted a theology of priesthood not dependent on the pastoral role. The primary duty of the priest was to celebrate cultic and sacramental functions; pastoral duties, if necessary, came after. While distinguishing between the celibacy of the clergy and that of the monks, Clichtove interpreted celibacy as an essential part of the cultic demand that priests be separate from the people. Eventually Clichtove even taught that priestly celibacy was based in the natural law as well as the divine law, and that legislation from the church merely sanctions these ordinations. Consequently, he insisted, the pope could not dispense from the church's law regarding priestly celibacy.

Influenced by his teachings and building on the decrees related to celibacy from the Lateran Councils, the Council of Trent became the locus for the third great effort to concentrate clerical control in the hands of celibates. If the Reformation represented a reaction against the cultic priesthood and the imposition of celibacy and monasticism in its various power manifestations, the counter-reform led by the forces gathered at Trent seemed to reinforce these dimensions. The counter-reformers reiterated the ban on marriage for priests and the superiority of virginity to marriage, again for reasons of cultic purity. Marriage and priesthood were mutually exclusive in that the former represented the profane; the other the sacred. Marriage involved the world; the cultic priesthood demanded separation from the world.

The majority of those who attended the Council of Trent did not subscribe to Clichtove's contention that the law of celibacy was divine in origin; for them it was a matter of ecclesiastical law. Yet there was a great deal of difference of opinion regarding its juridical status, especially in considering the possibility of exemption from the law or the vow. In the end, on November 11, 1563, two critical canons (9 and 10) were approved:

> If anyone says that clerics in sacred orders or regular clergy who have made solemn profession of chastity can contract marriage and that the contract is valid, despite the law of the church and their vow notwithstanding, and that the opposite opinion is nothing but a condemnation of marriage, or if anyone says that all those who feel that they do not have the gift of chastity (even if they have vowed it) can contract marriage: let him be anathema. For God does not deny the gift to those who petition for it in a correct manner, nor does he permit us to be tempted beyond our strength.

> If anyone says that the marriage state is to be preferred to the state of virginity or of celibacy, and that it is not better and holier to remain in virginity and in celibacy than to be joined in marriage (see Mt 19:11f; 1 Cor 7:25, 38, 40); let him be anathema.[27]

One of the unique wordings emanating from the ninth canon of Trent was the notion of "gift" in connection to celibacy. The council marked one of the first times official teaching indicated that God would grant the grace of perseverance in celibacy to those who asked. Consequently the clergy were expected to ask for the gift. Trent declared anathema any who said that clerics who felt they did not have the gift of chastity could marry. This teaching prevailed for centuries. It was codified in the 1918 Code of Canon Law.

The Code of Canon Law also connected celibacy to the ritual (and personal) purity of the priest. It declared that higher clergy were "forbidden to marry, and are bound by this obligation to observe chastity so that, in offending against it, they are guilty also of sacrilege."[28] In other words, if a priest would have genital relations, his body would be soiled. Being a soiled person, he would thus commit a sacrilege by celebrating the divine mysteries. The body of a priest must be culticly pure.

A result of the juridical nature of Trent can be found in the ever-increasing concentration of power and control among the people in the hands of the clergy, among the clergy in the hands of the hierarchy, and among the hierarchy in the hands of the pope. Crichton notes that, with this centralization of authority increasingly away from the laity, "the juridical emphasis became ever greater and the growth of the pyramid church ever more irresistible."[29] With Trent, the clergy came to be increasingly identified more with power and control than preaching and proclaiming God's reign.

That all said, possibly the most significant result of Trent's solidification of power in the celibate clergy came, not from the promulgation of codes about it, but in its decision that initiated the seminary system for the training of priests. The decree ordered that the bishop of every diocese where no university existed should establish a seminary to train boys and young men for the priesthood. According to J. D. Crichton, this decision was critical in effecting the professionalization and prestige of the secular clergy:

It can be said with a fair degree of truth that whereas in the middle ages it was bishops (often very unpastoral) and religious who held the field and dominated the scene, after Trent it was the priest in his parish. Over the centuries his professional competence, his spiritual quality and his pastoral zeal steadily grew and, with whatever limitations, he became a preaching minister of the Church. All this and indeed much more must be credited to the seminary system.[30]

From the seventeenth century on, inspired by the "French School" of leaders like Pierre de Berulle, the identification of a priest moved from a stress on his cultic role to his mystical representation of Christ himself. Berulle's influence was great in redefining the notion of the priest as someone set apart from others. Probably the most well-known representative of the French School was Jean Jacques Olier, the founder of the Company of St. Sulpice (the "Sulpicians").

Another force arising from France was the Enlightenment which reached its peak in the French Revolution. The post-revolutionary period represents the last time a general dispensation from clerical celibacy was authorized. According to Beaudette:

The Revolution was not only in many ways the implementation of the Enlightenment; it also moved the question of clerical celibacy from the theoretical into the practical arena. When the Constitution of 1791 provided that no profession could debar a person from marriage and that no public official or notary could refuse to ratify a marriage on such a ground, the French clergy was split in two, with marriage being considered a pledge of loyalty to, and continued celibacy a silent protest against, the new regime. After the Reign of Terror, one of the first efforts at reorganizing the church was directed at the restoration of celibacy. Following the signing of the Concordat with Napoleon, which left the internal discipline of the church to itself, 3224 priests and religious petitioned either for reinstatement or for the regularization of their marriages. Of these over 2000 chose the latter. The arrangement at the end of the French Revolution reducing clerics to the lay state and validating their marriages marked the . . . last time in modern history that the church has authorized a general dispensation from the discipline.[31]

I find quite striking the parallels between the post-revolutionary period and the years since Vatican II. In both cases one must first ask the motivation of those who sought ordination. Was it for power and prestige due to being part of a clerical caste that influenced men to join? Was it to be part of a clerical caste that one would be willing to take on celibacy? It would seem that these possible rationales helped people forego marriage, until marriage came to be valued from experience (as with the Revolution) or in better theology (as with Vatican II). In both cases, the result was the same: a mass exodus from the clerical to the married state. This "exodus" leads us to the present period.

Post-Vatican II Priestly Celibacy as Defining Boundaries of Control

At Vatican II Pope Paul VI insisted that any public discussion of celibacy at the council was "absolutely inopportune." His declaration was not challenged seriously by the conciliar fathers. However, what did get challenged at the council, at least by its non-use of the notion, was the time-honored justification for clerical celibacy through the appeal for cultic purity. By that time, enough good scholarship had penetrated the ideology of those writing the documents and proffering rationales for priestly celibacy, and the argument lost its former credibility. With its renewed stress on the priesthood of all believers and the value of the world, the very notion of a clerical caste also became more anachronistic. Though the *Decree on the Training of Priests* still urged candidates for the priesthood to "recognize the greater excellence of virginity consecrated to Christ,"[32] it did not clearly state that this "greater excellence" established virginity above marriage.

Vatican II stressed the sanctity of marriage, which limited further the connections that identified the reason for clerical celibacy with the need for cultic purity. But even this was not achieved overnight. Despite the council's newer approach, the notion of cultic purity for priests demanding celibacy still got resurrected as a main rationale for the discipline of celibacy. In his statement of February 2, 1975 the pope referred to the fact that priests and members of the consecrated life were celibate to maintain a "purity of the body."[33]

Allowing for this seeming slip back to the former rationale, the ultimate rejection of the cultic purity reason for priestly chastity had an unforeseen consequence. If the main reason used to justify a practice is discounted, what will the rationale be to continue that practice? Hanz-Jurgen Vogels has argued that the illogic of the rationale—which was used for centuries to justify the discipline—now calls into question the disciplinary laws that were made based on this justification.[34]

Specifically commenting on the former rationale based on cultic purity, Vogels asks, "Can the celibacy law then bind the conscience when its original basis and moral aim, the 'purity of priests,' has been recognized as mistaken and has seemingly not been replaced by any new basis on which to justify so far-reaching an obligation?" Arguing from the dictum that states, *cessante causa cessat lex*, Vogels concludes: "If the objective of keeping priests from 'impure' activity within marriage has disappeared—and in fact nobody dares to repeat the original motivation of the law—then we have to ask whether the law has any compelling force at present."[35] If the core reason for a law no longer holds, that law seems to lack juridical foundation.

At this point it is important to understand the underlying issue which prevails, despite the fact that the arguments around preserving clerical celibacy to maintain ritual purity no longer prevail. The core of the celibacy issue remains connected to the need to preserve clerical control. The need to preserve clerical control demands that some other justification be found if it is to be preserved and if the system of patriarchal clericalism is to be maintained.

Until Vatican II, when the institutional church had effective control over the minds and hearts of its members, clerical celibacy represented an unquestioned part of the culture of hierarchical control. In fact, the specific culture of the Catholic church in its Latin Rite could be defined as a celibate culture with the cleric at the center of the community. Clerical celibacy was pre-eminent in the minds and hearts of all. The leaders and laws which constituted the core of that Catholic culture could define its clerics as celibate and few disagreed. Those lay people who did voice dissent were labeled "Protestant-thinking." Priests who dissented were disloyal at best. Those who "left" the priesthood were selfishly sexual at the worst. "Good" priests did not "fall." Shame controlled the dynamics and the discipline. Silence controlled any deviations.

With the discrediting of the "cultic purity" arguments and the Second Vatican Council abrogating the "virginity is better than marriage" argument with its universal call to holiness, a new rationale to justify priestly celibacy was needed. As Mary Malone explained: "much of the old argumentation . . . [about celibacy was] wiped away by contemporary biblical exegesis, the human sciences and the theological re-evaluation of marriage."[36] But, again, where would the new argument come from?

It seems the rationale proffered at Trent would be resurrected. This revolved around the notion of God giving the gift or charism of celibacy. Now Matthew 19:11-12—with its notion of celibacy being "given"—was invoked in a conciliar decree. Nobody declared, however, that this passage was written before anything such as priests as we know them existed! Be that as it may, now priests were told to ask God for the grace of the gift to fulfill their promise to live a celibate life. This argument underlies the rationale proffered by the Second Vatican Council. It admitted that celibacy is not "demanded by the very nature of the priesthood, as is evident from the practice of the Eastern Churches" and that the council "in no way intends to change that different discipline which lawfully prevails in the Eastern Church." However, again appealing to the Matthean and Pauline texts, the *Decree on the Ministry and Life of Priests* concluded of celibacy:

> In the Latin Church, it was imposed by law on all who were to be promoted to sacred orders. This legislation, to the extent that it concerns those who are destined for the priesthood, this most holy Synod again approves and confirms. It trusts in the Spirit that the gift of celibacy, which so befits the priesthood of the New Testament, will be generously bestowed by the Father, as long as those who share in Christ's priesthood through the sacrament of orders, and indeed the whole Church, humbly and earnestly pray for it.[37]

Like previous arguments, this new rationale which considers celibacy to be a "gift" appears to be fraught with internal contradictions. The first contradiction deals with the difference between something imposed and something offered freely, between something institutionally mandated and something chosen because of a sense of call. The second contradiction can be termed a *deus ex machina* or a *post hoc, ergo propter hoc* argument which, in effect, states that even if it is not connected and yet demanded, someone asking for the grace will get it. It's as if we can control God to give a grace because we ask for it, even when it may not be God's chosen grace for us!

When the council asks the priest to pray for the gift, it seems an assumption is made that the gift cannot come through the law but through the prayer. Thus, if one who is a priest does not pray for the gift, from where will the "gift" of celibacy come? From the law? The contradictions in this rationale seem abundant. What we have here, in the words of Wulf, "seems not to be an answer" but "an uncontrollable reliance upon the Spirit."[38]

This "ask and you will receive" celibacy rationale that seeks to find a resolution to the law-gift dichotomy has led Vogels to conclude:

> But the Spirit has already shown us, in scripture and tradition, where we have to look for a solution to the crucial problem of gift and law. According to the New Testament, the charisma cannot be obtained by prayer, and this was confirmed indirectly by the Council of Trent when it did not expressly include the ability to obtain it by prayer in its definition.[39]

The New Testament understanding of charism notwithstanding, because of the law imposed by those with power to interpret the scriptures, priests are told they who ask will receive the gift. Somehow the gift of orders to the priests, along with their prayer and the prayer for the gift by the whole church, will make it happen. Somehow, the gift will magically make it happen.

In 1983, with the Revised Code of Canon Law, the heart of the matter about priestly celibacy was stated clearly: "Clerics are obliged to observe perfect and perpetual continence for the sake of the kingdom of heaven and therefore are obliged to observe celibacy, which is a special gift from God."[40] A breakdown of this sentence reveals two main threads: one addresses an ecclesiastical demand; the other deals with a scriptural warrant. Clerics are bound to observe perfect and perpetual continence and are obliged to live in celibacy. This continence is for the "sake of the kingdom;" the celibacy is "a special gift from God."

While these attitudes have changed in the minds of most laity, the vision of the old Catholic culture still seems to prevail in the Vatican. In speaking of Pope John Paul II and his insistence on celibacy for secular priests, Gordon Thomas wrote in *Desire and Denial: Celibacy and the Church* (1986):

> The Pope has repeatedly stressed there can be no argument about a decision originally made at a time when the Catholic Church was a totally dominant institution and had no difficulty in enforcing its holy writ. He insists that celibacy remains nonnegotiable. For nine centuries the Church has maintained its hold over both clergy and sisterhood by commanding that "service in moral leadership" depends on the total sacrifice of all sexual desires.
>
> But modern scholarship and, in the wake of the Second Vatican Council, a growing informed critical attitude among young priests and nuns have meant that the word of Rome, and particularly the view of Pope John Paul, are not accepted with the blind obedience of old.[41]

With the underpinning arguments which historically have been used to justify clerical celibacy de-legitimated, we face a crisis. We could revert to the situation a millennium ago when the papacy decreed that nobody could discuss what Paphnutius allegedly argued at Nicaea. That approach has already been used related to discussions about women priests. Fortunately, whether in the tenth century or the twentieth, papal decrees for silence cannot quell the debate about sex and women, marriage and clerical control.

In an effort to change the focus of the debate, the papacy now says the crisis of clerical celibacy is not with clerical celibacy but in the decadent culture wherein it must be lived. That our culture, embedded as it is in capitalist forms of control, is decadent will get no argument from me. But another culture that has its own share of decadence (if decadent means dying) can be found in the clerical culture itself. As Philip Sheldrake has concluded in his *Celibacy and Clerical Culture*, celibacy's "crisis" cannot be linked simplistically to supposed psycho-sexual problems in contemporary society. Rather:

> Many people now realize that it is traditional clerical culture that is at issue. This easily became like a men's club— the Masonic lodge or the officers' mess—safe environments

where men can "be themselves" without outside interfer-
ence. If celibacy is to survive as a viable and accepted
option it must be detached from the historically conditioned contexts within which it has existed for so long.[42]

As long as celibacy is used in the Roman church as a means of
control, it will be evident that the hierarchy's underlying goal is
not about feeding the flock the eucharistic bread. Rather it will
seem that it is willing to deny people the eucharist in the face of
evidence that a change in the celibacy laws would bring in more
candidates for the priesthood. According to Dean Hoge, the ordination of married men would solve the clergy-shortage problem:

As we have seen, the celibacy requirement is the single
most important deterrent to new vocations to the priesthood, and if it were removed, the flow of men into seminaries would increase greatly, maybe fourfold. Therefore this
option provides a solution to the shortage of priests. As we
said earlier, if celibacy were optional, probably the number
of Catholic priests would increase over a period of years
until it hit a financial limit, that is, until as many priests
were in service as the Catholic community could financial-
ly support.[43]

The obligation to provide the eucharist is more critical to the
life of the church than the obligation to maintain celibates for the
eucharistic celebration. In this sense, the words of Karl Rahner, in
his "Open Letter on Celibacy," ring true:

"If the church everywhere or in certain areas is unable to
find enough clergy unless she abandons celibacy, then she
must abandon it; for the obligation to provide enough pastors for the Christian people takes precedence over the
ideal, legitimate in itself, of having a celibate clergy."[44]

Rahner's conclusion about the priority of the people's need for
the eucharist over the need of some in the institution to preserve
clerical celibacy brings us to a deeper issue as we conclude this
chapter. The first three periods regarding the institutional church's
approach to celibacy found it promoted because of faulty grounding in the scriptures and approaches to liturgical celebration as
well as the need to address deviations among the clergy. However,
we now live in a fourth period marked by ever-decreasing numbers of priests and ever-increasing numbers of Catholics. Why do

we maintain a demand for clerical celibacy when we have discovered what the scriptures truly mean about it and when ritual purity has been discounted as a rationale for priestly celibacy? It has become increasingly clear to me that the current situation cannot be attributed to the clergy, their abuses of celibacy, or anything else, as much as to the leaders who refuse to enable the church to celebrate its identity as the Body of Christ. To paraphrase Paul to the Corinthians, if they and their supporters continue to keep God's people from coming together to celebrate the eucharist by insisting that only male celibates can preside, they bring judgment on themselves.

3

The Internal Contradictions
Resulting from Imposed Celibacy

An expanded understanding of the scriptural foundation for celibacy indicates that Matthew's Jesus considered it to be something applicable to a very few. Yet, paradoxically, celibacy has become something a few have made obligatory for many. Although the rules related to mandatory celibacy might reinforce elements of control in our particular Latin tradition, they actually undermine the deeper call of Jesus to "do this in memory of me," especially regarding the celebration of the eucharist.

This reflects a situation of control which has bound up many, with very few leaders apparently trying to lift the heavy burden the hierarchy has imposed (see Mt 23:5). Wrongly and unjustly, a celibacy requirement has become the norm for key positions of ministry in the church. The words of Jesus to the leaders of his religious institution who abused their power thus seem apropos: "So, for the sake of your tradition, you make void the word of God. You hypocrites! Isaiah prophesied rightly about you when he said: 'This people honors me with their lips, but their hearts are far from me; in vain do they worship me, teaching human precepts as doctrines'" (Mt 15:6-9).[1]

Because of this tradition and the ideological justification used to reinforce mandatory celibacy (especially for diocesan priests and homosexual Catholics who believe no charism of celibacy has been "given them"), we now face a host of what I term "internal contradictions" in the present approach to celibacy. This chapter attempts to address these internal contradictions, and to enunciate the historical and cultural conditioning which gave rise to them. Although the emphasis will be on diocesan priesthood and homosexual Catholics, I will begin with some contradictions that must be acknowledged regarding celibacy among "consecrated" members of religious congregations. My remarks refer especially to men in these three groups in places like Western Europe and North America, Australia and New Zealand.[2]

Implications for Members of Religious Congregations

In 1966, toward the end of the Second Vatican Council, I worked at Franciscan Communications Center in Los Angeles. I lived with the Franciscans at the St. Joseph Friary, located next door in the heart of the inner city. Among the interesting constellation of members in that community, perhaps the local superior (or "minister" as we Franciscans call our leaders) was the most unique.

Almost daily, to any who would listen, the local minister would voice his concern that the council fathers did not seem willing to address the issue that he had uppermost on his mind, namely, mandatory celibacy. With each recitation of his thoughts on the matter his feelings seemed to intensify. Whether because of his authority in the community or his passionate articulation of his views, few felt willing to challenge him. Being naive, and also quite self-righteous, I decided one day to take him on.

"I'm all for optional celibacy for diocesan priests," I said. "But I don't know why you seem to be so emotional about this issue. You are a religious. We have freely chosen to be celibate." "Not me," he countered. "I wanted to be a priest. I wanted to minister as a priest. The Franciscans were the only priests I knew when I was growing up. So I entered them. I ended up being a Franciscan because it was all part of the package." "Well, if that's the case," I responded quite righteously, "I think you could sit down today, write your letter asking for a dispensation, and the Vatican would give it." Soon after this, the man did indeed leave the Franciscans and the priesthood.

This Franciscan's conflation of religious life with priesthood was well expressed a few years later by John Jay Hughes, who found parallels throughout clerical religious congregations of men. Writing in 1969, he described a situation that still prevails more than we religious, especially we clerical religious, would like to admit:

The current debate over clerical celibacy manifests much confusion of thought and not a little naiveté. During a recent American lecture tour the writer was told of a public opinion survey which contained the question: "Should celibacy be abolished only for the diocesan clergy, or for religious priests as well?" And the presence of religious, who unlike the diocesan clergy have taken a vow of chastity, in the vanguard of those clamoring for abolition of the present discipline is hardly a sign of vigorous spiritual health in the religious orders to which such priests belong. It would seem that many of these orders have failed to imbue their members with the conviction that their vocation is different than that of the secular clergy, and that their contribution to the church's life and work is a distinctive one. Many, perhaps most, religious priests in the Untied States are, one suspects, religious by accident only.[3]

Besides the conflation of priesthood and religious life that took place in the past, there was another operational ideology that affected many candidates for orders such as mine. Simply put, it was the idea of "being better." In 1959 when I joined the Capuchin branch of the Franciscans, I never thought of entering the separate novitiate the province operated for lay brothers. I just assumed I would become a priest. So, when I visited the Capuchin contact-person asking for entrance into the novitiate, the only clarifying question he asked me was: "Why don't you want to be a diocesan priest?" My response was straight and simple: "Because religious priests go all the way."

Not only did he never challenge my "reasoning" on the issue, this attitude was reinforced in my years of formation through the teachings I received both directly and indirectly. Priesthood was held as the closest one could get to Christ. And religious priesthood seemed to take the call a step higher, to the highest state of perfection.

Today we know the contradictions and the theological futility of pursuing argumentation in support of religious life as pertaining to "something more" or "a better way." The Second Vatican Council expressed the universal call to holiness for all Christians and the role of religious life within that call. But in those days before Vatican II those former notions were formative for me.

My way of thinking in those years was complicated by another dynamic related to the church discipline and practice at that time which virtually limited any and all ministries and positions of leadership in the church to those who would embrace the diocesan priesthood or religious life. Thus, the *most effective* way one could respond to the baptismal mission was to become a priest or religious. Any other "calling" seemed second-best.

In addition to theological and pastoral reasons, there were some practical supports to reinforce one's commitment to be a religious, especially a religious priest. It was considered prestigious in that generation to "choose" to enter the priesthood or religious life. The wider Catholic community honored members who did so, especially if the community was ethnic. For others, joining the seminary or "the monastery" also represented a way of becoming upwardly mobile. These institutions offered better educational opportunities than those in the secular world, especially for the poor or women.

At any rate, in the late 1950s when I entered the seminary, the contemplative congregations were flourishing. Almost every apostolic congregation found itself building a novitiate or some kind of formation house. The groups considered monastic added new wings. Dioceses inaugurated massive development drives for the expansion of their seminaries. However, within a little over a generation, the novitiates have become retreat centers, the monastery wings have become retirement houses, and the expanded seminaries have become chancery offices. Concurrently, the daily prayers in the liturgy for "vocations to the priesthood and religious life" are multiplied, vocation recruiters burn out, and the remaining members watch helplessly as the median age increases. Meanwhile, the "young ones" come, stay for a few years, and leave. Bishops scour the Philippines and Poland recruiting priests for vacant parishes.

This lack of numbers today leads us to a type of "blame the victim" mentality that fears there must be something wrong with us. Rather than even consider that there may have been something wrong in the past expressions of celibacy, spurred by the memory of huge numbers in the religious life, we cling to notions of the "good old days." We deny the need to interpret in a new way the signs of the times. In the process, our dwindling resources find us preoccupied with creating new vocation programs geared to sustain a way of life that probably will never be again. Failing to listen to Jesus' own interpretation of celibacy as we find it in Matthew, we forget that when his vision is implemented there will be few celibates indeed. Did he not imply that it was only natural that few would accept celibacy? Why do we still insist that our way can be the exception to this?

In the autumn of 1994 the Eighth Extraordinary General Synod of Bishops met in Rome to discuss "The Consecrated Life and Its Role in the Church and in the World." When I read the "working document" for the 1994 synod, I was pleased at the inclusivity it manifested. I liked the way it incorporated contemporary writings on the "consecrated life." This term, stressed by the document, is used to cover celibacy and the other "evangelical counsels." It applied the notion to many different groups—from traditional religious orders to hermits, and from societies of apostolic life to consecrated virgins (as long as all have been given "church approval").[4] The statement noted the amazing numbers of these entities:

> Today there are approximately 1,423 institutes of women religious of pontifical right and 1,550 of diocesan right. Among the religious institutes for men there are 250 of pontifical right and 242 of diocesan right. There are approximately 165 secular institutes of pontifical or diocesan right, including those of priests, clerics, or groups of lay women and men. There are also 39 societies of apostolic life of pontifical right. To these we must add a growing number of consecrated virgins, of consecrated widows and widowers, hermits and hermitesses and other groups that have initiated the process of canonical recognition.[5]

The document noted also that, the "members of the institutes of consecrated life and societies of apostolic life number more than a million, but they are a minority within the people of God. In statistical terms they amount to only 12% of the members of the Catholic church."[6] And, of course, the numbers continue to dwindle. This seems verified in statistics for the United States. In 1968 there were 174,464 sisters; in 1991 101,911. In 1968 there were 22,984 ordained religious; in 1991 19,488. In 1968 there were 12,054 religious brothers; in 1991 6,896.

For various reasons, raw numbers of those choosing celibate lifestyles in the church may increase in developing nations for approximately the next decade. However, with the breakdown of castes, rising economic mobility, and new opportunities for ministry, I believe we gradually will witness these numbers leveling off. In the not too distant future the developing nations will also begin to experience the "diminishment" already being experienced in Europe, North America, Australia, New Zealand, and other areas of the Catholic world. Since the end of the Cold War, decreasing numbers of recruits are being reported in places like Poland and Yugoslavia where religious life did not need to be "underground" during the Cold War.

The Vatican's "working document" reflected the latest in the theology of the consecrated life. Yet, as I read it, I found myself comparing it to the last call before the curtain goes down on a great and beautiful play. With its stress on mission and "the new evangelization" the document articulated a form of life which once had great meaning; I know it provided much support to me. But its run is almost over. People already are wondering who will turn out the lights when the curtain comes down.

The evangelical counsels of poverty, chastity, and obedience were the common thread the document used to link the disparate forms of the consecrated life. Being evangelical, their basis has to be found in the life of Jesus as detailed in the gospels. However, the more one probes the gospels, the more I question whether the forms of obedience and poverty prescribed for those in the consecrated life truly have parallels in the life of the Jesus of the gospels. Increasingly I wonder whether "evangelical counsels" can be found in the *evangelion*. This seems especially true when it comes to the "evangelical counsel" of obedience.

First, our obedience as religious differs vastly from that of Jesus. His obedience as an adult was to no human being (as is ours), but to God. Neither did he obey God through any human surrogate, as do we. Furthermore, his form of obedience represents the form of obedience due God by all the baptized. Our form of religious obedience embraced by the vow or promise is within the institutional church. It is made to its variously-accepted religious leaders. The document makes it clear that all religious must obey the pope, the successor to Peter. I don't recall Jesus obeying Peter anywhere. So, if our obedience is "evangelical" because it is grounded in Jesus' example of submission, and since he submitted to no human being or religious leader, we will look long and hard before we can find examples of such "evangelical" obedience in the gospels.

Secondly, on a more practical level, when one compares the expression of obedience as undertaken by vowed religious with that of married people, the latters' degree of obedience on a day-to-day basis appears to be much more demanding. This fact was made clear to me by a perpetually-professed Jesuit who left his congregation to marry. Once married, he realized that obedience is not a once-yearly or once-every-six years matter connected to a transfer. Neither is its observance limited to the submission of an annual budget for approval. Rather, in a healthy marriage, obedience constitutes the core of the marriage vow itself; it demands daily accountability, loving submission, and an ongoing revision of life. He said: "The day I made solemn vows, in effect, I became responsible to no one. A major liability for those who are religious is that they never really feel the demands of being accountable to anyone." So, if obedience is viewed as responsibility and accountability, it hardly is "evangelical" in the way we religious seem to be living under its yoke today.

Thirdly, I believe that religious obedience today faces a crossroads. In communities where various forms of individualism have undermined the communitarian dimension of obedience, I think few would disagree with the notion that the obedience of diocesan priests to their bishops often can make more existential demands than that of a religious to a superior. As religious, many of us have been able to define our own ways of living. Though we may have submitted these lifestyle choices to be approved by superiors, we knew that the superior would give approval with a rubber stamp. This practice does not seem to occur very often with diocesan priests. Besides being changed every so many years, they must submit not only to bishops but personnel boards of their peers as well as periodic evaluation of their life and ministry.

The scriptural warrants for poverty as an evangelical counsel also raises some serious questions about its intended meaning. The continually proffered scriptural passages like Matthew 8:20 and 19:21 which have been used to justify a vow of poverty actually have more to do with basic requirements of discipleship. At least in Matthew, the discipleship that demands a re-ordering of one's life toward the poor is not a counsel; it is a *sine qua non* for all baptized Christians. When one seeks discipleship, solidarity with the poor is an inseparable dimension. Discipleship demands a re-ordering of one's life on behalf of the poor. Any poverty one might experience as a result, flows from the baptismal commitment to follow Jesus.

Furthermore, in the sources the scriptures identify with Jesus, especially those from Isaiah, the "evangelical counsel" which seems more critical to him than poverty is justice. In fact, as the parable of the Last Judgment points out, being "just" toward the poor will be the sign of one's sharing in the reign of God (Mt 25:31-46). Perhaps, in light of the injustice so rampant in our world—including poverty—justice is more at the heart of being an evangelical person today than poverty. But few religious today are involved in social justice work, and those who are often find conflicts with church authorities when they link issues of justice with aberrations in the institutional church.

Consequently, as I read the scriptures, the only real counsel of the traditional "three evangelical counsels" seems to be that related to the option for celibacy. In fact, I believe that celibacy must constitute the heart of any and all forms of consecrated life. My conclusion seems echoed by Edward Schillebeeckx, as well: "Strictly speaking, there is only one evangelical counsel in the gospel . . . therefore Christian celibacy is the only evangelical counsel properly so called and is left entirely up to the will of the individual Christian."[7]

Unfortunately, when you ask people questions related to how free they were when they embraced this counsel, their candid responses make one question the degree of freedom truly involved. In 1966, when I responded to the local minister in Los Angeles that I was free, I truly thought I was. It took me years to learn how wrong I had been. In fact, it was not until I actually encountered a woman I cared about deeply, that I realized how unfree I had been. In the future, I firmly believe, people will join the consecrated life primarily to be celibates. But in the last centuries this was not so, and it does not appear to be so now.

Much of my ministry involves giving retreats to diocesan priests and members of groups fitting the description of the consecrated life. For the last years, whenever I give talks on celibacy at these retreats, I have started out by asking how many became priests, or how many entered the consecrated life, to be celibate. Thus far, not one man has raised his hand. Only one woman has answered in the affirmative.

Unfortunately, the data shows that people still join religious congregations for the same primary reasons they did in the past: for the sake of becoming involved in ministry with the support of a community.[8] Thus it is little wonder that the Vatican's latest statement envisioned this same response. However, when the primary motive for joining (and remaining) is linked with mission, and the core reason that has made the consecrated life unique (celibacy) is not really addressed or supported, problems will arise.

Sandra Schneiders calls these "secondary" issues that have defined celibacy as *instrumental*. Dynamics like ministry and community serve as a means, not an end. She comments:

> What all of these situations have in common is that they are choices for relationships and/or ministry in communities which happen to be celibate, rather than a choice of celibacy as either the expression of one's own spiritual experience or as the way of directing one's own life energy.[9]

Increasingly, I am beginning to envision celibacy and "consecrated life" from the perspective of a paradigm that has shifted. Paradigms reveal basic ways of interpreting one's experience. According to Lucien Roy, when applied to church settings, paradigms involve three key components: 1) underlying theology or *story*, 2) interpersonal relationships or *style,* and 3) organizational makeup or *structure.*[10] According to Roy, any new paradigm will not function effectively until the three separate but interrelated components find sync. When this happens, a paradigm shift has occurred.

Paradoxically, just as the "working document" (from the 1994 Synod of Bishops) revealed an understanding of religious life which showed that the structure of the church has finally found sync with the story and the style operable in North American forms of religious life, the paradigm has begun to change. Just when the Vatican seemed open to embrace the story and the style with acceptable structures, a more radical story has begun to emerge. It is too early to even imagine what the style and structures are that will flesh out that story. However, I believe this new story represents the seeds of a new paradigm for celibacy. In the future its styles and structures will be very different. I believe that some of the story and style has already been put in place in that paradigm.

I am sure some will disagree with my analysis about many of the contradictions contained in the "consecrated life" and celibacy. I would love to be alive in a hundred years to see whether my understanding will find an echo in the consecrated life that will be common then. Of one thing I am convinced: while celibacy must be seen as the underlying link that has always constituted the essence of the consecrated life and always will, celibacy must be de-linked from its mandatory identification with the diocesan priesthood if the church will be faithful to the message of Jesus.

Implications for the Diocesan Priesthood

During the research for this section, a resigned priest sent me an article from the June 18, 1994 issue of *America*: "Statistical Reflections on Priestly Celibacy." A study of 1,810 active Roman Catholic adults in the United States and Canada responded to a questionnaire which included the statement: "I support the requirement that priests live a celibate life." Less than one-third of the respondents agreed.[11] Meanwhile hard evidence makes it clear that there will be a forty-percent reduction in the number of U.S. diocesan priests in the forty-year period between 1966 (when there were 35,000) and 2005 (when there will be 21,000). At the same time, the Catholic population will have expanded sixty percent (from 45 million to 74 million) during the same period.[12]

Despite such statistics, a July 21, 1993 issue of *L'Osservatore Romano* featured the text of a general audience address of Pope John Paul II on the rationale behind priestly celibacy. The headline for the talk declared: "Church Committed to Priestly Celibacy."[13] The "church" of the people in the United States and Canada, as well as other places where little support for priestly celibacy continues, represents a vastly different "church" than that envisioned by the pope and the Vatican.

Many in the hierarchy seem to view "church" and themselves as synonymous. Pope John Paul II has even referred to himself as "the church!"[14] Such images of "church" revolve around a notion of the institutional expression of church that is defined by patriarchal clericalism. This represents what I call "the church of Matthew 16." This hierarchically-defined church is distinguished from "the church of Matthew 18" which represents the collegial dimension.[15] As the data consistently shows, Matthew 18's church has a different vision about priestly celibacy. However, because the church of

Matthew 16 makes the rules, it controls not only issues related to compulsory priestly celibacy, but seems to believe its control will be supported by grace from God for the diocesan priest. All the priest need do is ask for the gift of celibacy; somehow, by a church edict, God will be obliged to give the gift. Unfortunately such *deus ex machina* theology has yet to make the problems around celibacy go away.

In 1972, a dissertation successfully defended at University of Notre Dame discussed *The Differences between Priests Legally and Personally Committed to Celibacy*. Personal celibates were defined as those having a balance between their inner psychic spiritual life and the outer discipline of the institutional church. Of the 1,256 priests who were surveyed, the results showed a marked difference between priests living celibacy because of the law and those who did so from free choice. These men viewed themselves as part of the "participation mystique within the organizational church."[16] A legal celibate was defined as "a mere conformist or as one who is being expelled from the participation mystique and beginning to question the meaning of celibacy."[17]

The data showed:

1. Priests identified as legal celibates had a higher score on anomie than priests identified as personal celibates.

2. Priests identified as legal celibates had a lower score on belief in celibacy than priests identified as personal celibates.

3. Priests identified as legal celibates had a lower score on attitudes towards celibacy than priests identified as personal celibates.

4. Priests identified as legal celibates had a lower score on the personal cost of changing the celibate commitment than priests identified as personal celibates.

5. Priests identified as legal celibates had a higher score on "dating behavior" than those identified as personal celibates.[18]

The priest-author of the dissertation concluded that, because celibacy is a graced gift from God, it "cannot be legislated for an entire group without risking the exposure of a good number of individuals to serious psychological problems." Noting that celibacy offers value for individuals only when it is freely chosen and freely lived, he concluded: "Psychological growth is the result of choice, and choice requires a clear, conscious evaluation of the options."[19]

In a twenty-five-year study of clergy, Richard Sipe discovered that of those priests he counseled or interviewed for his research, only ten percent admitted to no problems with celibacy. He also learned that half of the American priests suffer from psychological immaturity or sexual difficulties.[20] While Sipe's methods as well as his conclusions have been challenged by some, they seem confirmed when church leaders privately speak from their hearts. For instance, while I wrote this book, I spoke with someone who just had left the office as provincial of a large group of religious men. He had ministered in a province with a small, but significant, group of priests and brothers who had been accused of various kinds of sexual abuse. "I'm convinced," he said, "that eighty to ninety percent of the men have not been celibate at least for some period in their lives."

At this point it might be good to examine one of the main reasons priests and religious men give when seeking dispensations. One of these revolves around the "psychological immaturity" which prevented them from making a free choice. Most of the 80,000 priests who have left the active ministry between 1965 and 1990 have been granted dispensations by the Vatican. This rationale must have merit in the eyes of church leaders in the Vatican, in order for men to be granted dispensations in those numbers.

Instead of addressing the hard facts about priests who have left and young men unwilling to enter seminaries, people connected to the Vatican seem to have developed their own rationale for the celibate priesthood. Some of this can be found in "studies" such as Ignatius Press's *The Apostolic Origins of Priestly Celibacy*.[21] The book's purpose is meant to demonstrate that, based on apostolic tradition, celibacy is inherent to the nature of the Christian priesthood and that married clergy are governed by a law of perpetual continence. The argument has been resurrected, despite the fact that the late Jean Cardinal Danielou, who directed the research for the book (which originally was a doctoral dissertation at the Institute Catholique de Paris), recommended that the work not be published.[22]

Despite Pope John Paul II's arguing that celibacy has grounds in the call to discipleship and that the "ideal was affirmed" with increasing consistency throughout the church's history, he has not seemed to find anything contradictory in accepting converted married clergymen (primarily Anglican and Lutheran) to become Roman rite priests and still remain married. Under Pope John Paul II's papacy there have been more married priests than in any other period since the twelfth century. Yet even in this practice of admitting married clergy from other Christian churches, there have been contradictions. I discovered this personally when I met, for the first time, one of these converts. This very talented man was from the Episcopalian tradition. He always believed reunion would take place between the Anglican and Roman Catholic churches. Expecting it to occur, he married, became a priest, and raised a family. However, when reunion failed to materialize and, with his heart ultimately in the Roman Catholic tradition, he asked for full communion with Rome. It was granted. However, a stipulation of his ministering as a priest and remaining married was that he could not have "full-time care of souls." Consequently he was assigned to a parish where he would regularly help out with liturgy, but his full-time ministry would be counseling in a Catholic high school.

In chapter two it was argued that the former cultic reasons that once justified priestly celibacy no longer hold. More recent attempts to provide alternative reasons have not proved logical or credible either. Thus any laws based on such faulty rationales will be weak indeed. In the words of I. Morsdorff, "In order for a law to have obligatory force, it must be a reasonable ordinance. With regard to whether it can be followed, a law is reasonable when what it commands is not merely physically but morally possible, and that with regard to the capacity of the person affected. *Ad impossible nemo tenetur.*"[23] Building on Morsdorff's insights, Heinz-Jurgen Vogels concludes:

> Since the charism, the "capacity" for a celibate life, is not at the disposal of the individual affected, the law exceeds the capacity of many persons subject to it. For all those who do not have the charism, no legal obligation comes into force. Since, however, the law is intended to be binding on all priests, but not all priests have the charism . . . the law cannot reach its objective of obliging all priests to be celibate. It must, therefore, be repealed as an "unreasonable, irrational law."[24]

Even the staunchest defenders of celibacy for diocesan priest-hood would agree that the greater part of our church history has found celibacy separated from the priesthood. It is not my purpose here to further question the Pope's scriptural basis for his argu-ments, nor to rehash the history of the current discipline. Rather I want to offer a few more reasons why the present discipline appears to be out of control. This demands that we examine the internal contradictions that reveal themselves when one forces a gift, or in other words, when a charism is mandated, and when a choice of one reality is linked to something else. Some of these con-tradictions were outlined in an "op-ed" piece in *The New York Times* by Paul E. Dinter, a diocesan priest and New Testament scholar. This former campus minister at Columbia stated:

> Being a Roman Catholic priest is increasingly uncomfort-able. As a group, our image suffers as we endure what seem to be weekly disclosures that yet more clerics have engaged in sexual activity ranging from standard lust to outright perversion. . . .
>
> Despite recent assurances by church authorities about the careful screening used in the selection of seminarians, the hierarchy still uses silence and suppression in its battle against the world, the flesh and the devil. Because manda-tory celibacy has been declared necessary, defining it has become a blind ideology. To question it means disloyalty to the clerical establishment and exclusion from a leadership role in the church. . . .
>
> Those in authority should drop their pretensions at hav-ing an adequate theory of sexuality, openly rethink the mystery of sexual differentiation and seriously consider lifting the edict on clerical celibacy. Most men and women are meant to seek holiness by enacting their sexuality, not by avoiding it.[25]

Violence has to do with any force that inflicts injury. Where force controls, there can be no full nor authentic freedom. Where there is coercion, there is control. Where one must submit to anoth-er without freedom, autonomy is jeopardized. Liberty gets com-promised whenever constraint undermines choice. All of these contradictions result when people are compelled by a law that is compulsory. Such is the case with compulsory celibacy for priests; it represents a canonized form of institutional violence.

Despite all of these arguments, men still enter seminaries. But many also leave. And one of the main reasons is celibacy. U.S. data shows that the "desire to marry is one of the main factors leading seminarians to quit studying for the priesthood."[26] In fact, the most-stated reasons for leaving offered by (former) seminarians referred to negative attitudes toward celibacy and a desire to marry.

Meanwhile more and more Catholics suffer, unable to celebrate their identities as eucharistic communities. Also most efforts to effect change run into stone walls of resistance and subterfuge. This seems clear from an experience with the Vatican in my own archdiocese of Milwaukee.

In 1991 Archbishop Rembert Weakland, wrote a pastoral letter on the future of local parishes in Milwaukee. In the draft which was submitted to the people for comment, he wrote: "It seems inevitable that we will in a few years, if not sooner, reach a point when the number of priests will not be able to handle the 285 parishes and missions of the archdiocese. We cannot be assured that all parishes will have full eucharistic celebrations or Mass every Sunday." Seeing "no other way out of this very difficult situation," he presented a possible alternative—the ordination of married men—if certain conditions would be fulfilled:

- if a parish that cannot have a regular Mass on Sundays because of the shortage of priests remains faithful in assembling each Sunday for the Liturgy of the Word, presided over by a lay minister or a deacon, and with the distribution of holy communion outside of Mass only on rare occasions such as feasts, lest it become habitual and be seen as a normal substitute for the Mass;

- and if the parish continues to have all the characteristics described in the first section of this document, namely, worship and a sacramental perspective that is a part of their theology and practice whenever possible, education at all levels, and outreach to the needy;

- and if the parish has an active vocation program for the celibate priesthood;

- and if it seems that this state of affairs may continue for many years, perhaps into the next decade, then I would be willing to help the community surface a qualified candidate for ordained priesthood—even if a married man—and, without raising false expectations or unfounded hopes for him or the community, present such a candidate to the Pastor of the Universal Church for light and guidance. In such a case we would have done all possible at the local level and could feel that we had been responsible stewards of God's goods and graces. If the strength of the Church then should diminish here because of the continued lack of ordained priests and sacramental opportunities for the faithful, our consciences could remain in peace. We had done our best.[27]

One recipient of the archbishop's January 1991 "draft" was the Holy See. In the final form of the letter published in November 1991, the archbishop noted what he had proposed about being "willing to submit to Rome a married man who is a qualified candidate for priesthood." He quoted the text above and then gave the Holy See's response: "I was informed by the Vatican Secretariat of State that my suggestion of proposing a married man was regarded as 'out of place.'" The Secretariat noted that: "As a result of the recent Synod, an appropriate Apostolic Exhortation is under preparation in which the Supreme Pontiff will offer the universal church orientations and directives to face adequately the same delicate issue. We look forward to the publication of that document."[28] To this day, it is unclear what, if any, official statement on the issue has been made, except the periodic statements by the Vatican against married priests.

In 1994 the prediction of the archbishop proved true. Three non-clerics were installed as the archdiocese's first non-clerical pastors for three local parishes. If this was adequate it is hard to explain what "adequacy" means to those parishioners who will be without a resident priest and regular access to the eucharist.

The Vatican's nonaction on the subject of the same "delicate issue" of "eucharist-less" parishes has not been "adequate" for the needs of the people of Canada either. Some years after the Vatican promise, a group of Canadian bishops went to Rome for their *ad limina* visit. Some went realizing that the men serving as missionaries in their sparsely-populated areas were dying or leaving and were not being replaced. They also knew that fewer numbers of their own diocesan priests were available for many remote areas. So they brought their case directly to Pope John Paul II. "We

explained our plight to him. And we gave all our reasons why the
people have a greater right to the eucharist than we have in limiting the priesthood to celibates," Bishop Remi De Roo explained to
me. "And all he said was, 'Deus providebit' (God will provide)." He
then commented: "But God has not provided and God will not
provide. Somehow the pope seems to think that by saying Deus
providebit, the problem will go away. Well, it hasn't gone away and
we are left with the eucharist-less communities. Whose problem is
it? God's or the pope's?"

The Canadian bishop indicated how, what he perceived as
blindness in the Vatican on the issue of married priests, raises a
serious question. How can people believe that they possess all
truth? A consequence of this attitude, he noted, gets expressed in
the worst forms of fundamentalism. "When people believe they
alone possess the whole truth and that God gives them that power,
are they not in effect inclined to play God? So 'God' has to support
what they say or make right their wrongs. It's all so contradictory,"
the bishop said. We are led to ask ourselves the question: Is this not
what ultimately leads to fanaticism? Fanatics totally believe what
they alone say is true. Their truth is true. But it may be true only
from their limited viewpoint. The greater truth requires the dis-
cernment of the entire community of believers.

Another contradiction in the compulsory celibacy rule was
made clear by another Canadian bishop, Denis Croteau of the
Mackenzie-Fort Smith diocese. He also made note of the "very
spiritual" approach Pope John Paul II has taken regarding the
priest shortage. Somehow the Pope's belief that God will provide
the church with the priests it needs without a change in the celibacy rule seemed to suffice. He introduced the point that in some ethnic communities (e.g., among the Inuit and Dene peoples of
northern Canada) an unmarried priest is unable to be a leader:
"The idea is that these people have a family value in their culture
that, unless you are married, you're not a leader and people won't
listen to you." He noted further that, "If you have married and
raised a family, then you're an elder, a man of experience. Then
you can talk and people will respect your position."[29] Rather than
make an exception by having married priests in such a culture, it
seems the Vatican is willing to lose certain native peoples in order
to preserve clerical celibacy. Cardinal Jozef Tomko, head of the
Congregation for the Evangelization of Peoples, reportedly said

that any exception granted in Canada "could not remain an exception" and would open a floodgate of similar requests in Africa, South America, and elsewhere.[30] In any case, the rule stands, even at the expense of certain cultures.

Another related example of the internal contradictions and confusing messages from the Vatican related to celibacy can be found in the demand that all permanent deacons promise not to get married should their spouses die. While writing this book I met a very young-looking permanent deacon. Though he was very involved in his parish ministry, at the same time he was quite outspoken regarding many things happening in the institutional church, especially related to women's issues. Yet, it appeared he did not seem to apply some of the unfair rulings of the institutional church to himself and his own situation. When I pointed out that the rule requiring him to promise celibacy if his wife died made him a victim too, he looked surprised. He said he had never really thought about it.

"Why did you promise not to remarry if anything happened to Helen?" I asked.

"Well, I guess I just love her so much I couldn't imagine myself ever marrying anyone else, so it was easy to make the promise," he responded. Then he got quite pensive. He added: "I guess I just bought the package too. I so much wanted to help people as a deacon that I never really thought about the consequences for me and my own future as a man."

A week later I had dinner with two other permanent deacons and one of their wives. I asked them why they accepted not being able to remarry when they committed themselves to be deacons. One of them said: "I am so involved with my wife, that, at this point, I just can't imagine having anyone else but her in my life. So making that promise, given my situation, was very easy." It was almost an echo of the younger deacon. The other one said: "I believe my promise was just part of the package. You have to relativize it."

The more I listened to them talk, the more I discovered some deep internal contradictions in this discipline for deacons as well. The greatest dissonance is this: When he is ordained a deacon, the man who is married receives the fullness of grace to be faithful to that ministry in the church, precisely as a married man (who is assumed to be having genital relations with his wife). However, should his wife die, it is presumed that the man gets another grace from God to be celibate. Thus celibacy is not the "gift" given at ordination to married men who become deacons; it somehow appears at the deaths of their wives.

Implications for Homosexual Catholics

After many communications related to homosexuality from various U.S. bishops,[31] in 1986 the Congregation for the Doctrine of the Faith (CDF) issued a letter to the bishops of the Catholic church on "The Pastoral Care of Homosexual Persons."[32] The letter's title indicated that the Vatican seemed willing to admit that homosexuality represents the reality of some persons in the church. This letter was reinforced with another statement in 1992. An earlier, 1975 "Declaration on Certain Questions Concerning Sexual Ethics," recognized that homosexual persons were "definitively such because of some kind of innate instinct or a pathological constitution judged to be incurable."[33] The 1986 letter achieved something of a "first" in a Vatican statement. It stated that the homosexual reality in people may be a "given," not something they have chosen (even though a 1976 letter of the U.S. bishops already accepted the "through no fault of their own" argument).[34]

The 1986 and 1992 statements both declared that the homosexual orientation "must be seen as an objective disorder,"[35] and that the condition of being a homosexual is "a more or less strong tendency ordered toward an intrinsic moral evil." Since one's sexuality is constitutive of one's personality, these statements strongly imply that homosexual persons are constitutively disordered. Furthermore, they implied when one is sexually (and, therefore, personally) constituted toward someone of the same sex, that person is objectively ordered toward intrinsic evil. The consequence of these teachings for homosexual people sincere about their discipleship was articulated by William Shannon with devastating honesty:

> Whether one agrees with this position or does not, it is not difficult to see the psychological damage that could be done to a person by telling him or her that his or her very person was ordered toward intrinsic moral evil. It would be like telling someone that he or she is carrying a moral time bomb. It would be to say that such a person is a constant proximate occasion of sin to himself or herself.[36]

In the same context of saying that the homosexual orientation is an "objective disorder," the CDF statement makes it clear that homosexual persons have an "intrinsic dignity" that "must always be respected in word, in action, and in law."[37] Commenting on this part of the letter in light of its overall thrust, the National Board of the Conference of Major Superiors of Men declared: "This most recent statement is neither helpful nor enlightening."[38] I would add it also is confusing, condescending, and contradictory.

How can anyone having an "objective" disorder also have an "intrinsic" dignity? What's the difference between "objective" and "intrinsic?" Don't both words refer to the constitutive dimension of one's very self? Doesn't anyone or anything objectively disordered lack some kind of intrinsic dignity? Furthermore they imply that when one's sexuality (and therefore, personality) is constitutionally oriented toward persons of the same sex, one is objectively ordered toward an intrinsic evil. Also, if one accepts the divine activity in the creation of every person, then has God created homosexual persons with an objective disorder? Admitting the all-pervasiveness of original sin, why are homosexual persons alone created with such an alien constitution? Are only heterosexual persons images of God without any objective disorder?

What do the CDF conclusions say about God's "choice" process? If God has chosen this group to be created with an objective disorder and with an orientation naturally ordered toward moral evil, could not God be accused of discrimination? How could God choose to create homosexual persons with "a more or less strong tendency ordered toward an intrinsic moral evil" in such a way that "the inclination itself must be seen as an objective disorder?"[39] More than saying anything about a creature being "disordered," it would say more about the disordered ways of the Creator!

Other Apparent Contradictions in the Notion of Call and Need for Community

According to the *Catechism of the Catholic Church*, chastity represents a fruit of the Holy Spirit: "The *fruits* of the Spirit are perfections that the Holy Spirit forms in us as the first fruits of eternal glory. The tradition of the church lists twelve of them: charity, joy, peace, patience, kindness, goodness, generosity, gentleness, faithfulness, modesty, self-control, chastity."[40] However, the *Catechism's* understanding of chastity is not clear. It seems to reflect the same meaning as its meaning for celibacy: that is, not to have genital sex. Yet all three groups—those in the consecrated life, diocesan priests, and homosexual persons—are "called" to celibacy. To expand on this contradiction, consider the following argument:

First off, the *Catechism* makes it clear the consecrated life involves a call. It states:

> The perfection of charity, to which all the faithful are called, entails for those who freely follow the call to consecrated life the obligation of practicing chastity in celibacy for the sake of the Kingdom, poverty and obedience. It is the *profession* of these counsels, within a permanent state of life recognized by the Church, that characterizes the life consecrated to God."[41]

In another place, the *Catechism* also says that priests, those in our second group, are "called" to celibacy as well:

> All the ordained ministers of the Latin Church, with the exception of permanent deacons, are normally chosen from among men of faith who live a celibate life and who intend to remain celibate "for the sake of the kingdom of heaven" (Mt 19:12). Called to consecrate themselves with undivided heart to the Lord and to "the affairs of the Lord" (1 Cor 7:32), they give themselves entirely to God and to men.[42]

It might be expected that the notion of "call" would solely be identified with the celibacy of religious and even secular priests, given the current institutional theology. However, and surprisingly for the first time (to my knowledge) and in an official document of the magnitude of the *Catechism*, homosexual persons also seem to have received the call. "Homosexual persons are called to chastity" the text declares simply and definitively.[43] This leads me to ask: Is this chastity the same as celibacy in the eyes of the teaching church? If so, does this mean homosexual people have been "raised" to the level of priests and religious? Is this some kind of new status the institutional church has ascribed to those who are homosexual? Is the call to be celibate the *same* for religious, for priests, and for homosexuals? Why do celibacy and chastity get identified with a vow for one, with a request for it for another, and a constitutive imperative for a third?

Another problem that indicates some discrepancy can be found in the notion of the community that is needed to sustain a celibate life, be it for religious, priests, or homosexual persons. As will be shown in the later chapters of this book, an individual cannot be an authentic celibate without some kind of community. However when we examine the communal support systems that should be nourishing the celibate vocation for the person belonging to a religious order, a diocesan priest, or a homosexual person, again we face many more apparent contradictions.

I have written before about what happens when one applies a family-systems model to the current institutional manifestation of Roman Catholicism in its Western expression.[44] Following the family-systems model developed by Dr. Harry Levinson of Harvard University, we can see why any form of celibacy will face more problems when people expected to be celibate do not get their familial needs addressed.

Each person, according to Levinson, has the potential for having three families or family-like units in his or her lifetime wherein meaning can be found. The first is one's *primary* family. We are part of this "first" family in our infancy and childhood. Ideally it constitutes the context for experiencing love and nurturing, correction and challenge, and support and education from caring adults. It signifies the family of children who have parents.

Marriage establishes the former child's *secondary* family. In this constellation of reciprocal relationships between two people, the setting is created for new children to experience another *primary* family. What makes something a family of the second type is that two people create the conditions for a primary family to take place for others. This type of family is precluded by celibacy. To compensate for this void we often hear phrases related by or about celibates such as "the world is my family," "my parish is my family," or "your family is now your congregation." Sometimes scripture is even used to buttress this argument (e.g., Mt 19:29).

A *tertiary* family is not a blood or adoptive family as in the first two types of familial relations. Rather it consists of work or ministry-based relationships. However, given many of the familial-type dynamics that take place at this level, it rightly can be termed a kind of family. For instance, as a middle manager (an associate priest, for instance), I may treat a person in authority (the pastor or even the institution itself) as if he (or it) were my father. When this occurs various kinds of transference may not be far behind. As the psychologist Kenneth R. Mitchell has discovered of priests and religious:

> If I have what are loosely called authority hang-ups, they derive, in all probability, from my relationship with my father. These same hang-ups will be exercised in my relationships with the boss or the institution he represents. The translation to bishop or to Mother Church is not hard to make.[45]

Mitchell, who treated many clergy persons at the Menninger Clinic, notes that when the three kinds of families are compared with the life patterns demanded of some in the Roman Catholic church by the institution, "we come up against a strange problem in the lives of celibate clergy." He concludes: "Whatever the strengths and weaknesses of celibate life may be, one fact is clear: the priest's secondary family is a severely altered or compromised one, as is the nun's. And this fact has consequences."[46]

The first obvious consequence is directly opposite of what has been touted as a benefit of not having a secondary family. While one may be free of responsibilities connected to it, one also receives no gratification from nourishing life in the concrete way that this dimension of family entails. Consequently it is easy for such people to seek the gratifications of having a family in a rectory setting, religious life, or support groups only to find they really come up short of one's expectations. Others have tried to find this family by adopting children. It has happened more than once in my own province and diocese. This can have some consequences for a religious not only for celibacy, but for the vow of poverty as well! Still others are told or believe they can find this third kind of family when they minister to a world in need. However, while this has some merit, here too, one often takes on responsibilities without matching forms of gratification. I find this to be increasingly true in many parts of the Western church today where celibates minister in a culture that no longer supports them in their "commitment" or may even doubt it is being lived authentically.

This leads us to consider another consequence evidencing more internal contradictions in current church teaching related to celibacy. Gratification in a secondary family that gets expressed in such forms of intimacy as touch is not easily available in substitute forms like rectory living, religious community, or support groups like Dignity or Courage. Almost all gratifications of touch that represent an essential part of what I will call sexual intimacy—holding, caressing, embracing—seem to be out of bounds for most people except in their secondary families. This makes even more demands on males than females. A male can be immediately suspect in our culture if he touches another person "too long." A Jesuit canon (no. 35) stated: "No Jesuit shall touch another, even in jest." In my novitiate the "no touch" taboo even extended to animals. We were not allowed (under obedience) to touch the kittens that played outside our windows. We were told this might be a way of compensation and could compromise our celibacy.

Having developed some notions addressing just a few of the contradictions connected to celibacy and the denial of the secondary family, Kenneth Mitchell's conclusions serve well as I close this chapter:

> All of the foregoing is important because it points to the fact that, although the priest may live in a social structure which has characteristics both of secondary and tertiary families, there are aspects of secondary family life, psychologically important aspects, which are out of bounds for priests. Furthermore the worlds of living and work are not easily separated. The tension of such living is likely to be much higher than in ordinary secondary family structures, and the loss or distortion of the secondary family structure becomes a serious problem in the priest's world of work.[47]

4

Buzzards in the Sanctuary

The week of May 25 to June 1, 1994 proved to be a pivotal period in my life. That week's experience not only reinforced my decision to risk writing this book, it also helped me understand to what degree, and at what expense, the present dispensation regarding celibacy must be critiqued from the perspective of control. My unique social location as a North American has influenced my understanding. But it has been reinforced by my visits to many other parts of the world, in this last case, a trip to Panama. My Capuchin brothers ministering there had asked me to share with them on a retreat. Three active priests and one lay brother minister to an area the size of Delaware, with nearly 40,000 people. One priest must stay near the parish center in Chepo because his recurring back problems make it impossible for him to travel the Pan American Highway which in most places in this district is nothing but a dirt and stone road full of potholes. The other two priests divide up the rest of the territory into areas with seventy to eighty chapels in each. Some of the local communities receive only one visit from a priest in a year.

Although the people are lacking in their experience of eucharist and the sacraments, many lay ministries have tried to offer what support they can. Many communities have "delegates of the word," catechists, and even young lay people called "missionaries" who stay with the people for weeks at a time. These young people instruct and catechize the people, including preparation for the sacraments which will be celebrated when the *padre* comes. The numbers of lay people involved in different ministries is quite large. For two days, I attended a training course for over fifty of them, some of whom had walked days to get there. The theme was "discipleship;" the participants' enthusiasm was palpable.

After witnessing this style of church, I was not prepared for another experience I would have of the church in Panama toward the end of my stay: the installation of the new archbishop of Panama. The ceremony, which occurred on Wednesday evening, May 25, 1994 in Panama City, was a study in contrasts with what I had recently witnessed. It would begin my "week that was."

Pomp and Circumstance

I'm not one to concelebrate, but I wanted to support my Capuchin brothers in Panama. I got the distinct impression that I'd be doing them a favor if I would join them around the altar with the new archbishop. When I agreed I did not realize how much the ceremony would be a celebration of the male, clerical church at one of its peak moments. It was the closest thing to being at the Vatican for one of those Christmas Midnight Masses I've watched on television. As the ceremony progressed I realized it didn't matter where I was. I could have been in the Vatican or Panama City or anywhere else; I was part of a celebration of an all-male club. The ritual of the archbishop's installation could have taken place anywhere in the world. It just happened to be here.

Three of us Capuchin priests and a lay brother, as well as two young adult volunteers from the Chepo parish, arrived an hour before services began. On the steps of the cathedral stood the new archbishop, José Dimas Cedeño. He was flanked by the apostolic nuncio, Archbishop Osvaldo Pailla. They were in full crimson attire. Over their cassocks were beautifully laced surplices. On their heads they wore crimson birettas.

As I watched, more and more priests and deacons appeared on the steps. Next a large group of students from the major seminary arrived. (Not too long before, some kind of sexual scandal had occurred allegedly involving some faculty and students of the seminary. The culprits had been dismissed and the incident had been kept relatively quiet.) Then more bishops came, some escorted by police. Inside, the cathedral was filled with many invited guests.

I found myself getting a very queasy stomach, so much so that I thought I might be getting sick. Never having participated in such a gathering of the triumphal, male, clerical church, and aware of my promise to participate, I didn't quite know whether to run or to hide. I felt ashamed about my complicity in something I no longer believed in. I wanted to flee. Human respect and my disease of codependency instead found me submitting. I felt I could not go back on my promise to be part of the ritual.

In the vesting room very gracious women eagerly offered to help the priests put on our albs and stoles. Again I thought of resisting, but the kind insistence of the woman appointed to help me (who even spoke English) found me succumbing again. Noticing the nonchalance of many of the others being vested around me, it seemed that this service by women helping dress the priest was just taken for granted.

As we were organized for the procession into the church, cars arrived carrying the Panamanian president, Guillermo Endara and the president-elect, Ernesto Pérez Balladares. They were promptly escorted to the front rows of the cathedral. Members of the cabinet and the diplomatic corps already had been seated. It was politically important for them to be seen at the ceremony. Panama is a "Catholic country." Its leaders know the importance of keeping in the good graces of the church. The entire ceremony was being televised by all the Panamanian stations.

Once we processed into the cathedral, I found my seat near one of the side altars to the left of the main altar. Others higher in rank than me were more strategically placed near the main altar. Once in place, we spent the majority of the first hour listening to official proclamations related to the authority of the new archbishop. When the apostolic delegate from Rome spoke (for nearly twenty minutes) I kept listening for him to say words like *Dios, Jesús*, or *Christo*, which would seem to have something to do with the occasion. However, none were spoken. I did hear him refer once to the *Salvador* ("Savior"). Instead, I noticed with what great frequency some other words were used. These dealt with authority in our church, its source, and its extension. Words for "archbishop," "bishop," and the "Holy See," and other parallel images tended to dominate his talk. Though my Spanish is poor, I did not recognize anything that sounded like "good news" or words of hope addressing the needs of the people of Panama.

Needless to say, I found myself quite distracted. As I looked around, I found out I was not alone. By now many eyes, including mine, had become transfixed on something else in the sanctuary

besides the apostolic nuncio. High above the main altar and overlooking the nuncio, flying between the two domed areas, were two
large buzzards. Unable to escape from their predicament, they
would perch on one cornice for a while, look around, and then fly
to another. Their perch above the whole scene, needless to say,
invited many amused comments descriptive of their significance
to the occasion. Somehow their presence and predicament seemed
symbolic of the event better than any words of the pope's representative. I decided that the image of buzzards in the sanctuary
symbolized well what is happening with our triumphal, male, celibate, clerical church. As we clerics continue celebrating our rituals
of arrival and entrance, of upward mobility and status, the buzzards hover as silent sentinels signaling the start of another story.
Though our body is not quite dead, the buzzards have already
begun to gather. Yet most fail to read the signs.

The next day, I did not hear one person speak favorably about
the event. With all major television stations in Panama City covering the ceremony from beginning to end, people witnessed a display of ecclesiastical pageantry more geared to the cathedrals of a
dying church in Europe and North America than to the vibrant
communities like ours in Chepo, Panama. A great teachable
moment had been lost. The fact that I had been just one more cleric in that cathedral, whose presence added to the pomp and cir-
cumstance, only made me feel more terrible. I too had been one of
those male, celibate clerics who had contributed to the bankrupt
image by my presence and involvement.

Thankfully, the next day, my negativity and my feelings of
guilt and shame gave way to a sense of hope and joy. Watching the
evening news that Thursday, I heard that the Vatican was preparing a document on the *shoah* (the Hebrew word for the Holocaust).
According to the press report, it would declare that the Roman
Catholic church "confesses that she bears co-responsibility for the
shoah."

I couldn't believe what I was hearing. I sat dumbfounded. This
church of mine, whose institutional expression I have critiqued
quite publicly, now seemed willing to face its past, to admit its
part in allowing sins like the *shoah* to continue, and to repent of
its wrongdoing. I found myself thinking: if it is willing to admit
something it had denied for so long, like the *shoah*, maybe it
will do the same in confessing the way it has been linked to

control systems, to authoritarian dynamics, to abuse against women, to complicity in its rejection of homosexuals. I wondered what the implications might be if representatives of the institutional church acknowledged the sinfulness of depriving people of the eucharist by its insistence on maintaining a celibate priesthood in the Latin Rite? What if the Vatican asked forgiveness of those people it had silenced? My mind raced at the possibilities for healing and cleansing that could occur.

As I listened to the news, I learned that I was not alone in being dumbfounded at the report. My surprised incredulity was shared by many others, including Rabbi David Rosen, the director of interfaith relations and Vatican relations for the Anti-Defamation League in Jerusalem. When asked about his impression of what the Vatican would say, he did not respond with something like, "We've always told you so." Rather he expressed his own simple sense of wonder regarding the amazing about-face this admission of guilt on the part of the institutional church revealed. "It's not just important, it's mind-boggling," was all he seemed able to say.

The next day, Friday, May 27, however, brought me back to reality. Any positive feelings I or others like Rabbi Rosen may have had, were dashed with the arrival of the morning paper. Not only did the Vatican unveil the new sexist version of the English edition of the *Catechism of the Catholic Church*,[1] it had disassociated itself from the Holocaust document. The paper noted that the draft presented at a meeting of a liaison group of Jews and Roman Catholics in Jerusalem, "in no way [was] a projected document of the Holy See."

Somehow all the positive steps that were recently made—from the efforts of Pope John Paul II with Jews in Rome to the Second Vatican Council's condemnation of anti-Semitism—seemed hollow. The *shoah*, which occurred with a virtual conspiracy of silence from church people—from Pope Pius XII and the German bishops to German theologians and people in the pews[2]—was still not admitted as a sin by the church's institutional representatives. There would be no repentance; there would be no need for the institutional leaders to seek forgiveness. If there had been any sin, it was committed by the people, not the hierarchy, much less the papacy.

When buzzards perch they are just waiting for the last gasp of a carcass to be breathed. But many times the one clinging to its last breath is too preoccupied trying to survive to admit what's about to happen. But the buzzards know; that's their nature. I learned that the many other carcasses strewn in the desert of history attest to their wisdom.

Pedophilia in the Sanctuary

The next day of this defining week was Saturday, May 28. I returned to Miami to spend the weekend with Andres Martinez. Andy had been a Capuchin seminarian. I lived with him and other Capuchins in Berkeley while getting my degree. He had left the order, gone to Miami, and now worked for a men's clothier. His job found him taking clothing samples to successful businessmen in their offices. On one of his calls a customer he outfitted had told him an incredible story of being sexually abused by priests and seminarians when he was in his mid-teens. Andy thought I should hear his tale. So, immediately upon my arrival in Miami, Andy took me to listen to one of the most frightening personal stories of sexual abuse by clergy I had ever heard.

Before I relate this story, I don't want to leave any impression that only Roman Catholic clerics (or religious) are pedophiles. This is definitely not the case. In fact, the first male person convicted of pedophilia I ever knew was a young man in his twenties. "John Smith" was a 6' 6" sailor who fell in love with "Nina Bussalanti." She belonged to our parish at St. Elizabeth's in Milwaukee. When John came to Mass with Nina, I never saw a man in church so demonstrative with affection for his beloved as he.

I was at the altar when John and Nina made their vows to each other in front of God and God's people. After he left the Navy he got a job as a fireman for the city of Milwaukee. They had two boys. John loved them as much as he loved his wife. The family seemed perfect. Everything appeared to be normal. But there was a dark side to John none of us ever imagined. It came to light one evening while the Smith family was having dinner. Two policemen arrived at the door to arrest John for repeated solicitation of sex with minors. Later John confessed his crime, was convicted of pedophilia with pre-pubescent girls, and went to prison. Nina divorced him. John lost his wife and two sons.

My experience of knowing John represented my first contact with anyone accused of being a pedophile. Since then I have met others. But, far more than this limited number of perpetrators, I have met many, many victims of perpetrators like him, in and out of the clergy.

The man Andy introduced me to in Miami is in his early thirties now. "Steven" owns a very successful electronics business with three stores in the greater Miami area. Between conversations with prospective customers he told me his story.

It seems that when Steven was fifteen years old a young priest had just come to his parish in an upper-middle class neighborhood in upstate New York. His parents were happy that the priest took such an interest in the youth; he was thought to be a good influence who would help keep the teens out of trouble. "Father Tony" had built a cabin in the woods about an hour from their city. Often he invited different boys to help him work there. One day he asked Steven if he'd like to go. His parents gladly gave their permission; Steven needed this kind of attention from "a man of the cloth."

Once there, the two worked for quite a few hours in the woods. They cut down trees, chopped the wood, then trimmed and corded it. The work was long and hard. But it was made easier by the friendly bantering the two enjoyed.

Father Tony had built a sauna at the cabin. When the work was done he asked Steven if he would join him. When he replied affirmatively, the priest told him he could not wear a bathing suit. "House rules," he explained. The fifteen-year-old entered the sauna after his mentor had gone in and sat down. Soon after Father Tony said, "I dare you to turn out the light." Thinking his challenge was silly, Steven asked, "Why would I want to turn out the light?" Instead of answering him, the priest kept repeating the challenge. So Steven accepted the "dare." He turned out the light. What happened next resulted in Steven's loss of his virginity; his first experience of sodomy. Before this occurrence, Steven said, he had never thought of himself as homosexual. Now the experience resulted in his feeling that somehow he just must be. Later, when he challenged Father Tony about his behavior, the priest showed no regret. "I knew you were homosexual. All I did was help you discover what you would have to admit to one day anyway."

The sauna experience would not be Steven's only sex-encounter with a priest. Before he was eighteen, he had had sex many times with Father Tony. In addition, Father Tony introduced him to six or seven other priests and seminarians with whom he would have genital relations as well. All of these encounters took place with adults before he was eighteen. One time in his presence, four of the priests talked of going to Miami where they could engage in genital sex without any chance of being caught. "It was like they were part of a ring," he explained to me.

In describing the various encounters he had with these priests and seminarians, Steven said: "What I learned from all of this is that they made sex so cheap. It was totally dissociated from their ministry as priests. Thirty seconds before Mass, I'd be ready to go out and serve. Just then, Father would grab me in the crotch. Then he'd fold his hands, and go out to celebrate Mass." Another time Father Tony came over to church as Steven was preparing music for the Youth Choir he directed. It was Saturday night and time to close the church. "I always wanted to have sex in the confessional," the priest said, asking Steven to join him in the confessional. The high-school student declined his associate pastor's offer.

I was amazed at the calm way Steven detailed to me the events that had occurred. I found no sense of anger or resentment, no feelings of rage or righteousness in his comments. He didn't seem revengeful in the least. He didn't even seem incensed that the priest who had taken away his virginity when he was a freshman in high school was the main concelebrant at his father's funeral liturgy a couple years before our meeting. Steven (who never told his parents what had been done to him by the priest they almost idolized) didn't even seem overtly bothered by the fact that the other two priests concelebrating the Mass of Resurrection for his father also had had sex with him. He seemed willing to let the events of the past go unchallenged. He saw no value in demanding any kind of accountability, much less compensation, for the abuse they had done to him. He had no desire to expose their deeds and detail how they had abused their positions of power in the church and trust among the people to satisfy their sexual desires at the expense of young men like himself.

Having heard his story, I strongly urged him to go to the chancery in his home diocese to report what had happened, even though it had occurred fifteen years ago. Steven's reply was all the more sad: "Parents of other friends of mine who were abused did go," he said. "All the diocese seemed to do was to transfer them someplace else. I don't know if my friends got paid off, but those priests are still functioning." When I insisted that they might still be abusing other young men, his reply was even more pathetic.

"It's no use, the diocese won't do anything. It would do no good. Nothing is going to change," was all he could say.

Next he rejected my suggestion that, precisely because he had no bitterness, was not looking for money, nor had any axes to grind with the priests, that he'd be an excellent case to present his story to the media in an effort to change the structure. "If I knew my testimony would do something to change the system, I would do it gladly. But the system is not going to change. This stuff involves too many people. And many now have moved to high places," he said.

Recognizing the difference between priests who do to minors what some did to him, and priests who are celibate homosexuals, Steven also concluded that homosexuality was rampant in the priesthood: "Every priest I met in the diocese was gay. I am firmly convinced that every priest is gay. Everyone who enters the seminary or the priesthood is either gay or a repressed homosexual." When I tried to question the extent of his percentages, it was no use. His experience told him differently.

Celibacy Out of Control

I left our meeting wondering how many other young people like him have suffered at the hands of priests and religious who abuse their position and power in our church. How many more "Steven stories" could be told? Again I wondered why there is so much resistance among church leaders even to initiate a study on the dynamics related to celibacy among seminarians and priests. How can they refuse to examine the problems connected to the forced imposition of celibacy upon its priests and yet insist on its value?[3] The more I reflected on the issue, the clearer it became: celibacy has not been just a matter of exercising clerical control, it now is out of control. The numbers of those accused of ephebophilia (a psychological term dealing with sexual or genital attraction to post-pubescent minors), the revelations of legal pedophilla (a legal term dealing with sexual or genital attraction to legal minors),[4] the rise of repressed homosexuals into positions of church leadership who seem unable to play by consistent rules, is frightening. (This is not to say that homosexuality is the cause of these abuses; it is simply the particular context in which it takes place.) But an institutional layer of denial hangs over it all. And as long as a disease is denied, no remedies can be equal to the task of healing. Dishonesty then determines our procedures, even if our policies say something else. Meeting Steven reminded me that the system is as sick as its secrets. I left our meeting sad indeed.

The next day, Sunday, Andy and I went to Mass. The priest who presided definitely *presided* at this feast in honor of the Holy Trinity. His every move seemed studied. When the altar server brought him the book, or the water and towel, or the gifts, he nodded with just the right liturgical nod: not too low and not too slow. His homily was purely didactic, absent of any pastoral application. As he told us how splendid it is to contemplate the triune God, his gestures were liturgically perfect. Not one concrete example was used, no familial references were made that might have helped the people in the pews to understand the Trinity. We didn't even hear about St. Patrick and the shamrock!

At the end of Mass, as the presider prepared to offer the final blessing, the red-haired pastor made his appearance in the sanctuary. Resplendent in a cream-colored, brocaded cope, he stood near the altar railing. As the ministers and the priest began leaving the sanctuary, he began to walk back and forth inside the sanctuary. He held his clasped hands close to his chest, all the while giving the look of an approving shepherd toward his flock outside. That day I saw no buzzards flying above this sanctuary in this affluent section of Miami. Somehow I sensed, however, they couldn't be far away.

I left Miami for Milwaukee on Monday, May 30. It was Memorial Day in the United States and a memorable day in the church. This was the day that Pope John Paul II issued a letter to the bishops declaring "that the church has no authority whatsoever to confer priestly ordination on women and that this judgment is to be definitively held by all the church's faithful."[5] The wording of the statement revealed a new dimension of statements that had come from Rome: anyone dissenting invited possible dismissal from the church itself.[6] Cardinal Joseph Ratzinger explained that anyone who did not give obedient assent to the statement "obviously separates himself from the faith of the church." Any more discussion on the issue was ruled out; there would be no more debate on the subject. The case was closed. Later his comments would lead *The Tablet* of England to editorialize:

> The cardinal has a duty, of course, to make clear the status
> of the Pope's letter without ambiguity, but it sometimes

seems that the Catholic authorities do not understand how this language of centralizing control and imposed authority, which has become characteristic of the present Roman tone, is heard inside and outside the church, and what sort of impression it gives. The present emphasis is on a comprehensive and complete system of doctrines enshrining the faith and a complete system of prohibitive laws which oblige under all conditions.[7]

Early Tuesday morning, I read portions of the previous day's statement in *The New York Times.* "On Reserving Priestly Ordination to Men Alone," as the apostolic letter was called, reiterated the Vatican position that the priesthood had to be limited to males. The main argument for a male-only priesthood was stated quite simply and emphatically: Jesus chose only male apostles. This represented the will of Jesus. This revealed God's eternal plan. Consequently it was God's will that only men be priests.

In this letter Pope John Paul II also referred to previous statements issued by Pope Paul VI. The latter argued for male-only priests from the fact that Christ chose only men as apostles, the constant practice of the church which imitated Christ in choosing only men, and the church's "living authority which has consistently held that the exclusion of women from the priesthood is in accordance with God's plan for his church."[8]

One might note that Pope John Paul II's words refer to God's plan for *his* church. Somehow such reference describing God ("his"), which limits God's identity to the male form still has yet to be recognized as culturally conditioned and historically determined. Thus, even unwittingly, the wording of the apostolic letter shows how deeply the patriarchal cultural conditioning has penetrated the minds and language of the hierarchy. The depth of the resulting inability to see also becomes quite clear when Pope John Paul II again insists, with Pope Paul VI, that "Christ's way of acting did not proceed from sociological or cultural motives peculiar to his time."[9] Given the depth of the power of language to influence stereotypes, these popes were not able to recognize how—in referring to God as *he* —their own words reflect sociological and cultural conditioning. Consequently their own interpretation of the Jesus of history seems bound to be conditioned by that very limited perspective as well.

With such "nonculturally-conditioned" reasoning offered as a rationale for the people's unconditional assent and non-debate on the issue of women as priests, a Vatican overview of the apostolic letter concluded:

> Therefore, since it does not belong to matters freely open to dispute, it always requires the full and unconditional assent of the faithful, and to teach the contrary is equivalent to leading consciences into error. This declaration of the supreme pontiff is an act of listening to the word of God and of obedience to the Lord on the path of truth.[10]

The link in the declaration of the Pope, supreme pontiff, with "path of truth" strongly intimates some kind of infallible truth in the pronouncement. However, given the patriarchal foundation of this "truth," its limitations seem increasingly clear: in the Pope's own words, it represents the "truth of man." As I have noted elsewhere,[11] unfortunately this seems to be limited precisely to this: the truth of "man" rather than the fullness of human truth which comes from the truth of man *and* the truth of woman.

One can also draw this impression from Pope John Paul II's encyclical, *Veritatis Splendor*. It stresses the "truth of man" in such a way that its defense of moral objectivity reveals an all too visible male point of view and a tendency to resolve genuinely difficult questions by resorting to authority.[12] Besides, limiting this truth to that of man, yet projecting it as universally true, removes any possibility of dialogue. It would be the same as limiting a discussion of truth as regards church authority to Matthew 16 without reading the accompanying response from Matthew 18.[13] Obedience demands mutual listening if it is not to be coercive. As someone once said to me: "Where there is no dialogue, there can only be violence." When coercion exists, violence is its shadow. In this case, the pope's "truth" will be seen to represent his own perspective rather than an articulation of the faith and belief of the whole church.

Returning to the Scriptures for Meaning

Having read the quotes in Tuesday morning's *The New York Times*, I gathered at 7:30 a.m. with my Capuchin community in Milwaukee to spend our usual hour praying the morning prayer of the church. It would provide for me a fitting reflection on the past week's experiences that began six days before at the installation of the new archbishop of Panama.

We entered into our usual "act of listening" to the scriptures of the day. We found it particularly interesting that the gospel was from Mark 12:18-27. This pericope narrates the exchange between Jesus and "some Sadducees, who say there is no resurrection." Jesus is asked his thoughts about a woman who married seven brothers. None of the men "left children." Consequently, the question the Sadducees posed was: "In the resurrection whose wife will she be? For the seven had married her." Jesus' words said as much to their question as to the questions raised in me the last six days:

> Jesus said to them, "Is not this the reason you are wrong, that you know neither the scriptures nor the power of God? For when they rise from the dead, they neither marry nor are given in marriage, but are like angels in heaven. And as for the dead being raised, have you not read in the book of Moses, in the story about the bush, how God said to him, "I am the God of Abraham, the God of Isaac, and the God of Jacob"? He is God not of the dead, but of the living; you are quite wrong."[14]

At this point I want to propose that there are at least two layers in Jesus' words that relate to this topic. The first is that God's reign reveals an entirely different dynamic related to sexuality and genitality than those understandable or acceptable to the average believer. The second is that Jesus' own response belies his own sociologically and culturally conditioned male-defined reality that excluded women. It is understandable that Jesus spoke this way, not because it was God's will, but because he lived in a society where only men "counted" (Mk 6:44). This was the same society in which, even for Jesus, the God of the living was not only a *he*, but the God of men like "Abraham, Isaac, and Jacob."

If one would take the present way of thinking coming from many in Rome as it is applied to Jesus' "choice of males" for priesthood, every *choice* must include a non-choice. This would be tantamount to Jesus saying something like "I choose to be the God of Abraham but not Sarah, the God of Isaac instead of Rebecca, and the God of Jacob rather than Rachel." The argument from silence around "choice" used to justify the "non-choice" or exclusion of women from roles previously limited to men thus appears not only illogical, it does a disservice to the culturally limited realities that the text itself reveals in such situations. However, in the papal argumentation, no such culturally conditioned dynamics affected Jesus' choice of men instead of women. The simple declaration that something is thus, does not make it so.

Sad to say, it became clearer as we prayed, that the Markan Jesus' response to the Sadducees might also be the response we might make to such ways of thinking among some of our church leaders today: "Is not this the reason you are wrong, that you know neither the scriptures nor the power of God?"

I know of no scholar of reputation in the academy of scripture scholars who has defended the scriptural argumentation of the Holy Father about women and the priesthood. I do know of some who say they will obey his order to be silent on the matter, but they are equally silent about defending the logic of his argumentation. The same holds for bodies of bishops, like the National Conference of Catholic Bishops in the United States. Well over a year after his statement I found no ringing endorsement of his position from the NCCB. Unfortunately, in his letter the Pope proffered a rationale to support the arguments for his conclusion, instead of merely saying something like: "The case is closed. There will be no women priests." The fact that his reasoning is illogical, inconclusive, and, ultimately inconsistent with the truth itself, makes one ask if this statement truly reflects the "power of God" or, rather, the possible misuse of power of someone—acting in the name of that God—who uses the scriptures consciously or unconsciously in a way which justifies the continued abuse of women in the household of faith.

At this point, some reader of this chapter may wonder how Pope John Paul II's statement on the ordination of women has anything to do with the issue of celibacy. The link I find revolves around the need of *male*s to control others, especially women. This control is at the core of the patriarchal clericalism which represents the heart of many dysfunctional dynamics in the Roman Catholic church.[15] In the process, I feel, our effort to control also represents just one more gasp of patriarchal clericalism before the buzzards pick the carcass clean.

It would be unfair if I would leave any impression that the effects of patriarchy are isolated in the ecclesiastical family represented in institutional Roman Catholicism. While the Roman church in its structures stands as an ideological bastion of defense of patriarchy's ways and interests, the ecclesiastical bureaucracy and its operating ideology merely reflect as an icon the deeper patriarchy that can be found throughout most institutions. Jeff Hearn has made this clear in his seminal study *Men in the Public Eye: The Construction and Deconstruction of Public Men and Public Patriarchies.*

Hearn has discussed the historical consequences that occur when the men are "public" and the institutions are patriarchal. He addresses issues related to men, masculinity, and patriarchy on the one hand and gender, sexuality, and organizations on the other. From this approach he has concluded that "dominance/public domains/public men/men are in a mutually reinforcing relation" and that it is precisely these configured relationships which create what he calls "part of the problem of public men." Hearn never mentions the "public men" represented in the clergy of the Roman Catholic church as key to the preservation of its patriarchal organization. However he does show that the fact of being a "public man," being in a "public domain" or institution, and "patriarchy" interrelate, nourish, and depend on each other. He also has concluded, despite the rise of feminism, that "power and dominance of the public domains and public men appear to be historically on the increase, at least in its potential."[16]

The fact that these dynamics are on the increase, should not be surprising at least in the Roman Catholic church. This seems evident in the two incidents that greeted me upon my return from Panama: the Vatican's insistence on male language in the English version of the new *Catechism,* as well as in the intensity of the statement of Pope John Paul II about women.

How the Pope's statement on the non-ordination of women and the parallel demand for silence about it reflects patriarchal clericalism in the institutional church and how this relates to the need for celibate males to control women has been well-articulated by Sebastian Moore. Himself a cleric, he writes of the dynamics of patriarchy:

> *Control* is the name of the game. And if we ask how the theologian interpreters of the Genesis text achieved the unanimous corporate oversight of seeing *loss of control* as the primary consequence of the Fall where the text is saying that *awkwardness between the sexes* is the primary consequence, we surely have our answer: the text is being read

with the eyes of the patriarchal mentality, for which man is
the center, woman the hazard, and control the name of the
game.[17]

Moore shows that our present age is witnessing the beginning
crisis of our past patriarchal forms. It faces increasing irrelevance
as women begin the quest for their own identity and find support
for this goal from sympathetic men. As the institutional church
begins to be aware of this breakdown as well, there should be little
surprise when its leaders strive to preserve old forms for the sake
of their traditional power. I find Moore's conclusion helpful in
understanding Pope John Paul's statement about women's non-
ordination:

> In the middle of all this, we have the Catholic Church,
> which, institutionally, is the most patriarchal body there is.
> Its *idea* of sexuality, shaped by generations of male celibates
> and prescribed by a male celibate magisterium, is very
> much that of the patriarchal age, its implicit theme, "Men,
> control yourselves (and control the women too)." Hence, I
> am sure, its failure to touch people today, even people of
> the best will in the world.[18]

So the buzzards in the sanctuary wait. They watch the last ves-
tiges of a once-powerful body whose patriarchal blood has become
toxic. They know that there is no magical transfusion on the horizon that can revive the collapsing corpse.

Our extended prayer-reflection on the abuse of papal power
that Tuesday morning brought us to our final consideration from
Mark's gospel. We listened to Jesus' words to the religious leaders
of his day. He addressed the Sadducees on the precise issue that
kept them trying to maintain control: "You know [not] . . . the
power of God." The leaders had no higher power beyond themselves.

Power represents the ability to influence. Yet in itself, power is
neutral. The way one uses power to influence is the only way to
determine whether or not power is positive or negative. When
power gets expressed positively its manifestations are found in
nurturing and challenging, as parents do with children and teachers with students. These forms of power are exemplified as *care*.
On the other hand, when power is expressed negatively, its influence gets expressed in exploitation, manipulation, or domination.

These manifestations of power are synonymous with forms of *control*. Since the reign of God is revealed in power, and since God's power is not exploitative, manipulative, coercive, or dominative, we "know" the power of God in forms of care. This cannot be confused with power exercised "in God's name" under one of the other forms of control. Rather, those negative exercises represent an ungodly and abusive manifestation of power. This fits well the definition of abuse offered by the U.S. bishops in their document on domestic violence considered in the first chapter: "any kind of behavior that one . . . uses to control another through fear and intimidation."[19]

This form of power—which makes its authority felt—was expressly rejected by Jesus when he compared his form of authority (as care) with that of the Roman rulers and their surrogates who used their power as a means of control: "You know that the rulers of the Gentiles lord it over them, and their great ones are tyrants over them. It will not be so among you . . . (Mt 20:25-26).

The week of May 25 to June 1 showed me how far all of us in the church still have to go until we listen actively to these words of Jesus in a way that will make *them* non-debatable. When that day comes, there will be no need for dissent. There will only be an unconditioned, "Amen."

5

Celibacy and the
Crisis of Meaning in the Church

In the mid-seventies I participated in a "think tank" discussing issues related to the future of religious life. One of the attendees was Alan McCoy, O.F.M., the president of the Conference of Major Superiors of Men. At one point Alan and I were privately discussing the problem of many numbers of fine people leaving our congregations. We agreed that the overwhelming majority had left because of issues related to celibacy. Most had left religious life to get married.

Alan said something that stayed in the back of my mind until years later when I witnessed his prediction coming true: "If we thought we had an exodus before, wait until the next one takes place. The next one will not be a crisis related to celibacy; it will be a crisis of faith itself."

In the years since they were first spoken, Alan's prophetic words have been realized. Today, as people continue to leave the priesthood and religious life, many are no longer doing so simply for reasons of celibacy. Rather, many seem to be leaving for a totally unrelated reason. Although it gets articulated in different ways, the basic explanation is: "It doesn't mean anything any more." The system that once gave their lives and celibacy meaning no longer provides the impetus it once did. Why stay in something that no longer gives life or meaning, or is something in which you have lost faith? One sign that verifies this rationale is that a good number who leave have no intention of marrying, nor do they get married.

I believe a strong link exists between the crisis of faith Alan McCoy envisioned and this deeper crisis of meaning many in our church today experience. I sense many are losing faith in structures that impose things like male priesthood and mandated celibacy to the point that the structures themselves no longer mean what they used to. Thus the crisis of faith does not reveal something merely personal; it is institutional as well. And, as Philip Sheldrake notes, the crisis goes even beyond the institutional: "What we confront is a crisis of meaning for an ecclesiastical *culture* that has depended on a complexity of symbols and on an ideology of separation and superiority."[1]

In our contemporary culture, the notions of faith and meaning should intersect each other in ways generative of life. Instead, all too often, we watch a gradual death take over. The fact that only a quarter of U.S. Catholics attend Sunday Mass says something about peoples' crisis of meaning and loss of faith in the power of the institution to dictate their patterns of worship.[2]

Trying to separate faith and meaning will hinder efforts to understand why celibacy is in such a crisis in the lives of individuals, the institutional church, and in the culture of the church that has had a clerical form of celibacy define its meaning for so many years. When one has a crisis of meaning that is not only personal but institutional and cultural as well, the individual's crisis will be three times as difficult.

Earlier I quoted from a study of priests which compared the attitudes and behaviors of those defined as "legal celibates" and "personal celibates." The data from that study showed clearly that legal celibates had higher scores around the issue of meaninglessness ("anomie") than their peers who were personal celibates. Anomie results from unclarity, unrootedness, or a vacuous sense related to something in which one formerly believed. One may enjoy one's work—as seems to be the case with many older priests and religious today—but anomie relates to the living of one's life. There can be a great difference in priests who are satisfied with what they do, but not the way they are living.[3] This difference and dissonance is measured by scales defining one's anomie or sense of meaninglessness.

One of the best articulations regarding the connection between personal faith and meaning has been proffered by Sharon Parks, a developmental psychologist at Harvard. For her, meaning-making is an activity of faith. She writes:

> If we are to recover a more adequate understanding of human faith in the context of present cultural experience, we must be clear that when we use the word faith we are speaking of something quite other than belief in its dominant contemporary usage.
>
> Though faith has become a problematic [issue in our culture], the importance of "meaning" has not. Modern people can more easily recognize that the seeking and defending of meaning pervades all of human life.[4]

Meaning-making, according to Parks, involves the activity of seeking some kind of pattern, order, form, and significance to one's life and one's surroundings. It represents the desire to make sense out of things and to discover fitting connections, especially in the surroundings where one finds himself or herself. She writes: "It is in the activity of finding and being found by meaning that we as modern persons come closest to recognizing our participation in the life of faith. It is the activity of composing and being composed by meaning, then, that I invite the reader to associate with the word *faith*."[5]

Parks also makes a connection between faith and meaning and one's environment or culture. For her, a culture is composed of the forms of life by which a people cultivate and maintain a sense of meaning. It represents that which gives shape and significance to their experience. This culture depends upon the ability of human beings "to learn and to transmit learning [regarding meaning] to succeeding generations."[6]

Prior to Vatican II, a well understood Catholic culture provided meaning for people willing to be celibate in order to minister in the church. It gave shape and significance to their experience. It offered particular rewards and nourishment for people like me as well who sought religious life. But those days represent the end of an era. In their stead we find a more secular, less Catholic culture that still wants to make sense out of things, yet without undue reliance on external referents such as church authorities. This generation no longer blindly accepts fiats from authority figures. Given this social climate, it should not be surprising that people in such a culture increasingly find celibacy to be quite senseless and meaningless.

This difference of the generations is evident in a study prepared by psychologist Donna Markham, comparing attitudes toward religious life of women religious and other women in three age groups: twenty-one to thirty-five-year-olds, college-aged, and high-school. The study, created for the Quinn Commission (which was the U.S. bishops' response to Vatican concerns about U.S. religious life) asked participants to respond to the statement: "If I were a single woman, I would consider entering a religious congregation." Women religious responded significantly more positively (65.8 percent) than the other groups. Negativity among the other respondents increased as age decreased. Only 9.7 percent of the twenty-one to thirty-five-year-olds, 3.2 percent of college women, and only 1.3 percent of high-school girls said they would consider entering religious life.[7]

This data finds echoes in the attitudes of people today toward those indicating a desire for priesthood and religious life. In my generation the culture praised you for your self-sacrifice; now they wonder what might be wrong with you. I have found this attitude even among many of us who still remain. One of the first things we ask about possible recruits, is "why" would they want to enter. What are they hiding? What haven't they dealt with in their lives? Is there something wrong with them?

Consequences of the Crisis of Meaning

In a parallel study of women and men religious, Donna Markham discovered that the disparity between the perceptions of younger people and vowed religious, along with the latter's resistance to face such data, indicates some kind of malaise. She noted:

> The continuance of celibate religious community life (as we know it) beyond the present generation is questionable. Younger persons do not find religious life attractive. Among the small group of persons who apply, there is evidence of considerable emotional distress, especially among male applicants. Members of religious congregations are, themselves, unclear about their mission in the church and in the world. The lack of internal clarity and the presence of marked negative regard and criticism from external sources result in stressed organizational functioning characterized by depression, denial, and unconscious attempts to cover over critical concerns.[8]

My own experience corroborates Markham's data and conclusions. She points not only to a malaise that has enveloped religious congregations but also to a kind of anomie. This meaninglessness has become a pattern of life for all too many individual members in the religious congregations I am familiar with. I believe parallels can be found in many dioceses as well.

Ever since the pioneering work of Victor Frankl, psychologists, developmental counselors, and spiritual directors have understood the importance of addressing issues of meaning-making with their clients and directees. Today it's generally expected that people in seminary formation and initial vows, at some time will simultaneously be participating in some form of counseling, often seeking an answer to questions around faith and meaning. Many of the rest of us have spent many hours in therapy trying to figure out what has happened. Given this phenomenon, one might well ask if the countless hours of counseling and countless monies spent really might be somewhat futile as long as the underlying issue of meaning that rests at the heart of our search is not addressed in our therapeutic encounter. Although we continue to spend thousands of dollars on therapists, the nagging question of meaning still remains.

Challenging the therapeutic approach of people like Freud and Skinner, Frankl wrote in his *The Unheard Cry for Meaning* that, even when a neurosis "could be removed, more often than not *when* it was removed a vacuum was left." Frankl's "vacuum" represents the lack of meaning. In discussing the limitations of other therapeutic approaches, he finds their failure linked to questions of meaning:

> The patient was beautifully adjusted and functioning, but meaning was missing. The patient had not been taken as a human being, that is to say, a being in steady search of meaning; and this search for meaning, which is so distinctive of man, had not been taken seriously at its face value, but was seen as a mere rationalization of underlying unconscious psychodynamics. It had been overlooked or forgotten that if a person has found the meaning sought for, he is prepared to suffer, to offer sacrifices, even, if need be, to give his life for the sake of it. Contrariwise, if there is no meaning he is inclined to take his life, and he is prepared to do so even if all his needs, to all appearances, have been satisfied.[9]

In most everyone's life some crisis of meaning seems inevitable, especially in one's mid-years. However, the assumption shared by most therapists is that when one's search for meaning takes place within a wider and supporting environment, the process can turn out positively. However, the crisis of finding one's personal meaning system is compounded when the system or the culture in which one is a member itself no longer offers meaning. Today this necessary support system is less available in the present forms of priesthood and the consecrated life. This multiplies our problem of meaning.

All meaning involves relationships. When one's life relationship within a system or culture is such that it no longer offers its members support in its meaning-system, the crisis of personal meaning is all the deeper and more conflicted. Thus it is for those who took on celibacy, had it placed on them, or are expected to be celibate because of their sexual orientation. When the rationale that once justified one's personal celibacy is so filled with inconsistencies, when it no longer gives meaning, when its failed rationale also applies to the institutional environment established to provide meaning, then faith in the system as well as oneself gets further compounded and compromised.

Building on Frankl's thoughts about the lack of meaning and the option of suicide, I would submit that the institutional church's insistence on celibacy as a requirement for its priests and for homosexuals has had more of an effect on suicides of people in these groups than we would want to admit. (I still believe unresolved issues of sexual orientation led one of my confreres to commit suicide.) And, even if such insistence on celibacy may not result in individual people committing suicide, I still suspect that many suicides among both groups relate to issues related to identity and meaning, if not celibacy itself.

The lack of meaning connected to institutions will have cultural consequences which we have already noted. This is taking place in the slow but steady decline of our traditional Catholic culture. This systemic strangulation is occurring precisely because the institution with its meaning system, as well as the Catholic culture, no longer provide sufficient significance nor offer strong enough sanctions to invite the necessary sacrifice that celibacy demands.

In *The Non-Suicidal Society*, cultural biologist Andrew Oldenquist notes that, if we take seriously biologically based knowledge about the communitarian side of human nature, we will recognize the immense importance of "group egoism"—i.e., our need to belong to a group that cares about us, wherein we can find meaning, and in whose future we have a stake. Only such a group will be that in which we may make at least moderate sacrifices of self-interest. Otherwise we will be forced to live as part of a suicidal society. Oldenquist defines a suicidal society as one:

> whose social ethics, family and community structure, procedures for rearing children, physical layout, educational and juvenile justice systems, are so counterproductive or ineffective as to produce unacceptable numbers of hostile, wretched, useless and dangerous citizens.[10]

Oldenquist finds the seeds of the suicidal society not in the elders of a society but in the young people. These represent the ones reared in an environment that is "counterproductive or ineffective" in producing the kind of people which will enable the society to grow and be a source of growth for others. With so many younger religious and priests as well as many seminarians seemingly angry or unhappy, one can only wonder about the consequences for the future. Who knows how many "useless and dangerous citizens" we will have in church leadership in the future.

The Mass Neurotic Triad and Its Expression Among Celibates

When one feels empty of meaning, when one loses faith in a previously-accepted life-giving system, or when one feels like an alien in a heretofore welcoming culture, a void is left at the core of one's being. Frankl calls this "the existential vacuum." From his experience this sense of personal alienation, meaninglessness, or anomie can be detected in various symptoms. He describes the symptomatology of the existential vacuum as the mass neurotic triad. It comprises depression, aggression, and addiction.[11]

I find it does not take a degree in psychiatry, psychology, or counseling to detect strong resemblances of this "mass neurotic triad" among diocesan priests and members of religious orders today. However, by failing to change the meaningless "meaning system," people will continue to take on celibacy, only to find it never was a true option for them. Their consequent loss of meaning will then find many of them entering one or the other forms of the mass neurotic triad. And the institutional dynamics which helped create the pathology in the first place will suffer more by having to find ways to meet the consequences of its failed norms.

Depression

The first symptom of lack of meaning or the existential vacuum is various forms of depression. This understanding of depression refers to clinically-defined depression which represents a pathological mood disturbance that is accompanied by various thoughts, feelings, and beliefs people have about themselves or their world. It is also characterized by the low-level depression that reveals itself in a lack of enthusiasm, happiness, and joy. It can have other manifestations that fall somewhere between clinical and low-level depression. Often these manifestations seem to have some links with sexuality (and celibacy) as Freud himself showed.

I first became aware as a young priest of the depression-celibacy connection and how a lack of integration could lead to dysfunctionality. I was assigned to an ethnically changing parish—from white to black—where there were many conflicts. Racism seemed everywhere. Increasingly I became aware of how whites exploited blacks. I was depressed at being a part of the group of white people who did this. We Capuchins also had conflicts among ourselves. Some friars wouldn't even talk with one another. My depression increased.

I coped by concentrating on my work during the day and then returning to my room at night. One night, however, I decided to go to the "Ad-Lib," a strip-joint in downtown Milwaukee. I had never been to such a place before, so I didn't know quite what to expect. Inside the dark room a few men sat at tables. Almost all of them, like me, were white. Most were sitting alone. Like them, I sat and watched the women on the stage take off their clothes while the music played. Most of the women were black. Every now and then, when I'd look around, I saw the men ogling the women. They were paying money for these objects to perform. For some reason this led me to think of the slave auctions. The more I thought about it, the more I realized that I was just part of this sexist, racist system that uses people and drops them when they can't perform. By my presence there I was contributing to it. Seeking a release, I found myself bound up even more. Now, even more depressed, I left. As the song goes, I was "looking for love in all the wrong places." Especially when I was afraid of doing what I needed to do—to find that love within myself.

Later, as I wondered why I had gone to such a place, I realized personally that sex is just one way we try to escape from depression. Casual and uncommitted sex is one of the ways people use to forget about their pain or sense of deprivation. Such sex is our effort to fill up the hole in our heart in one way or another. However, as I learned, when we seek unhealthy ways to alleviate the pain, we usually feel guilty. The guilt makes the pain stronger. So we seek stronger relief. This often leads to seeking release in many of the same dysfunctional ways that caused us the guilt in the first place. So, as we repeat the behaviors, we get more deeply involved. Finally an addictive pattern evolves.

While this form of acting on depression has its many victims among us, there is another form that has even more victims. Among my contacts with bishops and major superiors of congregations dedicated to the consecrated life, I increasingly hear considerable discussion related to a kind of "low-level depression" among their members. This phenomenon gets expressed in various ways: low energy, low productivity, general feelings of being ill-at-ease and unhappy, a lack of spontaneity, and feelings of futility. This phenomenon cannot really be termed "burn-out"; it seems to reflect something deeper.

Most often these attitudes never get addressed. When enough members of a community witness such behaviors and a decline in morale, the tenor of the place takes on characteristics found in many residences which house senior citizens. On the one hand the residents find no meaning in their lives. However they have yet to accept or embrace the inevitability of their approaching deaths in a way that might give them peace. So they feel condemned to a way of life they really don't choose. These dynamics reveal a kind of "low-level depression" that characterizes the experience of people in places of death.

One time I lived with "Barry," a young man in temporary vows. As he neared the time to request making a permanent commitment, I found him more and more unsettled. His concern was not just about making a celibate commitment that would limit his possibility of genital expression; it had a communal dimension. This got expressed in a saying he repeated frequently: "I don't want to grow old and live with a bunch of grouches." Barry's fear was not without foundation. It arose from simple observation. While he saw his share of happy, peaceful, and involved Capuchin Franciscans living in our province, he also found enough "grouches" to make him worry what might happen to him.

One evening I heard him say it again, "I don't want to live with a group of grouches." So I asked him, "Why don't you be concrete so I can better understand what you mean? You must have come to this conclusion from observing something happening in the province." The more we talked, we decided to classify the behavior and attitudes of the twenty or thirty men living in our Milwaukee communities as either a "grouch" or a "grower." At the end, we shared our observations. We were surprised to discover we had exactly the same number of friars in each category!

Low-level depression reflects a lack of meaning. Its influence gets compounded for individuals when the environment of priesthood and religious life reflects a parallel depression. While some would argue this seems less the case with diocesan priests,[12] it appears to be very much at the heart of problems facing religious congregations. In discussing the significant discrepancy in women religious' cognitive and affective evaluations of themselves, Donna Markham's psychological profile concluded that it "is suggestive of diminished morale and a kind of 'corporate depression' which is highly defended against through the use of denial and reaction formation."[13] Our individual low-level depression gets aggravated in an environment of institutional depression, especially when it is accompanied by institutional denial.

Aggression and Anger

The second symptom of lack of meaning is aggression. As with depression, I believe connections can also be made with sexual deprivation or denial. The interconnectedness among deprivation, frustration, anger, and aggression is clear to most everyone. When I was growing up people often talked about "frustrated bachelors" and "angry old maids." People instinctively connect someone's aggression with sexual deprivation. The pattern of aggression is quite clear: some goal, need, or desire is experienced. A barrier to those is encountered, resulting in a sense of deprivation. The sense of deprivation creates frustration. The frustration triggers feelings of anger. The anger leads one to act out aggressively, especially toward the perceived source of the frustration or deprivation.

Some psychologists have gone so far as to say that deprivation always causes aggression and aggression is always grounded in some kind of deprivation. Regardless, between the two of them we will always experience frustration and anger.[14]

When one's need for intimacy meets institutional barriers such as compulsory celibacy, the sense of deprivation can easily find people frustrated under its yoke. The resulting anger, often toward the authority figures within that institution, becomes more understandable once we understand its cause. I find it interesting that the most common emotion expressed by seminarians in a 1994 study was anger, and that the anger was often expressed toward authority figures in the institutional aspect of the church.[15]

Martin Pable, a fellow Capuchin and psychologist, has found that one of the most manifest ways celibates exhibit aggressiveness is in what he calls "low-key hostility." He writes:

> In my experience, the most frequent syndrome I have found among priests and religious is what I would call a "low-key hostility." These are not angry people; they are quietly and passively resentful. They resent the burdens of celibacy, the ineptness of religious leadership, the confusion of theology, and the ingratitude of the faithful. Their prayer life—or lack of it—will often reveal that the low-key hostility is also directed at God; somehow he has let them down.[16]

Aggression (which differs from assertiveness) can be passive or active. Passive-aggressive behavior is often more controlling than active aggression. For example, a person can keep others at a distance as much by silence as by shouting. People also react to deprivation and frustration passively when they withdraw, become overly submissive, or manifest behaviors connected with classic codependence. Scratch such external manifestations of passive-aggression, and you will usually find someone who consciously or unconsciously feels deprived and angry. Brenda Herman, who works among church professionals, has described well at least a partial cause for such passive aggression:

> Passive-aggressive behavior is used by a person who stores anger. Fearing the implications of expressing anger, the person acts in a passive manner in an attempt (often not effective) to control the environment without and the rage within. Other persons involved in the situation perceive the person's passiveness as an aggressive attitude. Constantly

being late, not showing up, holding back information, and using silence or escape into asceticism are ways in which some people deny their anger and aggressively seek to control a situation through passive behavior.[17]

In institutional settings, where people feel they have no voice, passive-aggressive behaviors often exist, especially toward those in authority or toward systems representing unaccountable authority. And in cases in which people and systems representing authority are linked with forces of control that result in a person's (un)conscious sense of deprivation, the passive-aggressiveness is doubly hard to address. Psychologists have discovered that members of a group that have become accustomed to authoritarian leadership can often direct an aggressive stance toward a single victim (e.g., a woman employee). Other frequent manifestations of passive aggression occur in the subversion of projects, the undermining of others' effectiveness, jealousy, and envy, as well as a tendency to sabotage common efforts. For example, I knew of one leader in a religious congregation who seemed to undermine any group agreement if the idea was not his. He is a bishop now.

Between frustration and aggression is anger. In fact, anger probably reflects the ordinary way most people manifest their aggression. Like all emotions, anger can be used in a positive or negative way. It can be constructive or destructive. I've met priests and members of religious orders who have used their anger to challenge injustice in very creative ways. I know of others who have used it to control those around them. Repressed anger is a third manifestation. Its results are often directed to and experienced by the very people who are closest to us.

We also find a tendency to project our own repressed anger onto others. Somehow when we label people "angry," they can be dismissed more easily as being "out of control." Typical of this expression we find those ecclesiastics who seem to make it a habit of using the adjective "angry" in identifying many feminists in the church. However, what is said about others' "anger" in such cases often reveals more about what is unacknowledged and repressed in the labelers than those being labeled.

A close examination of one's anger usually reveals unfulfilled needs or wants, or some sense of having one's rights or personhood violated. Janet Malone's defines anger as "a psycho-physiological response to a perceived personal or social hurt or injustice."[18] This is an especially critical point to understand when relating to people who feel they've had no real part in the key decisions (e.g., the demand to be celibate) which affect their lives. This may explain the anger of so many people in the church, including men and women religious, secular priests, and homosexuals. Where unfulfilled wants or needs seem to be the experience of one's life, the resulting sense of deprivation, incompleteness, and pain can only add to the angry outbursts, the aggression, or the depression.

Anger can have many links with depression (as well as addiction). Carol Tavris, turning a truism on its head stated: "Depression is not 'anger turned inward'; if anything, anger is depression turned outward. Follow the trail of anger inward, and there you find the small, still voice of pain."[19] Chief among the expressions of anger of many repressed celibates are various forms of rage, a need to control, and a certain hardness or stand-offishness.

Many times anger results from a sense of betrayal. Thus Jesus' anger in the Temple was at the religious leaders for violating the responsibility entrusted to them by allowing disreputable commerce to take place on Temple grounds. I think this may have represented the kind of anger that arose in me at the Dubuque Airport. There I realized I had been "duped" or "betrayed" into thinking celibacy was, somehow, God's will for me, only to discover this was part of the teaching of an institution intent on controlling me (and others) through its discipline. Perceiving this as unjust, I became angry.

Many times, when people speak against a sense of perceived wrong arising from some injustice (such as the present dispensation related to celibacy), they themselves are defined as "the problem" and labeled as "disloyal." Or they can be dismissed as being "angry." Meanwhile the system—that has betrayed the gospel understanding of justice (in this case, celibacy) by mandating something unjust—goes unscathed. When this happens, it seems to evidence a kind of "blame the victim" mentality. The focus is placed on the "angry nun" instead of the abuse experienced by women in a patriarchal church. We wonder why "Father isn't happy," instead of seeing the problems of mandating celibacy as a requirement of ordination. We scapegoat gay people who desire to make a public commitment of their monogamous love. In this sense, Janet Malone's insights about the causes of anger in familial relationships make great sense:

> The sources of most of our anger arise out of relationships in which there is some type of intimacy and interdependence. We become angry with parents, partners, siblings, friends, and colleagues. Anger can arise in professional and social or church situations in which there is interdependence, or at times dependence, because of an unequal balance of power. Anger occurs when we have been hurt by significant others in our lives, whether personally, professionally, societally, or ecclesially.[20]

The anger generated by hurt reflects not only a sense of betrayal in relationships; increasingly, I am finding that this betrayal also is closely connected to a loss of intimacy and interdependence. Many times the loss of intimacy gets idealized or intellectualized as a way of coping with the pain. However, in a trenchant insight that connects the loss of intimacy and betrayal of relationships with intimacy and interdependence, Carol Gilligan finds yet another element beyond the anger and rage that often flows from these feelings: depression, or what she calls "sadness."[21] While her notions are related more to women, the Dominican psychologist Joseph Guido, finds similar parallels among seminarians: "Like Gilligan's young women, these men are prone to idealize what they have lost and to rage against their sadness for what they want but cannot have."[22]

Addiction

Frankl's third leg of the "mass neurotic triad" that stems from a sense of meaninglessness is addiction. Elsewhere I have defined addiction as "any object or dynamic that controls, at any level, behavior, emotions, and thinking in such an obsessive-compulsive way that it leads to increasing powerlessness and unmanageability (at that level), and ultimately death."[23] These addictions find many priests and members of the consecrated life as well as homosexuals exhibiting attitudes and actions around substances, processes, and relationships in numbers comparable with their lay or heterosexual counterparts. However, as with the other symptoms, individual addictions get compounded when the institution is addictive and remains in denial about its own and its members' addictive ways. The possibility of personal recovery is thereby diminished since the addiction's presence and the institutional reasons to sustain it are often denied in order to preserve the existing arrangements.

The most evident form of addiction affecting the people considered in this book refer to substances such as food, alcohol, nicotine, drugs, and other chemicals. As with the issue of celibacy, a denial by church leaders exists regarding problems related to addictions. In his study of alcoholism among the clergy, Joseph H. Fichter, stated: "There is a large difference of opinion, not only among the clergy alcoholics but also between them and church officials, on the current trend in clergy alcoholism. More of the alcoholics (31.3%) than of the church officials (9.8%) think that alcoholism is increasing among the clergy."[24]

Fichter published his book in 1982, the year after my last term on the Capuchin provincial council. During that term alone, the council intervened in at least twenty-five cases of alcoholism among the 275 men who belonged to the province at that time. Because of the province's persistent efforts to address substance abuse addictions, we regularly have at least fifty men in some form of recovery. While our province may have been progressive in addressing addictions, I don't think the percentages of our members with addictions are dissimilar to those in other congregations of religious or among diocesan priests. The question for me is not so much why we have so many substance abusers, but whether their reason for "using" can be isolated only to their own biological families; could there be factors within the ecclesiastical family affecting their addictions as well? Despite the fact that no solid data exists comparing the incidence of alcoholism among the clergy in relation to the wider population, the experience of my own province indicates that our addictions are *at least* as prevalent as in the rest of society, and may be significantly higher.

The second classification of addictions refers to what can be called "process addictions." These include gambling, shopping, working, exercise, and even an activity like playing the stock market. I discovered the latter tendency in myself when I oversaw some invested funds for another group. I was in California where I could get a "rush" two times a day. I could open the morning's *Wall Street Journal* to get the final reports from the day before. Then

I could work myself up in anticipation of the afternoon's trading that was picked up in the *San Francisco Examiner*. And the money wasn't even mine!

Other priests and religious have serious gambling addictions. This certainly proved to be the case with one of our brothers and it had implications for our congregation. He admitted his problem but never sought help. Although they knew about his problem, the leaders did not demand that he get help until it was too late. His gambling with money found parallels in the way he gambled with the presence of the province's ministry in an Islamic country where he and some of our other brothers worked secretly. When he was discovered by that country's customs officers sneaking in religious articles, all of his baggage was checked. This revealed detailed notes about the nature of the Capuchin mission there as well as the names of the men involved. He was placed under house arrest. Finally he and the other men had to leave the country.

We all knew of this friar's proclivity toward gambling. But nothing was ever done about it. Only when he gambled with the lives of others, and of our interests in that country, did we take action. It wasn't until he returned to this country that he was sent away for treatment for his disease.

The third form of addictive behavior that affects priests, religious, and homosexuals in a significant way, I believe, deals with relationships, sexual dynamics, and genital expressions. People can be "relationship addicts" in the way they use other people based on their utility. Others might be "sexual addicts," using people as objects for their sexual pleasure. Sex addicts are controlled by obsessive thoughts and feelings and compulsive genitally-oriented behaviors with themselves or with others. While the tendency may exist for one or more of these forms in all of our lives, the problem arises when these forces take control in such a way that they undermine our integrity and commitments.

Because so many professionals in church ministry find identity in their roles and in what they do, their resulting inability to be intimate can easily result in unhealthy relationships where others get used and abused. This method of control can lead to a relationship addiction. I know of one priest who was expert at raising money, until his benefactors became aware of his method of operation. The only times they would receive letters or calls from him were connected to a request for monies for this project or that program he was coordinating. Whenever they needed something from him, he was conveniently not available. Sooner or later they grew tired of being used by him. His addiction undermined the effectiveness of the ministry itself.

Some relate to others in ways that feed unhealthy sexual addictions, even though they may never have genital sex. The manifestations of any sexual addiction have been well-described by Patrick Carnes, a pioneer in the study of this form of addiction:

> Sexual arousal becomes intensified. The addict's mood is altered as he or she enters the obsessive trance. The metabolic responses are like a rush through the body as adrenaline speeds up the body's functioning. The heart pounds as the addict focuses on his search object. Risk, danger, and even violence are the ultimate escalators. One can always increase the dosage of intoxication. Preoccupation effectively buries the personal pain of remorse or regret. The addict does not always have to act. Often just thinking about it brings relief.[25]

Whatever the sexual object of a person's preoccupation, when actions defined by that object dominate one's thoughts, feelings, and deeds, the person is out of control. This can be true particularly in the area of sexual fantasizing and feelings of anxiety about whether or not to remain celibate. When such thoughts get expressed in behaviors, they can be myriad and destructive not only of self, but others as well.

Such is the case of a young religious I know. Given his good looks (and matching personality) women easily become infatuated with him. While these characteristics might or might not have played into their own possible sexual addictions, his "drug of choice" centered on happily-married women with children. At the point in the relationship where these wives and mothers would let him know they were willing to violate their chastity and break their commitments to their husbands and children by having genital relations with him, he would drop them.

Having led these women to "lust in their heart" enabled him to fulfill his lust. While admitting he gets a rush in leading them on the way he does, he does not admit his behavior might be addictive. So his recovery is stymied. Meanwhile more lives get broken in the process. And he considers himself an excellent priest.

Another form of relationship addiction involves genital expression in various compulsive forms of behavior. These get expressed in masturbation, cruising, visiting pornographic book stores, massage parlors, gay baths, etc. Interestingly, in light of my thesis about control and church hierarchy, Patrick Carnes includes in this group of addicts, people who are preoccupied by the need to repress their own or others' sexual and/or genital expressiveness.[26] Elsewhere I have called this form of repression a kind of "sexual anorexia."[27] This disease seems reinforced in the experience of Anne Wilson Schaef, herself an addictions specialist. She writes: "I believe that many of our most outspoken leaders of organized religions are themselves sexual addicts. They are so obsessed with sex that they make it impossible for church members to learn about healthy sexuality in the church. Often, the church makes sex the most important aspect of a relationship."[28]

Increasingly, I believe, sexual anorexia might explain many of the reasons for the obsession some in the hierarchy seem to have in preserving the present situation of celibate, clerical patriarchy in the institutional church. And, just as someone like the singer Karen Carpenter could die of anorexia, I believe sexual anorexia around celibacy can be suicidal for individuals as well as the institution.

Another form of sexual addiction involves exhibitionism and voyeurism (or a combination of the two). The latter can be especially evident among formation directors, counselors, and spiritual directors who probe their clients and directees for details regarding their sexual lives and experiences. Somehow this voyeurism gives them vicarious satisfaction. They may never act out or invade another's body sexually or genitally, but they do so mentally. This group of genital addicts also includes those who exhibit a pattern of indulging in indecent phone calls or exhibit a pattern of consistent, unsolicited liberties with others, such as touching, patting, or hugging.

Finally, there are the addictive genital behaviors of child molesting, incest, rape, and pedophilia. However, when these "level three" forms of genital expression are perpetrated by priests and religious, they usually involve people who have come to relate to their victims from a position of trust. Consequently, as we've seen so often with pedophilia, their behavior also involves the issue of power over others in some form of control. In almost all cases of pedophilia involving clergy and religious, the perpetrators were able to more easily escape critique and punishment of their behaviors because they occupied positions of power in ecclesiastical settings wherein their victims had first come to trust them.

When any of relational, sexual, or genital behaviors become truly addictive, one's life has become unmanageable. When institutions impose forms of control that can lead to such behaviors, the institutional life will be unmanageable as well. Is there any wonder then, that people increasingly are having not only a lessening (if not a crisis) of faith in priests and religious, but even more so, in institutional religion as well?

In conclusion, I have tried to show in this chapter that any individual crisis of meaning (faith) is compounded when key institutions and even culture itself no longer generate meaning or faith in that "something." Thus, as people increasingly experience their own personal crisis of meaning in celibacy, when celibacy in the institution is undermined, and when the culture that was once defined by celibacy no longer generates faith in celibacy, the individual celibate's crisis of meaning will be more severe. It is little wonder then, why we continually face in the Catholic church various forms of the "mass neurotic triad" of depression, aggression, and addiction. The next chapter will examine further unhealthy ways people cope with a celibacy that no longer gives meaning to them.

6

More Unhealthy Ways of Coping with the Celibate "Option"

Around the time I discovered I had little scriptural foundation for my professed life of celibacy, I met a woman to whom I knew I was sexually attracted. Before meeting her, I didn't have to confront the issue of celibacy. I even thought I had addressed it in a fairly healthy way.[1] The relationship I subsequently developed with my new friend presented me with my first sustained challenge to the "option" for celibacy I thought I had chosen freely. This relationship forced me to re-examine how I had lived until then as a professed celibate, how I would relate to her if I would remain a celibate, and whether I could truly live celibately in the future.

The experience also made me aware of how little I really knew about the true meaning of celibacy. Gradually, I discovered that my approach to celibacy had not always been healthy, much less holy. Under the new light of this relationship I also discovered that, to fill the emptiness compounded by my "choice" for celibacy, I had experienced more than my share of meaninglessness that got exhibited in more than my share of the depression, aggression, and addiction discussed in the previous chapter.

During this time, I closely re-examined my life. I recalled conversations with others in counseling, direction, and confession. I read articles and newspaper reports, and participated in clergy conversations. The more I did this the more I realized many other unhealthy ways I and other "professed" celibates have compensated for the lack of meaning that comes from the practice and nonpractice of being celibate. While these ways differed in expression, they had the same cause expressed in the depression, aggression, and addiction noted previously. Like these manifestations of the "mass neurotic triad," these other symptoms also reveal a deeper disease: the emptiness that accompanies the awareness that a traditional form of mandated celibacy no longer provides much meaning to many. These expressions also get aggravated further in a system which is becoming increasingly meaningless as well.

Depression, aggression, and addiction often represent key indicators of a life without sufficient meaning, especially for celibates. These other symptoms can be found in codependency, asexuality and ladder-climbing, intellectualization, workaholism and perfectionism, repression, acting-out, and disassociation. In this chapter, I will try to examine the dynamics of these other unhealthy alternatives to the celibate "option."

Codependency

Codependency, especially in younger seminarians and religious, is expressed in various forms connected to "external referencing." Here one's identity is measured by the expectations of others. The "others" in this case can be either individual persons or institutional representatives. Codependency can be expressed in a kind of mindless adherence to rules and rituals, as well as cultural norms and expectations. It also exists in older, career-type clergy and religious who have found their lives revolving around upward mobility in the system which depends on being accepted by those in control. The main characteristic of codependency for those of us who suffer from it occurs when our ways of thinking, feeling, and acting are defined by the thinking, feeling, and acting of forces outside ourselves. We are not self-defined; rather others control how we perceive ourselves to be and how we determine the direction our lives might take.

In the late 1980s I became increasingly aware of how codependent I am. I discovered that much of my self-identity revolved around other peoples' assumptions and expectations. Paradoxically, these "others" did not need to be defined; they were as easily institutionalized as individualized. I was a classic codependent insofar as their way of thinking, feeling, and acting effectively controlled my own.[2] My identity was not based in my own self; it was controlled by what others thought, felt, or did vis-à-vis my "self." I was codependent to the degree that my identity and meaning were defined by these "others." This did not mean I took on their ideas and theology, their desires and wants, much less their expectations or norms for my behavior. In fact, I learned that my type of code-pendency often expressed itself by reacting to these very things by thoughts, feelings, and actions that were directly opposite. Nonetheless the ideas, desires, and expectations of these others still controlled my own. Many times, I simply acted *against* them; yet they still controlled me.

It seems I am not alone. A 1991 study concluded that Catholic laymen view themselves as more independent than Catholic priests. Conversely, the study also showed that, as a group, priests presently view themselves as more dependent than Roman Catholic laymen.[3] I believe much of the reasons for our "external referencing" can be found in the fact that those of us who are priests and male religious are public figures. In addition, we minister in a public institution led by very public individuals. Consequently we clerics and religious in the institutional church do what all men are tempted to do—find personal meaning or identity in reference to outside "identifiers"—but we do it to an extreme. Victor Seidler has shown that, while "men often have a strong sense of identity within the public realm, this is often at the cost of a more personal sense of self." This male tendency has its costs in discovering one's authentic self:

> Because there is a strong connection between learning our masculinity and learning to be impersonal, rational and objective, we are often left with a weakened sense of individual identity. Often we are left estranged from our feelings and emotions, learning to read off our feelings from the world around us. This produces a false sense of objectivity, and we become so identified with the goals and ends we set ourselves, especially at work, that we are often blind to our emotional needs.[4]

While this tendency to be externally referenced for one's identity can exist in all males, it seems particularly the problem with us males who depend upon or seek acceptance and/or approval from the institutional church and its leaders for ministry within it. The cost of such other-defined thinking, desires, and expected behaviors is discovered in crises which inevitably will occur.

Dominican priest-psychologist Joe Guido wrote a fascinating and disturbing 1994 Harvard thesis on Catholic seminarians. His findings showed that three-fourths to five-sixths of the seminarians studied—who ranged in age from twenty-three to thirty-four—were not fully capable of self-generated meaning and values, but rather derived a sense of self, meaning, and values at least in part from the interpersonal and institutional contexts which constituted their environment.[5] In this they may not be different from other men of their age in this culture. Ninety-five percent of the seminarians studied were "not fully capable of constructing their experience and its meaning" at a level of personal integration and self-definition.[6]

However, Guido's thesis also revealed the high extent to which an adolescent level of consciousness still dominated in so many of these adult seminarians. He wrote that fully "one-fifth of these men may be relying upon mental capacities that more appropriately characterize late childhood and early adolescence than adulthood."[7] Furthermore he discovered that the overwhelming level of consciousness of almost all the seminarians was "inadequate to the challenges of adulthood." He concluded that healthy maturity for these men demanded that they "dis-embed" themselves from their present ways of thinking in a manner "commensurate to the demands and tasks and loves of adult life." If they do not, he determined, "they will increasingly experience a subjective sense of discomfort and an objective measure of inadequacy in the tasks they undertake."[8] Guido hypothesized that, in eight years or so after leaving such a controlled environment as the seminary, and left to their own resources to face these tasks, these (former) seminarians would experience deep crises as priests.[9]

Asexuality and Ladder-Climbing

Another symptom of behavior for those who have taken on celibacy can be found in various forms of asexuality. This means one's sexual feelings and needs do not get experienced, much less expressed. I discovered an almost classic example of the consequences of asexuality in a friend while I was studying in Berkeley. "Francis" had been in his congregation at least seven years. Previous to his arrival in Berkeley, Francis had studied for his doctorate in economics; his whole orientation had been geared toward the degree. Only after completing it could he move on to theology. Then he would be ordained.

Once Francis achieved his goal of the doctorate and came to Berkeley, however, he experienced a new world of ideas and feelings. He became able to perceive sexual needs and desires in himself that had been repressed. Free of his preoccupation with achieving something outside of himself—namely the degree—Francis realized he had unresolved sexual issues related to intimacy that had gone unaddressed for many years. He began to feel a strong urge to couple with a woman and to experience sexual and genital intimacy.

At the same time, increasingly conscious of his own needs, he became more observant of how some of his peers seemed to be addressing their sexual needs. He became aware of relationships among his confreres in community that opened his eyes to something else going on. He noticed some of the unhealthy ways some of his peers were expressing sexual intimacy. Some were living as gay couples. He never before realized that so many men in his order were gay, especially at the seminary level.

He articulated his surprise to me one day in words that jolted me as well: "I used to just assume that almost everyone in the order was heterosexual and that gays were the exception. But since I've come here and seen what I've seen, now I just assume the average seminarian I meet will be homosexual." Not long after, Francis left the order, started teaching at a university, met a woman there, and was married.

Another form of asexuality is acted out in a form of "ladder-climbing"—a kind of sublimation whose expression is power. This usually takes place well after ordination and occurs when a person becomes so "given over" to climbing the ladder of success that his sexual drive is repressed through power. Oftentimes that power is expressed in having influence over others in the form of control. It receives further reinforcement in patriarchal systems, such as the church. Herein the loss of meaning or intimacy receives compensation through various power relations. The personal loss of meaning is compensated as one seeks to find meaning in one's systems. What Jeff Hearn explains of men in the public eye, fits well the situations of priests and male religious who serve as public figures:

> The creation of more complex societies with more powerful public domain institutions provides the conditions for yet more powerful relations for men. Any possible feelings of "loss" for men—personal, existential, collective—may be more than "compensated" by new orders of men's power, both individual and collective. . . .While the movement to

the modern, and thence the postmodern, may involve loss, it also offers opportunities for men to gain power.[10]

A classic example of the asexuality expressed in power seems quite clear in a bishop I know. "Bishop Horatio" finds his identity in his role as bishop. Almost always he appears with his French cuffs and rabat. Everyone just knows that Horatio must always be addressed as "bishop." One time I was at a workshop for a group of bishops (including Horatio) and congregational leaders of religious orders. Since this gathering was an annual affair, relationships among the participants had become quite informal. No other bishop or leader wore his traditional habit; all went by their first names. But "Horatio" wore his official street clerics and everyone continued to call him "bishop."

In one instance during a discussion, one of the women provincials and he had a lively exchange on some issue. They disagreed strongly on the matter. Finally, the exasperated sister said something like, "But Bishop, how can you say something like that? You are a man!" Looking shocked at her challenge, and drawing himself up, Horatio proclaimed, "I am not a man; I am a bishop!" This man's identity was in his office, not in his person.[11]

I have known men who are priests and religious who have worked diligently to become bishops and congregational leaders. Sometimes their drive for a hierarchical role has been palpable. With one who became a bishop, you could just watch the ways he "schmoozed" with other power bishops in the church. Two of the bishops who have been involved in decisions to keep me out of their dioceses because of what I have written and said about *The Dysfunctional Church* have been promoted. Another time, during the election process in one community, I said to one of the candidates for higher office as we walked around during the chapter: "You really want to be elected, don't you?" "How can you say that?" he asked, somewhat embarrassed. "I can *feel* it," is all I could respond.

Intellectualization, Workaholism, Perfectionism

In the "Francis" example above, his preoccupation with getting his degree kept other issues from coming to the surface. He could resolve them in his head. In my own life, my ability to intellectualize even found me publishing quite a good paper on celibacy!

Intellectualization is another way celibates compensate for lack of meaning. Intellectualization is a great way to avoid dealing with our feelings, especially feelings about intimacy and sex. If I can keep everything at the level of facts, data, objectivity, truth, norms, etc., I can avoid moving beyond my brain to other parts of myself and my body. By staying at the level of the head, I can avoid dealing with issues of the heart and can stay in charge. I don't need to be defenseless, much less vulnerable. However, such mind games can be played only for so long.

Many times, I find a more permanent form of intellectualization alive and very apparent in many other priests and religious. We seem expert at keeping everything in our head where we can remain in control. Catholic celibates tend to be among the best at intellectualization and the most guarded about issues of intimacy.

Workaholism and perfectionism represent two more potentially debilitating ways to avoid issues related to celibacy and other situations which are found to be unmeaningful. A workaholic's identity revolves around what one does. A perfectionist's purpose gets identified in achievement. Such behaviors do not go unnoticed in a system based on achieving holiness and holy achievements. In the interplay between institutions and individuals which reinforces unhealthy behaviors when meaning is lacking, it is precisely these two dynamics which often characterize the truly loyal and successful person.

This is especially true in these days of shrinking personnel in the ranks of the clergy and religious life. Those who remain are saddled (or yoke themselves as good codependents) with extra burdens. A friend of mine finally left the priesthood when he discovered he was burning himself out trying to cover two or three parishes every week. Loyal codependent that he was, he felt a personal responsibility to bail out the bishop. Finally he realized the institution which honored him for doing this would just keep letting him do so until he broke. When it dawned on him that he was just being used to keep the system afloat, and how he was "codependent on the system," he left. The system would not change its way of thinking and its demands on him. So he changed *his* thinking and became free of its demands.

Perhaps more accurately, workaholism should be termed "work addiction." Work addiction better describes the true nature, as well as consequences, of this attitude, form of compulsivity, and behavior. While some church leaders decry the lack of productivity among the members of their dioceses or congregations (which may be the case with some), I don't believe this is the norm. Studies show that the sixty-hour week for clergy can be quite normal.

Consequences of celibates' creating lives centered in work have only become apparent in recent years. As a 1994 reflection on apostolic religious life from the Archdiocese of Milwaukee stated: "Long accustomed to an exaggerated work ethic, we religious have only begun to recognize the harmful tendency to define ourselves in terms of our capacity for uninterrupted work in God's vineyard."[12] In my personal life, I have found that my work addiction, especially in its previous expressions, often arose from feelings of fear. My fear had many faces: fear of intimacy which resulted in escape, fear of rejection which resulted in having to make things perfect, fear of losing control which made me do more things myself than I should, and fear of being isolated and unaffirmed, making me want to succeed and be recognized.

In his *Revisioning Men's Lives: Gender, Intimacy, and Power,* Terry A. Kupers coined a phrase, "pathological arrhythmicity," as the male counterpart to premenstrual syndrome (PMS). Reading about its symptoms, I realized the disease is endemic for many of us men whose lives have been defined by our presence in a patriarchal system. His description of its pathology seems to fit the job description of many a loyal cleric in the Catholic church:

> The coping styles we have evolved in order to succeed at work—working long hours without letting up, arriving at work each day even when not feeling well, hiding our true feelings, remaining vigilant before the prospect of attack from as-yet-undisclosed enemies—all depend on our ability to override natural cycles. It is natural to cry when hurt and laugh raucously when something appears very funny; thus, our practiced stifling of tears and modulation of laughter are just prominent symptoms of our arrhythmicity.
>
> There are other symptoms: an obsessional feeling one always has to be on schedule, an inability to let emotional experiences take their course, an inability to truly enjoy relationships and events that are not task-oriented, a refusal to admit when strong feelings interfere with the desire or capacity to continue what one is doing, difficulty

coping with illness (one's own and those of others), an inability to rest and take time to heal, and so forth.[13]

Paradoxically, work addiction, while supposedly being for "the greater honor and glory of God," often has little to do with God. Rather, it may have much more to do with the promotion of self for one's self-made gods and their ways. It usually has little to do with spirituality and self-transcendence. When this occurs, work addiction belies an inward emptiness under the mask of the holy. For instance, we create gods called "ministry," "availability," or "doing it right." These gods become the idols of our false or unfulfilled needs. Rather than serving the God revealed in Jesus Christ, our work becomes a false god in whom we (or our canonical superiors) are well pleased.

A deeper analysis of work addiction shows that a workaholic does not seek religious answers to the traditional religious questions regarding self, identity, direction, and ways of resolving difficulties. Rather the "answers" get resolved in religion-become-work. Answers found in work become stronger the more religious overtones can be connected with them. Benjamin Hunnicutt, author of *Work Without End*,[14] concludes that "The new work ethic is not Protestant; there is little or no God-talk associated with it. It is a distinctively modern and secular work ethic/religion."[15] In other words, much work—even that undertaken in God's name or in the name of religion—can reflect patterns having little or nothing to do with God. In fact, much of it often can reveal spiritual bankruptcy.

The lack of a God connection in workaholism demands that we realize how institutional religion is hurt, not benefited, by workaholism, at least in the long run. Leonard Greenhalgh, a psychologist at Dartmouth University's Tuck Business School, has offered a "taxonomy of workaholics." He finds in all individuals with a work addiction some deep attraction with the corporate level in which they work. This attraction to the corporate dimension for the individual workaholic can be apropos for us who work as ministers in the institutional church. For some, workaholism can be an escape from anything anxiety-related or from unfulfilled needs. According to Greenhalgh: "If somebody has a compulsion to keep busy, chances are there's something he or she is trying not to think about." Others become workaholics by avoiding some other kinds of problems but seek a "socially acceptable excuse for avoiding problems there." A third group has a deep need to control and does so by making sure everything is done correctly. "These are pretty good for the [organization] . . ." Greenhalgh says. "They are super organized, overcome obstacles, and are highly committed. The downside is that they're not easy to work for. They can't let others participate because they would lose a degree of control." The final type that easily becomes a workaholic is the one with a low self-esteem, who is depressed, who is externally referenced, and whose identity is defined by approval from others: "This is somebody with a low degree of self-esteem who needs to get a feeling of self-esteem from his work. Maybe his parents' approval was conditional on his doing well." It's not much fun being such a person, Greenhalgh says. "He's got a chronic low-grade depression. People label him 'overly serious.'" However, this kind of person is just what an organization's leaders would desire: "He really strives to excel; he takes on challenges because he's looking for approval, particularly from higher management."[16]

Since perfectionism relies more on performance than personality, and success instead of selfhood, a perfectionist's personal identity often rests in doing rather than being. A perfectionist becomes preoccupied with results rather than relationships. Indicators of perfectionism are low self-esteem and poor self-control, procrastination and fear of failure, and relationships that often can be short-lived or troubled. Many times the tendency or manifestation toward perfectionism can reflect reaction formations against self-imposed taboos, self-forbidden (or other-forbidden) attractions, impulses, desires, and motivations.

Great differences exist between persons who strive for perfection in a self-actualized way and ones who continually seem oriented to ever higher levels of performance or some unreachable goal. The former have a healthy pursuit of some end that serves as a point of motivation. The latter are compulsive and relentless in their strain to do better; they also expect of others goals that can't be achieved. The perfectionist can never be perfect. Neither can anyone else.

Like workaholism, perfectionism can be rewarded highly by an organization more preoccupied with performance than persons. "Making it" can replace meaning. "Doing it right" stands as a surrogate for right relationships. "Practice makes perfect" often means, "Do it my way." The "right way" can be "the only way."

Psychologists have found that perfectionism is a common trait among children of dysfunctional families. With many more people entering seminaries and religious life from dysfunctional families, the likelihood of many more cases of perfectionism cannot be far behind. A common attitude many of these perfectionists may have had as children—"If I get perfect enough, maybe Mommy or Daddy will help me"—often gets transferred to new ecclesiastical "father" figures. This dynamic, accompanied by external referencing, spells sure troubles in the long run for those driven by this obsessive need.

Perfectionism reveals a drive for achievement, prestige, and accomplishment. And when the patriarchal clerical system is based on performing in a certain way (determined by perfectionists outside of oneself), the perfection-demanding parents of one's childhood can get displaced by institutional authorities. Meeting their expectations or ideals (or other notions of "perfection") can easily become the norm for one's identity. Wilkie Au and Noreen Cannon have shown how religion often serves as an overlay to reinforce such nascent perfectionism: "While the perfectionistic attitude is so remarkably widespread that it can be seen as a cultural phenomenon, it is strongly reinforced for Christians by certain religious factors."[17] The first is grounded in the biblical command to be perfect as God is perfect (Mt 5:48), the second is the way the Christian message is portrayed by the churches, and the third arose historically from the rhetoric of religious life. In my own life, I certainly have become better aware of how all three function in my conditioning.

Another religious dimension of perfectionism can be found, I believe, in the way religious authorities have traditionally rewarded perfectionism with everything from perks to chancery positions and prelatures to sainthood. The effort to be accepted by such authorities or be befriended by them is often obsessive. Fear of displeasing them can lead one to an addictive form of perfectionism.

Repression and Acting Out

Repression represents another unhealthy way of coping with lack of meaning. Repression represents an unconscious process whereby a person tries to keep from conscious awareness certain thoughts, feelings, and experiences he or she is reluctant or fearful to face. Repression is synonymous with unconscious control. For one to be free or to consciously make choices is antithetical to the power of his or her unconscious processes. Not living under this freedom and seeking to repress it has a price. The priest-psychologist William F. Kraft has shown clearly the costs of such repression for celibate priests or religious:

> A person who categorically rejects a dynamic that is factually part of his or her make-up pays a price. Repression is a negative reinforcement; instead of expunging an experience, repression can increase its strength and promote pressure for expression. The ways a religious unconsciously copes with repressed sexual energy are usually not in the service of health. For instance, a sexually repressed religious may become frustrated, irritable, and angry. Or such a religious may automatically abstain from intimacy for fear of being sexually activated, and he may use celibacy to rationalize such avoidance. Or a religious may project or displace his own feelings by blaming others for immodesty, or perhaps achieve some vicarious satisfaction and shaky self-reinforcement by becoming the community "sex censor."[18]

In dealing with repression, I believe, there is a significant difference between how men and women respond to situations where they have never freely chosen celibacy, yet are publicly professed to be so. It seems that many women have something seminal in them or are conditioned in a way that enables them to sublimate celibately in a more healthy way than most men. I think that one of the reasons for this rests in the fact that women are socialized around relationships; men around sex.[19] What might be sublimation for a woman can be repression for a man. While the relationship itself becomes the concern with women, for men sexuality and/or genitality becomes the opener for the relationship. Even the physiology of men sends sexual signals in a stronger and more immediately physical way than women. Men usually feel physiological pressure to be sexually satisfied in a relationship before women, though women seem to sense it more deeply when they experience it. Thus, many women find it easier to repress sexual feelings; for men it's almost impossible.

The easiest way people escape the celibate lifestyle is to seek release from it through various forms of genital gratification or acting out. Masturbation is the most common form of genital gratification among celibates. William Kraft describes clinically what men know intuitively about masturbation and other forms of genital acting-out: the core motivation for the behavior rests in the sense of deprivation, loneliness, or hurt that one feels at the depths. Such persons "may engage in genital activity to escape the pain of his or her lonely emptiness," he writes. "Although this is humanly understandable, it is not healthy or good. When gratification of genitality is used to escape loneliness, there may be 'fulfillment,' but the fulfillment is only temporary."[20] I find it almost the norm that when priests and religious confess to masturbation their rationale invariably involves some kind of loneliness or sense of being misunderstood. It is done to fill up the sense of inner emptiness.

Genital gratification or acting-out also involves much of the way priests or religious can spend their free time. Many know just what they will do sexually or genitally during leisure time, on days off, when they visit a city far-enough-away from where they may work, or go on a vacation. In these situations, a person's thoughts and planning often get oriented to ways they can seek sexual or genital release. Sometimes we do this secretly; other times it is a matter of public knowledge. I once lived with a friar whom everyone knew went to pornographic movies on his day off. Others share among themselves where the gay cruising bars can be found in the nearest big city or where female prostitutes congregate. For those returning from their outings, the code seems to be: "If you don't ask, I don't need to tell."

In one of the places where I lived in the late 80s, there were many seminaries. I myself lived in a house of formation while there. At various times the seminarians would have parties, mainly feted at the houses of the various religious orders. One of the new brothers at our house had been told for weeks to look forward to his initiation into the party scene. When he finally did go, he discovered "twenty to thirty seminarians all over the place." In every room "something was going on." Wherever he went in the religious house he found at least some of the male seminarians kissing and embracing each other or some female guest. "I was given the distinct impression," he told me, "that, if I chose to remain, new levels would be available to me."

Such acting-out at the individual level often results in repression on the institutional level. I know of one bishop who said to his newly-ordained: "I know there will be times when you all need to do what you have to do. Just don't do it in this diocese." Also, a provincial I knew found himself dealing with deviant sexual and genital behavior by some men in his province. When I asked him how these celibates could justify their behavior, he said simply, "I just think they dissociate."

Deeper forms of repression occur when one excludes from awareness those experiences and impulses that would be anxiety-provoking if they were consciously expressed. This is known as dissociation. It represents thoughts, feelings, and actions that are incompatible with one's self-concept or self-image. This idea, as articulated by Harry Stack Sullivan, describes dissociation as a defensive technique whereby thoughts and impulses which would threaten one's self image and which are expected by society are screened from consciousness. It distorts the reality of the thoughts, desires, and behaviors that are incompatible with one's position in life.[21]

The Reluctance to Address the Issue of Homosexual Men in Church Ministry

Part of the experience of my seminarian friend at the parties noted above raises a very sensitive issue that has been repressed or dissociated at the institutional level for too long. I refer to the issue of the rising numbers of homosexuals in seminaries, the newly-ordained, and the priesthood, as well as the apparently even larger numbers entering and belonging to institutes of the consecrated life.

I tried to describe this reality as prudently and cautiously as I could in *The Dysfunctional Church*. Yet, with the publication of the book, I realized I had used an unfortunate word to describe the situation. I wrote:

> North American data suggests that among the clergy at least thirty percent are homosexual in their orientation. On the other hand, these increasing numbers of men must remain closeted and repressed—denying who they are—because of the climate of homophobia that comes from the Vatican. When the various unhealthy symptoms in a closed, dysfunctional family dominate (no-talk rule, internalized feelings, unspoken expectations, entangled relationships), it is no wonder bishops and major superiors

seem paralyzed by this phenomenon of ever-increasing numbers of homosexuals seeking admission to seminaries, priesthood, and religious life. They just deny the problem exists.[22]

The unfortunate word I used to describe the situation appears in the last sentence of the quote above. In speaking of the increasing numbers of homosexuals among the clergy, I said that bishops and major superiors deny the *problem* exists. To me, the increasing numbers of homosexuals entering the priesthood and religious life is not the problem. Rather I trace the problems connected with this issue to the ways denial and dissociation work in the institutional church and culture, that keep the reality from being addressed creatively, cleanly, and clearly.

One reason some homosexuals enter seminaries and formation programs, I believe, is because they have heard enough gay-bashing from the leaders of the institutional church that they co-dependently are attracted to the very forces that will abuse them more. Others enter with repressed homosexual feelings; without realizing it they are attracted to an all-male group. Still others come because they feel they will be supported to live in a way that will keep them from facing that which they reject in themselves. Other men, more honest about their homosexuality (and thus, more healthy), believe they will be encouraged in life-giving ways to deepen their celibacy. Whatever the reasons may be, once they enter, because the leaders fail to address the reality and offer healthy ways to help men live celibately in an all-male fraternity, there can be a tendency to be influenced by other elements including some of the negative elements in the gay subculture.

A tendency of oppressed groups to find meaning and support among their own members can be found in subcultures that exist in wider cultures of repression. While this can be very healthy and necessary, it also can contain a shadow-side in the form of exclusionary dynamics which undermine community. In such gatherings, boundary lines get drawn. When such dynamics take place, people out of the "in group" may either become homophobic or find their own homophobia "validated." Gay-bashing can result. Even when the sub-groups are not exclusive, they can be perceived as a threat because of homophobia and/or projection by others who have not addressed their own latent homosexuality.

Another consequence of having increasing numbers of repressed homosexuals in the priesthood and religious life has only begun to surface as our Catholic clergy moves from being defined as heterosexual to being increasingly homosexual. Social psychologists, aware of what happens when oppressed peoples use power when it is given to them, recently have pointed to a phenomenon already occurring in some religious groups: the arbitrary way some homosexuals or gays entering positions of leadership can exercise authority. A priest friend of mine who is gay recently told me about his own experience of mistreatment at the hands of some of the very men in the chancery who were closeted gays. This led him to fear the consequences, not only for people like him who were open about their orientation, but priests in general, having nothing to do with sexual issues: "I always knew where I stood with the old guard of 'Irish bucks,'" he said. "They played by the rules. But now, because they've been hurt by the old rules (about homosexuals in the church) that were stacked against them, and because they've been repressed for so long, these new people don't play by rules. There's nothing consistent. You are either in their favor or out of it. It all depends on whether they like you or not."

In too many instances, I find the institutional response to such data is one of denial, delusion, and dissociation. Once, after meeting with the North American provincials of an international group of religious men, the host-provincial expressed shock at learning that in my province some of the gay friars had organized themselves into a support group. At that time it was quite unique for any group of religious men to have such a "gay caucus." "All of us have gays and good numbers of them. At least our province admits it and tries to respond to it in a healthy way," I said. "We would never do anything like that in our congregation," he responded. "Why not?," I asked. "Because we don't have that kind of a problem," he countered. For some time, this man's province had gone without men in temporary vows. However, just a few months before, three novices had made first profession. One of them had come to the gathering of the provincials that I had attended. On the way back to his place of residence in another state, he was apprehended by the police. A young man, a minor, had reported that he had solicited him for sex. Just three months out of the novitiate, the newly-professed celibate was sent immediately to Jemez Springs, New Mexico for treatment for his sexual disorder. Ultimately he left, or was forced to leave, the congregation.

A few months later, during a workshop I gave, I stopped at the local community house where the other two newly-professed were living after novitiate. There I learned they were in the process of moving out. They planned on leaving the congregation. It seems they had fallen in love with each other and wanted to cohabit. Their departure would leave the province with no men in temporary vows. The lived reality was quite a contrast to the provincial's remarks!

Reflecting on his initial reaction about gays in religious life, as well as the reactions of others like him, I have concluded that there is no other way to describe this behavior other than denial. Possibly, because he had identified himself so totally with his office as corporate personality of the province, he could have been revealing some kind of corporate dissociation as well.

One of the greatest obstacles to honestly addressing the issue of homosexuality by ecclesiastical leaders involves the fact that many of them, provincials and bishops, may be homosexual themselves. While some may have admitted their orientation to a few close friends, they fear "coming out" lest they be rejected by their peers or the public. Still others have repressed their homosexual feelings. Whatever the case, some live in fear and intimidation that they might be "outed." Others fear that, if they address the issue in a healthy and constructive way, they may be challenged about their own orientation or past actions. So silence shrouded in secrecy sustains the shame.

Despite all the forms of denial, the need to address the situation of increasing numbers of homosexuals in the clergy and religious life, and the need to do so creatively and humanely, grows stronger. The resistance to making changes in the celibacy law that has begun keeping many heterosexual persons from entering priestly ministry, will not diminish the situation either. I have met too many heterosexual persons who resist the priesthood and religious life because they don't want to get caught up in an environment they perceive to be concerned more about issues having to do with the gay life than the spiritual life. They feel cheated.

As I conclude this chapter, I don't want to leave any kind of impression that the denial, dissociation, and delusion of the institutional church leaders is unique to those in the North American church. I have heard parallel echoes of it from bishops in other places as well. And, it would be especially wrong to say or imply that our problems in the priesthood and religious life can be isolated to the increasing numbers of repressed homosexual candidates and members.

While denial, delusion, and dissociation may characterize the institutional response to the crisis of meaning in the institutional church, Jesus had something to say about the underlying problem in such situations:

> The scribes and the Pharisees have taken their seat on the chair of Moses. Therefore, do and observe all things whatsoever they tell you, but do not follow their example. For they preach but they do not practice. They tie up heavy burdens [hard to carry] and lay them on people's shoulders, but they will not lift a finger to move them (Mt 23:1-4).

At times like these, Jesus' words in Matthew's gospel should not easily be forgotten.

7

Intimacy: The Only Healthy Way to Live Celibacy

While attending graduate school in Berkeley during the 80s, I took some time to return to Milwaukee for provincial meetings. These meetings were held at the residency house we had established for men interested in joining the order. One of the young residents was Fred Hickey, a twenty-nine-year-old whose goodness and accessibility affected all in the house. Although I had met him only briefly, from what I had heard about him, I was hopeful that he would join the province.

One evening as I sat alone reading, Fred entered the community room and took a seat nearby. "Mike, I've got something to tell you," he began. "I've really tried to connect with the Capuchins and really like you guys, but I've become convinced I just can't do it. I know I've got to be married someday." My first reaction was selfish: again we would be losing another fine candidate. But, since he had offered the best reason why he shouldn't be in an outfit like ours that professes to be celibate, I agreed that he had a very good rationale. His response, however, led me to wonder to myself whether a celibate group like ours really had a future. I found myself asking him: "Fred, do you think there's any room for celibacy in the future church?"

Fred's response was immediate, clear, and emphatic: "Oh sure!"

"Well, then," I queried further, "if there is going to be a place for celibacy in the future, what do you think it will take for someone really to be celibate?"

Without a moment's hesitation, this twenty-nine-year-old offered one of the best definitions of healthy celibacy I have ever heard: "Well, if people really are going to be celibate, they are going to have to find ways of becoming warm and intimate, and also to have a place in their hearts only for God."

Although his articulation assumed the part about being genitally abstinent, Fred's definition has become the core of my own understanding of celibacy: *the embrace of a divinely-offered gift inviting one to freely choose a life-commitment of abstention from genital intimacy which expresses itself in an alternate intimacy with God and others.* In other words, the celibate is a person who freely embraces the divine offer to refrain from genital intercourse and who, as Fred said, finds ways to be warm and intimate with others and who has a place in his or her heart only for God. According to Fred's definition, developing warmth and intimacy with some others, as well as maintaining a place in one's heart just for the Absolute, represented the only viable option for a truly healthy form of celibacy.

Struck by the wisdom of Fred's response, I found myself becoming quite pensive. I started recalling the unhealthy ways I had expressed my own celibacy. I also noted (as presented in chapters five and six) how others have dysfunctionally compensated for theirs. In fact, I realized those pathological expressions merely reinforce dysfunctionality and death in and around us. Because they erode life and nurture death in so many ways, they also compromise the effectiveness of the gospel that must be proclaimed in one's life as well as one's words.

Not one of these "options" discussed in the previous two chapters represents a viable, healthy way of living the celibate life. Not one represents a way of becoming warm and intimate. (In fact, as some have shown, they actually represent defenses which keep us from being intimate.) Not one invites people to have a place in their heart only for God. Yet, all too often, they have come to characterize the style of celibate living that too many have accepted. While these options may not have done permanent damage to some of us, oftentimes they have been permanent enough to do us and others harm.

Unhealthy Notions about "Identity" and "Intimacy" Learned from Our Church and Culture

When I entered the novitiate of the midwest Capuchins at age nineteen, among the first things the formation directors told us were the need for us to "die to ourselves" and to avoid "particular friendships." My class of thirty-one men ranged in age from seventeen to twenty-three. All but one of us had just come from seminaries. We entered the Capuchins seeking to respond to what we thought was God's call to the fullness of life. Unfortunately with a stress on "dying to ourselves," our budding search for identity itself was undermined. Furthermore, with fears about "particular friendships" our beginning efforts at developing intimacy were sabotaged as well. We were reminded constantly to avoid anything that might compromise our celibacy; this meant self-discipline, especially in the way we related to others.

I knew I was attracted to Frater Linus. I first met him when I came to the college seminary after high school. I looked forward to the chance of becoming friends with him during the novitiate. How wrong I was! Almost immediately, from the talks and conferences of the novice master, I was led to believe that there was something very wrong with being attracted to another man. Furthermore, if I'd choose to spend time with him, rather than some others, I could easily be headed toward a "particular friendship." Fearful of violating my budding "celibacy," I avoided ever becoming close to Linus. Little did I know that my attraction to Linus was something God-given to me as a sexual being. I did not know then that all authentic friendships must be particular. The only thing that makes something potentially dangerous for a celibate is not when a friendship is particular, but when it becomes exclusive.

The stress in our novitiate on avoiding particular friendships was repeated throughout our formation. It was replicated as the main course almost everywhere else in the institutional church at that time as well. Diocesan seminarians were warned about them, sister-postulants lived in fear of acting on their feelings, and people like me thought that if I did act on my feelings I would jeopardize my salvation. By its preoccupation with "PFs," as they were called, the institution actually undermined the possibility of candidates in the seminary and religious life developing a sense of intimacy. It almost seems that its unconscious goal was to create ministers who would be automatons rather than affective.

According to Erik Erikson the counterpart of intimacy is "distantiation." It meant for us, in plain words, "keeping your distance." Erikson defined it as "the readiness to isolate and, if necessary, to destroy those forces and people whose essence seems dangerous to one's own, and whose 'territory' seems to encroach on the extent of one's intimate relations."[1] The institution seemed quite ready and willing to be part of that destructive force. Continual warnings about getting physically or emotionally close to others and avoiding or ignoring natural feelings were means to that end.

At the same time, the "dying to ourselves" message was repeated over and over. The song had many verses, but this was its constant refrain. Being only nineteen, it was impossible to "die" to a self which had not yet been developed. Nevertheless I did my best to die to whatever that "self" was. Usually my efforts had something to do with avoidance of pride. The novice master also tried to knock whatever pride I did have out of me. His role, he once told me, was to "break" me. When I realized this meant he wanted to get me to cry in front of him, my counter-codependency went into high gear. I'd be dipped if I'd let him prevail!

Somehow, despite my codependency and intellectualization, the idea of dying to oneself, even then, troubled me. Why should there be all this stress on dying? What was there about God or God's reign, or whatever represented life, that would invite me to be willing to die to whatever I was supposed to die to? Maybe even then I was doing what I could to find a way to make room in my heart for God. I remember challenging the novice master on the issue after hearing one more time that we should die to ourselves. "But why don't you ever tell us what we are to live for?" I asked. Little did I know then my question was my way of seeking the "reign of God" within myself. I was told I was out of order: "Ours is not to ask the reason why, ours is just to do and die."

In today's society, at least in western Europe and North America, *intimacy* too often gets identified with genitality or the pursuit of some kind of illicit sexual pleasure. If someone asks another after an evening out: "Were you intimate?," it has commonly meant: "Did you have sex?" In this atmosphere, intimacy is more equated with orgasm than relationships. To experience intimacy in modern culture is to enter the arena of the forbidden and hidden.

How did all this conflation of intimacy and genitality begin? Maybe it started when clothes covering women's genitals began to be called "intimate apparel."[2] The message has certainly been reinforced in other modern media. Who really knows? The result, however, is clear. Intimacy has been conflated in our culture with genital intercourse. To try to understand it from any other perspective thus will be very difficult. To appreciate its nuances will be doubly difficult.

When I was growing up, having genital sex somehow equated with achieving one's identity as a "man." Even if you didn't "do it," you had to act like you did. The easiest way for a certain group of Catholic boys who went to St. Mary's Springs Academy in Fond du Lac to "do it" was by having sex with a certain girl from the public high school who was known among both schools as the one who "put out."

When I became a freshman at the Springs, one of the first things I tried to do was to get accepted into the elite group of guys in the class. One night it was decided we would go to "Donna's" house, pick her up, take her some place in a woods, and have sex with her. Fearing the wrath of hell, but wanting to be accepted in the group, I did not object. The closer we got to her house the more terrified I became. Now my anxiety not only revolved around committing a mortal sin. That was bad enough. My greater terror that night, I now have to admit, centered on my fear whether I'd know how to do it. And, if I did it, would I be as good at it as the others? I didn't have to find out. Donna's dad would not let her leave the house.

Another thing that seems different about the way many men my age first experienced sex compared to now, involves the public nature of our initiation. When I was a teenager, you would never let your parents know about it. Now teens are bold enough to have sex in their own homes. When a young man I know had sex for the first time, he announced his deed to his family at a Big Boy brunch after Sunday Mass!

Recalling his experience, I find it interesting that, despite all the official teaching of the Catholic church against pre-marital genital intercourse, the recent increase in the number of young people making commitments to remain celibate until marriage has not arisen from Catholic sources. It seems to be generating from other Christian denominations, especially Southern Baptists.[3] Increasingly, virginity and abstinence, chastity and celibacy are being embraced by young people belonging to these faith-expressions. They are offered as healthy values and virtues rather than as things to avoid because of fear, as was once the case in the church.

Because the identification of intimacy with genitality has become so commonplace, honest efforts to explain intimacy often get sidetracked in semantics or snickers. This is especially difficult when one attempts to discuss how a celibate person can be intimate. Kenneth Mitchell has described this issue—compounded with institutional barriers and phobias—well:

> We should not be deceived, therefore, into thinking that without direct sexual expression the celibate person cannot achieve a capacity for intimacy. Nevertheless, my colleagues and I agree that almost every priest with whom we have worked, young or old, fleeing or staying, satisfied or dissatisfied, was in terms of psychological developmental issues, bothered more by intimacy problems than by problems of personal or vocational identity. The formation of priests—or nuns, for that matter—takes place in a curiously constricted world in which the opportunity to work out the meanings of intimacy for oneself is either distorted or totally lacking.[4]

Chapters nine and ten will offer in greater detail a vision of another world, less constricted, wherein the contemplative and compassionate dimension of celibacy, as well as its necessary communal context will be examined. Having considered in the two previous chapters "intimacy problems," we will now consider intimacy possibilities.

Understanding Intimacy and Its Various Expressions

Intimacy involves emotions and relationships. It implies some kind of emotional and personal dependence in relationships. Authentic intimacy demands mutual disclosure, as well as some vulnerability that involves giving up the need to control. Because many people have been taught (or unconsciously choose) to deny their emotional needs and avoid relationships that might make us dependent or involve commitment, they often fear being intimate. Until a person, especially a man, is able to discover ways of overcoming the fear of intimacy, what Victor Seidler notes probably will be true:

> A fear of intimacy has held men in a terrible isolation and loneliness. Often men have very few close personal relationships; we learn to live in a world of acquaintances. We

grow up learning to be self-sufficient and independent, we
learn to despise our own needs as a sign of weakness. Often
we ask very little from others, though we do expect them to
do our emotional work for us. But since we are largely
unaware of these needs, we rarely appreciate others for
doing this. This becomes another part of invisible female
domestic labour. But since we have such little sense of our
own needs, it can be difficult for us to appreciate the needs
others have. This often makes us crude and insensitive in
our caring for others.[5]

Achieving intimacy is impossible in a dynamic defined by
individualism, isolationism, and institutionalization; rather, intimacy always involves the fullest meaning of relationships.
Intimacy represents something grounded in authentic communication and communion among persons. It takes one person
beyond himself or herself into the other who reciprocates in kind.
As someone once described it to me: "Intimacy is like a dance. You
have to have a partner. Without being able to be intimate with the
partner, you are just merely posturing."

For healthy integration, all authentic intimacy must involve
some sort of reciprocal self-revelation and self-donation that manifests itself in care and commitment. Committed care constitutes
the core of intimacy; that's why any form of control undermines
the possibility of the intimate life. You can't control intimacy. You
can't command it. The kind of intimacy that reflects one's personal
integration also involves something connected to freedom. To
impose a gift is a contradiction in terms. Where intimacy is forced,
it abuses both giver and receiver. Intimacy and abuse are mutually
exclusive. Given this understanding, it becomes all the more clear
why a celibacy that is coerced for any reason will represent abuse.
Thus, when someone is celibate only because of compulsion, to be
warm and intimate becomes a contradiction in theory as well as in
fact. In my mind, an authentic expression of intimacy cannot be
limited to the physical level, nor can it be imposed.

Intimacy, being connected to love, is primarily something spiritual. Thus, whether we speak of personal intimacy, sexual intimacy, or celibate intimacy, at the core of each expression there must be
something spiritual, loving, and of God in order for authentic intimacy to be achieved. This kind of intimacy involves three levels:
personal, sexual, and spousal/celibate.

Personal Intimacy

At the first and most basic level we are human individuals. My particular way of being a human individual separates me from the other individuals in my genus due to the fact that I am also a person. As a person I need an identity, an awareness of who I am and how I am different from other individuals who are persons. The factors that help me discover my personal identity originate in and are affected by my family of origin, socio-economic factors, and my ethnicity and culture, to say nothing of my religious dimensions. Since becoming an authentic person involves discovering one's identity, identity and intimacy are deeply connected. To be one's authentic self (identity) demands some kind of healthy interaction with another (intimacy). The reality that distinguishes a human person from a human individual is intimacy. This involves mutual relationships defined by self-acceptance, self-disclosure, and self-sharing.

There is some argument about which comes first: identity or intimacy. Some would say that one cannot have an identity without experiences of intimacy. Others say intimacy defines authentic identity. Erik Erikson found intimacy to be the task of discovering one's identity. His reasoning was quite simple: there is no chance to be intimate with another if I have not discovered my own identity and become at ease with it. However, Erikson's theories no longer have the sway and support they once did. Many psychologists have discovered that it is not quite so easy to show how identity and intimacy relate.

Mary Elizabeth Kenel attempts to find a compromise to the argument. She writes:

> In the process of learning to be intimate, one must first acquire intimacy with one's own self, growing to an awareness and appreciation of one's own identity, uniqueness, and value as a person. To achieve this, it is essential to recognize the true or authentic self, the "real me," so to speak, rather than maintain a view distorted by the denial or repression of essential elements.[6]

One thing does remain certain about any connection between identity and intimacy: there is no way one can be self-disclosing (which is the beginning of intimacy) without having basic self-awareness. Selfhood is what makes an individual a human. Self-awareness makes a human personal. This involves some kind of relationship with other self-aware persons. Only the self-aware person can be other-aware and thus relational. Only in relationality can we be open to the possibility of intimacy.

For me to be a person who can say, "I am who I am," I need to be in relationship with others who can also say, "I am who I am." How individuals become *authentically* personal is defined by the way they experience relationships of personal intimacy with some other(s). To be who I am, to be a person, demands relationships; but to be authentically who I am necessitates relationships of intimacy with other persons who are equally self-defined. The development of a truly mature personality requires loving interaction and identification with another person. In other words, I cannot be a true person without intimacy with another. And this intimacy demands a certain degree of self-disclosure and other-acceptance on my part as well.

Such personal intimacy represents the characteristic of a relationship of loving closeness, familiarity, and friendship that is marked by mutual disclosure, struggle with differences, and trust. By definition, all intimacy is personal intimacy. Thus, all definitions of intimacy must be grounded on the notion of "personal" intimacy.

Sexual Intimacy

Because, as individuals, we are either male or female, our personal lives are sexual by nature. Our sex will be male or female, but our deeper identity will find our maleness or femaleness expressed in some sexual way. One's sexual identity goes beyond just being a male or female. I cannot be who "I am" as a person without being who "I am" as male or female. However, our sexual identity goes beyond this identification. It not only involves our biological sex and gender, as well as the social roles and functions the culture associates with sexual identity (e.g., "a woman's place is in the home" or "big boys don't cry"). It identifies my "I am" in some sexual way that involves attraction to the "I am" of other persons. The self-awareness of who I am as a male or female enables me to be open to the possibility of a sexual relationship with another.

A major implication of self-awareness and personal intimacy is to discover and accept my "self" as having a body that is male or female with a concomitant physiology that makes me sexual. Thus only if an individual is personal can one authentically be a male or female who is sexual—if intimacy is to characterize either level of relationships. Sexual intimacy, then, builds on personal intimacy. When these two dimensions are integrated, one can be an individual who is personal *and* at the same time a male or female who is sexual. In other words we become a sexual person when we are able to be intimate, in a sexual way, with other persons. This chart shows how our bodily dimension is incomplete without the relational dimension which makes us capable of intimacy.

Levels of Intimacy	
Bodily Dimension	**Relational Dimension**
Individual	Personal
Male/Female	Sexual

Within male or female genders, a person will be oriented sexually to others, either heterosexually or homosexually, in varying degrees. For individual males and females to be authentically personal and sexual, they must have relationships wherein they can experience and express sexual intimacy as well. Just as I can't be an authentic individual without the socialization that makes me personal and just as I can't be authentically personal without relationships of intimacy with other persons, the same holds for the second level of our bodily dimension. I can't be authentically male (as women can't be truly female) without relationships of intimacy that enable me to be a person who is sexual and intimate. In the same way it means I must move from just being identified with being a male or female, gay or straight, to being a sexual person. As Mary Elizabeth Kenel has shown,

> Before such integration can be achieved, there must first be an awareness and acceptance of the self as a sexual person, a thought that creates so much anxiety that some people completely repress the sexual dimension of their lives. They fail to appreciate that human sexuality is a healthy and positive aspect of personality that has a broad, diffuse expression in all areas of living. In their efforts to remain separated from sexuality, repressed persons allow it to

assume a role of major importance in their lives as they become obsessed with sex, just as an anorexic, although as a starving individual, focuses on food. What is even more insidious is that the sexual/emotional detachment of the repressed religious or priest is often mistaken for spiritual detachment.[7]

Such spiritual detachment can be another term for "distantiation." This inability to be intimate with others, using the need to remain intimate with God as an excuse, was a developmental hazard I experienced in my own life. Now, on the other hand, I doubt that I can ever be intimate with God without some kind of intimacy with others. But it wasn't always that way. In fact I was once quoted by Sheila Murphy in her book on sexuality, celibacy, and relationships among Catholic clergy and religious as saying:

> I was always afraid of developing an intimate relationship with someone. I think I thought it'd automatically become genital. I've discovered this doesn't have to happen like it does in the movies. Now that I've pursued intimacy, I wish I would have done it earlier. It would have helped my growth as a human. [I regret] that I was "hung up" regarding past relationships and didn't trust myself or others to be sexual, intimate *and* celibate.[8]

When Sheila interviewed me for her book, I was ashamed of having to tell her of my stumbling attempts at intimacy. Now I don't mind admitting so. We're better for our experiences.

Men, it seems, can easily confuse the need for sexual intimacy with their sexual needs and desires. Thus men often conflate intimacy with sexual contact(s). And, when men seek these sexual contacts for the purpose of pleasure, the persons involved usually become objects of pleasure. Many psychologists find in this behavior a similarity with the separation between boys and their mothers as experienced in childhood. When boys are separated from their mothers, they identify with their fathers by repressing or "cutting off" their feelings and desires. The implications for celibates is quite telling, especially when the connection between our public image and *control* is made. Control "cuts off" the possibility of care; without care we are cut off from intimacy. Consequently what Seidler writes of men in general has particular relevance for male celibates:

I think this helps explain the ease with which we "cut off" from our ongoing relationships. We have learnt to compartmentalize our feelings so that we can carefully control them. But this very "cut off" quality can hurt our developing sexual relationships and make it difficult for us to learn to take initiative and responsibility for our relationships. Often it makes our relationships incidental and our feelings unclear. Because we grow up to assume that our masculine identity has to do with our individual success and achievement in the public realm, this constantly undermines our resolve to take more initiative and responsibility in our sexual and personal relationships. Even though we are often not aware of it, we often insist on controlling the terms of relationships we are in. We get irritable if things are not done our way and we resist giving up control.[9]

Building on Seidler's thesis, it seems clear that women and men relate differently precisely because they are male and female. Men and women experience their sexuality differently and thus will express it differently. Whether this difference, Christopher Kiesling notes, "is inherent in the nature of male and female or simply cultural is unimportant; at this time in history it is real and common."[10] The consequence of this is that the dynamics of sexual intimacy are experienced and expressed differently for men and women. Whereas a woman's experience of intimacy can involve a whole way of life, for a man, intimacy usually can be compartmentalized. This often leads to confusion and misunderstandings. For example, as Kiesling writes, a woman may face problems at the level of the core relationship of intimacy in not finding enough self-disclosure on the part of the man, while the man may struggle with his physiology wherein his experience of the intimacy is that it is moving rapidly to a very passionate level; consequently he may hold back in his self-discipline. These differences can be alleviated with healthy, clear communication. Whatever ways women and men communicate sexually with each other, if they make an effort to understand each other in the process they are likely to deepen their intimacy.

Given this understanding, sexual intimacy characterizes a non-exploitative and non-genital relationship of loving closeness, familiarity, and friendship that is marked by mutual disclosure, an effort to work out differences, which is expressed in affection, gestures, and physical manifestations of care. If I had to choose one word to summarize the dynamics that characterize sexual intimacy, I would use the word *friendship*.

I have always been fascinated by the notion of friendship; I even wrote a paper on the topic for a course I took at Berkeley. There I learned that women have different notions related to friendship than men. Men see friendship in its more Aristotelian sense of being useful for each other, enjoying one another, and having some common goal that bonds. Women stress connectedness, belonging, continuity, trust, and security.[11]

Without denigrating the male notions of friendship, it seems to me that the feminine expression of friendship is more applicable to crossing simple male-female categories to reflect sexual intimacy including self-disclosure and self-entrustment with others. This form of friendship involves sharing not just one's stories but one's self. It implies a kind of influence that supports care and rejects control. This friendship is grounded in mutual trust and loyalty rather than manipulative individualism and suspicion.

Given this understanding of sexual intimacy and friendship, it's easier to discover again how control-defined dynamics undermine the possibility of living a life of intimacy. This will become keenly apparent when we examine the notion of celibate intimacy.

Spousal and Celibate Intimacy

Given what has been presented thus far, I believe that only individuals who experience personal intimacy and who, as males and females, also have relations of sexual intimacy, can experience true spousal or celibate intimacy. Each latter form of intimacy is nourished and sustained by the former. Whether individuals will be authentically intimate at this third level (spousal or celibate), however, will depend not so much on whether they are genital or non-genital, but on whether their lives are grounded in the first two relations of personal intimacy and sexual intimacy. If their choice is limited to being simply genital or non-genital, they will never be complete just as an individual is incomplete without personal intimacy or males and females remain incomplete without sexual intimacy.

At this point, I think it would be helpful to expand the chart that we saw previously.

Levels of Intimacy

Bodily Dimension	**Relational Dimension**
Individual	Personal
Male/Female	Sexual
Genital Non-Genital	Spousal Celibate

As this chart points out, individuals who are male or female will be genital or non-genital. This bodily dimension of one's being constitutes the possibility of achieving authentic intimacy on the three levels. But this demands we go further than our bodily urges. Yet there is a tension between the dynamics of the bodily dimension and the dynamics of the relational dimension that tends to focus people to move prominently on the bodily side. However, only the relational pole will lead to authentic intimacy on the personal and sexual level, as well as the committed level of spousal or celibate intimacy. Whether or not one moves from the bodily dimension to the dimension of authentic human intimacy in its personal, sexual, and spousal/celibate expressions depends on people's maturity regarding their relationality and the character of their commitment.

Considering the third level of our chart, individuals who are male and female will be genital or non-genital. Limited to the bodily dimension, an individualistic, purely male-female approach will find one acting genitally in an animalistic or opportunistic way. People can be genital without any intimacy. In that case, one will be genital without sufficient consideration for the other person or consideration for being truly sexually intimate with that person. When this occurs, the "other" gets objectified. She or he is viewed simply for one's pleasure, to release one's sexual urges, or for mating purposes which one views as a right. Also, just because one is non-genital, does not mean that one will be intimate. It could simply mean the individual has made himself or herself non-genital out of depersonalizing motives such as fear, or the other unhealthy options discussed above. These "eunuchs" will be far from intimate.

Looking at the left side of the chart we see that in our bodily dimensions we are not only individuals who are male and female;

our genital capacity is likewise a natural part of our bodily existence. To be conscious of our gender identity is to be aware of our potential to be genital as well. But unlike individual or gender identity, genital activity is not a given. It is a potential which represents something which one exercises through his or her own choice.

As we consider the right side of the chart we recognize that we are also persons who are sexual. This relational capacity is the fulfillment of our bodily capacity. We have shown that to be fully individual we must be personal. To be fully male or female, we must be sexual. Yet, integration on the third level builds on the integration of the first two levels. Our capacity to be genital enables us to be truly faithful in spousal intimacy, and our capacity to be non-genital grounds our ability to be authentically celibate. This is so whether we make a public profession to be celibate or remain celibate due to life circumstances. To be truly spousal or celibate, we must be fully personal as well as sexual.

Just as a person in a committed, permanent relationship involving genital expression can be faithful only if there is intimacy in that relationship and in one's relationship to God, so too a person in a parallel, non-genital commitment will be chaste as long as one finds ways to be intimate in their relationships with others and God.

Most men and women express themselves in a genital way in forms of permanent commitment to their partner. When and where this is honored the result is a relationship of fidelity. Expressed relationally, spousal fidelity becomes a way of intimacy with God and the other that excludes genital intimacy with anyone but the one to whom a permanent commitment has been made. Spousal intimacy can be characterized as a relationship of loving closeness, familiarity, and friendship that is marked by mutual disclosure, struggles with differences, and trust expressed in affection, gestures, and physical manifestations of care between two people who accept the responsibility involved in expressing their communion through genital intercourse in a permanent commitment. In its fullest sense, all spousal genital intimacy is love-making. But love-making need not be limited only to spousal intimacy; it should characterize celibate intimacy as well. When this happens, both become manifestations of grace.

By nature, we have been made to be persons who naturally are sexual. We also have been made to be naturally oriented to express our sexual personhood through genitality. However this does not mean that every person must think, feel, and act genitally in order to be an authentic person or even an authentically sexual person. Neither does it mean that we all have to be genital in order to be human, or healthy, or holy. However, if we are going to be authentically sexual persons, it implies that we have found ways of being warm and intimate that are personal and sexual, even though they are not genital.

Negatively speaking, we have seen that some religious and priests use their state of "celibacy" as an excuse for not being intimate; others justify their repression of sexuality for fear of intimacy; still others engage in genital relations as an escape from intimacy. Whether one's sexuality is repressed or acted-out, all of these options, I believe, border on the abusive. The ultimate abuse may not even be to others, but oneself.

Sometimes those who act out are unable to be intimate. Others manifest a sexual and/or emotional problem of some sort. Other times, as Kenel shows, the relationship can be a narcissistic one. Here the sexual partner is exploited in order to meet the celibate's own genital needs which have been wanting because of a lack of intimacy:

> These needs are not simply a matter of physical lust or sexual tension but are often related to areas of the personality that have long been buried. Because of this lack of awareness, the religious often deludes himself or herself into thinking that the problem pertains to the domain of sexuality/intimacy, when in reality the operative dynamics are on a far different level of development. To achieve integration, such persons must acquire an awareness of what it is they are seeking through their sexual behavior.[12]

Whenever professed celibates act out genitally, they cannot integrate their sexual identity with their personal identity because, at its core, a caring, non-genital commitment to another has been abused. Consequently and ultimately, any genital expression will be a violation of the celibate's sexual personhood as well. Donald Goergen writes: "Christian wisdom sees genital love as an expression of affection within a committed intimate partnership. It is precisely such partnerships or marriages that celibate men or women choose not to make. This is not to say they choose to forego intimate relationships, but intimate love need not necessarily be genital."[13]

Having recognized what dysfunctional behaviors are in store when one does not integrate the dynamics of one's bodily dimension with one's relational dimension, we can now understand more fully what it means to manifest celibate intimacy. In my mind, celibate intimacy involves a relationship among people who have committed themselves to be non-genital in response to a divine gift, a relationship of loving closeness, familiarity, and friendship that is marked by mutual disclosure, struggles with differences, and trust which is expressed in affection, gestures, and physical manifestations of care between people. This commitment is permanent for some, temporary for others. For some it is articulated; for others it will be unconscious, but nonetheless authentic.

This definition of celibate intimacy is similar to the earlier definition of sexual intimacy. There is an important difference, however. When we speak of sexual intimacy we refer to relationships which, given the natural course of things, are open to the possibility of genital expression. When we speak of celibate intimacy we are describing relationships which, by the mutual consent and commitment of the persons involved, are not open to future genital expression. Likewise when we speak of spousal intimacy, our definition is the same as sexual intimacy, with the exception that in this case the genital expression of intimacy is between the two partners who have committed themselves to the relationship.

Authentic celibate intimacy can only be experienced or expressed when one's life is grounded in relationships that are conducive of personal intimacy and sexual intimacy. Without the first two kinds of intimacy, one will resort to genitality devoid of authentic intimacy; the genitality will be without commitment. Contrary to popular opinion, the refusal to be genital without commitment is not repression. It actually represents a way of expressing love. As Christopher Kiesling notes, "To restrain one's desire for a physical expression of love incompatible with the loved one's celibacy (or whatever state or condition the loved one is in) shows respect for the integrity of his or her chosen way of life."[14]

Authentic celibate intimacy builds on the willingness to enter into relationships that enable an individual to be personally intimate, and enable males and females to be sexually intimate.

Celibate intimacy with another or others represents personal relationships of trust and loyalty that generate the kind of caring commitment characteristic of friendship. This kind of caring commitment involves self-awareness (the personal dimension), self-disclosure (the relational dimension), self-entrustment (a trust/loyalty component), and self-commitment (the commitment component). It is at this point that we discover how spiritual intimacy is revealed in personal intimacy, for, at the heart of this intimacy rests the fullest meaning of the word "faith." In other words, I believe in the other as much as I believe in myself. I have as much faith in the other to whom I am committed as I do in myself. This "faith" is what now gives my life and my relationships "meaning."

From this perspective of faith it should be clear that there can be no such person as a celibate without community. As should be evident as well, this community need not be geographical; it all depends on one's relationships of intimacy. What this kind of community supportive of celibacy might look like will be examined in chapter nine. However, as has been intimated, there can be little or no authentic faith for us if it does not ultimately find expression in spiritual intimacy.

Spiritual Intimacy

All healthy human relationships revolve around intimacy of one kind or another. An authentic celibate is the person who knows how to make love in the fullest spiritual sense of the term. The truly celibate person is the one who is a maker of love, even if she or he has never had a genital experience.

Thus, if intimacy involves reciprocal relationships of care and commitment, only when care and commitment define the celibate choice will professed celibates be able to be truly intimate. Making love involves sharing myself with another in ways that are reciprocated. Celibate and spousal intimacy are both characterized by commitment. In its spousal expression this intimacy requires a commitment to one person (the partner). By definition, that choice means a restriction of genital expression to the one who has been chosen. Consequently such persons in committed personal and sexual relationships say by that fact that they will be non-genital with anyone but the object of their commitment. The celibate expression of this intimacy is likewise marked by commitment. On the personal and sexual level the celibate is pledged to non-exclusive, non-genital commitments of care. Such commitments represent the only way one can reach all three levels of intimacy: personal, sexual, and celibate. When either spousal or celibate intimacy are manifest in our lives, we automatically find spiritual intimacy: a relationship of loving closeness and personal familiarity with God that is expressed in compassion for others. At its core it is love-making (God in us) and making-love (compassion for the world). To paraphrase Fred Hickey: When we can be warm and intimate with others there will be a place in our heart only for God.

From this faith perspective, it should be clear that at all three levels of personal, sexual, and spousal/celibate intimacy, the assumption is that spiritual intimacy of some sort gives meaning to each dimension. As a person, the fact that I can say "I am" mirrors that One who said, "I am,"—Yahweh. To be able to say "I am" assumes an awareness of my self as a unique person made in the image of God. But as an image of God, who is love, I can only be who "I am" if I am able to experience and dwell in love. This involves an affective dimension that involves rapport, receptivity, and reciprocity. Personal intimacy, then, is spiritual by definition.

Next, as a sexual person, the fact that I am naturally attracted to some others reveals the natural attraction of the persons of the Trinity for each other. There is a desire to be with the other, to find one's "I am" in the embrace of the other "thou." Spirituality involves sharing this level of oneself with another to become a "we." It implies intimacy that is sexual. In this sense, Donald Goergen says we must ask how our religious identity and spiritual life are deepening in a way that impacts on the way I am sexual: "Spiritual life and sexual life interact and mature together."[15]

Finally, as a celibate sexual person, what also makes me spiritual is the way I do not spiritualize my relationships in the sense of being removed from being sexual and personal. Rather I am able to be intimate as a celibate precisely because I have discovered non-manipulative ways of being personally and sexually intimate with others. This is what makes me both celibate and spiritual. This is where celibacy and spirituality embrace in a sexually-embodied person. As a celibate, while I may be separated from other individual males and females in life by not being genital, spirituality is what enables me as a celibate to make love in a non-genital way. Making love in this way, as Jesus' incarnation shows (Jn 3:16), is the only authentic way to be spiritual and celibate.

8

Celibacy as Fasting: From, For, and With

Once when talking with a young man interested in joining our province he asked me how I viewed celibacy. I noted that, among other images, I had begun to consider celibacy as a form of fasting.[1] The day after our conversation, while praying with my brother Capuchins, the gospel passage happened to refer to the disciples' need to fast when the bridegroom had left them (Lk 5:33-39; see Mt 9:14-17; Mk 2:18-22). As our prayer over the scriptures developed, we also noticed a link between the traditional form of fasting related to food and fasting related to celibacy.

First we discussed the passage as it related to food in itself. The Lukan version we read quoted Jesus' response to the Pharisees and the scribes about his nonfasting:

> Then they said to him, "John's disciples, like the disciples of the Pharisees, frequently fast and pray, but your disciples eat and drink." Jesus said to them, "You cannot make wedding guests fast while the bridegroom is with them, can you? The days will come when the bridegroom will be taken away from them, and then they will fast in those days" (Lk 5:33-35).

Note that though the text quotes the Pharisees as doing the asking, it seems they are not connected to their disciples. The Pharisees here do not refer to their own disciples by saying "*our* disciples, [who] frequently fast and pray." Rather it is "the disciples of the Pharisees," as though they are speaking as observers, from a distance. For a scripture scholar, this offers strong evidence that Luke's version represents some issue his own community needed to address. It reveals redacted material which did not come as much from questions of the disciples of John and the Pharisees, nor even the disciples who walked with Jesus. The question needed to be raised to address an issue confronting the Lukan community. The bridegroom had left his disciples. Now, half a century later, Luke had to remind them about their need to fast and the reason for fasting. A deeper probing of the text shows such fasting would involve three dimensions: a fasting *from*, a fasting *for*, and a fasting *with*.

The *fasting from* and the *fasting for* notions of fasting are evident in the Pharisees' and scribes' query and Jesus' response. The disciples of John and the Pharisees "frequently fast." It is understood that this fasting represented the traditional fasting *from* food that people of that era did, often according to strict regimens. The fasting *for* notion can be found in Jesus' reference to himself as the "bridegroom." Jesus makes clear his disciples will fast *from* food when "the bridegroom will be taken away from them" (alluding to his death, resurrection, ascension). This fast would prepare them for his return. The third dimension is less evident. However, because they constituted his community, it goes without saying that his disciples would do their fasting *with* each other.

The gospel reveals Jesus explaining that his disciples need not fast as long as the bridegroom was still with them. However when "the time came" they would fast. In Luke, "time" is an important notion. The idea is used to indicate the beginning and end of Jesus' presence on earth; it also has a prophetic dimension referring to the new day or time of Christ's coming.

For instance, when the *time came* for Mary to be delivered of her child (Lk 2:6), Jesus was born. And when *the day* of Unleavened Bread *came*, on which the Passover lamb had to be sacrificed (Lk 22:7), Jesus was delivered up; but then, *on the first day of the week* (Lk 24:1), he would rise. After these things had occurred, Jesus' disciples would fast in preparation for the days of the Christ. This would be the time that the felt experiences and personal encounters of those who feasted with him at his banquets would not be so evident. Fasting would be a way to enable his physical absence to become consciously present.

This time for fasting represented the situation when Luke wrote these words. Adapting Mark's version of the story, Luke reminded his community of Jesus' disciples of their need to fast.

Why? Because fasting would help them remember Jesus' presence with them. Their fasting would re-create his presence in their midst in a way that would affect their lives, their relationships, and their witness.

We realized for the first time as we prayed that morning over this passage that any authentic fasting of our own needed to involve elements of fasting *from*, fasting *for*, and fasting *with*. Our fasting *from* will be incomplete and a burden without the reasons why we fast uppermost in our mind. Yet we cannot fast *for* something without fasting *from* something else. And because both fasting *from* and fasting *for* can be so difficult, support is needed. This is where fasting *with* each other can make the difference. Any wholehearted fasting involves expressions of these three key elements.

Consideration of these three elements of fasting offers another insight as well. Traditionally, authentic fasting involves giving up some good. However what is given up, while good, is not perceived by the one who fasts as of the same significance as the object of the fast. This implies some kind of purposefulness to the fast. What is fasted *from* is not perceived to be as important as what is fasted *for*. Finally, fasting does not represent an individual thing; it is has a communal dimension: "then *they* will fast in those days" (Lk 5:35).

This life-giving notion of fasting ultimately led us to take a community stance on the nuclear arms race. Each of us in the community had been working for disarmament in various ways. None of us had had much success. It made sense to us that the arms race was the "kind of devil" that could be cast out only by fasting (Mk 9:14-29). So we decided to join in the fasting effort to bring about new forms of nonviolence and peace in the world. We determined as a group that we would each participate in the fast to the degree we felt led. Furthermore, we would do our own fasting in solidarity with other groups in the Milwaukee area who also would be fasting. It had been decided that those able would meet each day of the fast at a local church for prayer in the morning, at noon, and in the evening.

All of us in our house started fasting totally from food and drink (except for lots of water). For various reasons, some stopped after a few days and created other forms of fasting. Along with Jacob, another brother in the house, I kept going. Whenever we got hungry for food, we'd just drink water. Whenever we got thirsty, we'd drink more water. After five days I began wondering why I was not experiencing greater hunger pains (especially for my chocolate) or cravings for my regular caffeine fix of coffee. Why wasn't I obsessing more about eating or drinking? Why wasn't I suffering from some kind of physical pain? Why wasn't I hungry or thirsty?

Instead of feeling starved I actually felt I was being *nourished*. Why? Probably because I was preoccupied with a more important value than food and water, namely the hunger and thirst associated with the desire for justice. This gave me a kind of purposefulness. It was not that important that I not eat or drink if peace could come with an end to the arms race. More nourishment came from being in solidarity with others who shared the same dream. With them I had a purpose more compelling and imaginative than eating as usual. Being committed to a higher goal with like-minded companions who chose to fast was more compelling and inviting than sitting down to another meal. I could fast *from* food and drink, *for* a purpose. This made it easier. But it became easier still because I could do this in solidarity *with* others.

With this experience as background, it became easier for me to understand how one could make parallels to celibacy as a form of authentic fasting as well. The following sections will develop how these three dimensions of fasting must be unified if one's embrace of celibacy is to evolve into more healthy forms.

Fasting *From*

We go to bed the nights before Ash Wednesday and Good Friday with as much food in our stomachs as any other night of the year (maybe even a little more!), yet we wake up more hungry than usual. What creates the disparity? Is it a physical reaction or does it have more to do with something taking place in our minds?

In the case of a Lenten observance that is legislated, if we have no reason to fast except to fulfill a "law" of fasting, it is no wonder we will be preoccupied with food for the rest of the day. If no other motivation touches our minds and hearts but the fulfillment of some law imposed from outside, in which we have no real stake, we probably will have problems. This insight about the negative dimensions of law-imposed fasting from food offers us new insights about what happens when celibacy is experienced as some kind of institutionally-imposed or culturally-conditioned expression of fasting *from.*

When I was a teenager, we'd often talk about being "horny." This meant that we were experiencing in our thinking, our desires, and our feelings, the absence of being able to be genital. While these emotions and passions predominate for some years following puberty, their ebbs and flows remain with us far beyond. Even when people get as old as I am now (and even older, they tell me), "there remains a fire in the furnace."

When fasting *from* overly defines our experience of fasting as compared to the other two forms, it leads to dysfunctionality and ultimately, to death itself. When fasting *from* represents one's approach to celibacy, as noted in previous chapters, it is easy to take on the characteristics of sexual anorexics. Unfortunately, given the way celibates have been formed in the past, and present modes of denial, I believe we have too many sexual anorexics among the clergy and religious congregations of women and men.

It has been my experience that when such sexual anorexics become leaders in the church, in a diocese, or in a congregation, their understanding of how to address the issue of celibacy is filled with commands like "don't," "can't," "not allowed," "mustn't," or "shouldn't." In the process, they reveal the undermining dimension of repression more than the possibly liberating form of sublimation.

Good therapy often can help people understand why they become sexual anorexics. However, even with therapy, as I noted in chapter five, when the meaning system breaks down, all the therapy in the world will do little good. When one feels compelled to be celibate without choosing it, and when no purpose except a law or promise made under compulsion is recognized as justification for the purging, problems will abound.

We've already seen in chapter five what happens when people fast from something without having anything to fast for: their depression makes them "grouches" instead of "growers." Barry discovered enough "grouches" in the province to alert him to what kind of community he might have to live in in the future. He wondered whether he too would take on the appearance of a celibate fasting "from" something but "for" little or nothing. And how did this relate to Jesus' caution about those who fast in such a way that their appearance manifests gloom (Mt 6:16)?

Many of us were taught that when we became aware of what we were fasting from, we should busy ourselves or think of something else. However, these were ways of suppressing our feelings or sublimating them to something else. Needless to say, suppression and sublimation represent two more possibly problematic ways one can fast from genitality.

Unlike repression, suppression involves a conscious or free awareness of an experience that is kept from being addressed in one's thinking, feeling, or acting. Where repression is a "no based on a no," suppression is a "no based on a deeper yes." In other words, because I have made this commitment to celibacy, I will not think, desire, or do anything that might jeopardize my commitment.

Sublimation has parallels to suppression. However, where suppression stresses a no because of a yes, sublimation entails redirected energy from one reality to another perceived to be better (a yes over a no because of a yes.) Like suppression, sublimation involves an acceptance of certain ways of thinking, feeling, and acting that one would naturally reject because of a conflict in values. However, unlike suppression, sublimation does not hold what has been accepted in check. Rather, it redirects these energies to other thoughts, feelings, and actions in order to support and sustain a commitment.

While both suppression, and especially sublimation, can have some value for the celibate, too often they focus on what one is fasting *from*, namely that which is repressed or denied. William Kraft has shown that unhealthy forms of suppression and sublimation can be based on a false philosophy of persons that separates body and spirit, genitality and spirituality. Equally they can be based on a Freudian vision of the person that posits pleasure as life's main motivating force. In this theory, one's thinking, feeling, and acting seek to serve the desire for pleasure. Consequently it will be understandable that any suppression or sublimation theory based on such a pleasure-defined force will maximize genitality at the expense of spirituality. In this spirit, Kraft concludes:

> Though suppression and sublimation are important and necessary, they are psychological ways of coping with genitality rather than direct ways of integrating genitality and spirituality in the person. To be sure, these psychological postures are congruent with and can foster integration, but

their relation to religious growth tends to be indirect. And a danger of these approaches is to consider genital desires only in terms of physical needs that are to be suppressed or sublimated rather than repressed or satisfied. Genitality, however, can have more than only a physical meaning. It can have a more direct and positive influence on the spiritual life of religious itself. Instead of seeing sex as an enemy or impediment, a deeper challenge for the religious is to experience sex as a friend and a help in living a celibate life of love.[2]

If one's understanding or experience of celibacy is limited to the negative or what is negated (i.e., thoughts, feelings, or actions) it will prove to be limited and unsatisfying. Men, especially, will concentrate on their inability to follow through on the drives that their physiology, evidenced in body-stimulus itself, shouts to them to be satisfied.

Also, just as we associate with women the experience of emptiness that comes with a sense that she will be barren, I think men have intimations of the same. At least I think it has happened to me. My experience of this sense of void came powerfully clear while I was in New York City studying for my masters in economics. It was the mid 80s and I was in the heart of my middle years. This is the time when sexual feelings are heightened and basic commitments get renegotiated. Certainly no textbook discourse was needed to make me aware of what I was fasting *from*.

One night when I returned from school, Meryl Streep was starring in *Sophie's Choice* on one of the movie channels. The story takes place in Manhattan. A young émigré named Sophie has fainted in the main public library. A young man assists her, takes her to a rooming house, where he stays with her and nourishes her to health. Because she is so indebted to him (and codependent on him), she starts living with him. However, the man also is a sociopath. At times he can be warm and intimate with Sophie; at other times he is violent and abusive. But codependent that she is, she stays, suffering his periodic abuse.

Meanwhile, in the room directly below theirs, a young man—Stengle—moves in. He is a writer from Atlanta. Immediately upon seeing Sophie, Stengle knows he has fallen in love with her. I found myself identifying closely with Stengle. He was in the bed below the one he really wanted to be in. And, as the movie progresses, it becomes clear that Sophie will be making some choices that will never include intimacy with him.

The movie brought on an overwhelming sense of emptiness. When I went to bed that night, I found myself saying: "You're never going to have anyone like Sophie; you're never going to have *anyone*, period." Laying there with that realization forcing itself into my consciousness, something deep within me started to express itself. Tears came to my eyes spontaneously. I knew what I would be fasting *from* for the rest of my life. I don't know if I've ever experienced the depths of loneliness quite like that night. The tears merely evidenced how deep the loneliness was.

However, at almost the same time as I felt the depth of the loneliness, something even deeper came to the fore: I found myself (a Franciscan, no less!) saying the time-honored prayer of St. Ignatius over and over: "Take, Lord, receive. *All* I have is yours now." It was *my* prayer, from a place deeper than where I was experiencing my loneliness. It was my prayer of abandonment to the One alone for whom I had made a place in my heart. Still, I found myself asking: "What if God isn't there?" And then, quite spontaneously, I found myself adding, "And *you* just better be there when I show up, or I am really going to be ticked!" Although I had intimations of what I was fasting *for* at that particular time in my life, it's quite clear now that what I was fasting *from* still dominated my conscious experience of celibacy.

Renunciation approaches such as these reinforce celibacy as a fasting *from*, sometimes in ways that can become debilitating. All too often the theology of celibacy has placed too much stress on this negative dimension. Certainly some of the understanding of celibacy in the late 70s focused on this dimension. Christopher Kiesling wrote in *Celibacy, Prayer and Friendship* at that time: "The celibates we are talking about in this book not only are unmarried but also endeavor to forego all directly willful indulgence in pleasures of genital sex, whether with others or alone."[3] Although the author does balance this definition with a very positive understanding elsewhere in the book, such a stress on this aspect of celibacy highlights the problems that we continue to face today when we limit the discussion of celibacy to the notion of abstinence in isolation.

At this point, before moving on to discuss what a celibate is fasting *for*, we might examine two seemingly opposite dyads and see in them a kind of midway point between fasting *from* and fasting *for*. These dyads are found in the differences between aloneness and loneliness on the one hand and estrangement and separation on the other. The former in each dyad concentrates on what one fasts *from*. The latter intimates a sense of what one is fasting *for*.

When I experience *aloneness*, I am "all one." I am totally into myself, if I can call that part of my individuality a "self," since self implies personhood. Aloneness conjures up images of abandonment, isolation, despair, and the "existential vacuum" about which Frankl speaks. When a celibate experiences aloneness, there is no one else. This, thankfully, is not the case of the celibate who experiences *loneliness*. One can chart the difference quite clearly:

> Celibacy from = aloneness = a sense limited to the self
>
> Celibacy for = loneliness = a sense extending the self to another

A celibate experiencing aloneness is an individual without personal intimacy or a male or female without sexual intimacy. Oftentimes the aloneness is grounded in an obsession that one is unable to be genital. Conversely, to be a celibate who knows loneliness is to be a person who knows intimacy; such a male or female has discovered friendship. Unlike the celibate who has nothing to draw upon, which can only lead the one alone into deeper forms of despair, the celibate who is experiencing loneliness can draw on a sense of presence. This presence has been celebrated, but isn't available to the senses at this time. This embrace of loneliness reveals something that rests at the heart of what it means to be an authentic celibate. As George Aschenbrenner writes:

> Most authentic, unself-conscious living of celibacy is born of responsible dealings with loneliness. The uniqueness of each individual person makes loneliness an inescapable part of the human condition. Celibacy, because of its disengagement and affective renunciation (surely never meant to be a renunciation of all affectivity!), often brings in its wake a distinctive type of emptiness and loneliness with great potential for fostering the development of a mature self-

possession and a richly intimate life with self, with others, and with God.[4]

Loneliness, by definition, implies longing. Longing for the other. Aloneness, as "all one" implies, indicates being by one's self, void of the other.

A second dyad reflecting the interim between experiencing celibacy as fasting *from* and fasting *for* can be found by examining the differences between *estrangement* and *separation*. One who is estranged is a stranger to others. Others are no longer welcomed. There is no hospitality, no dwelling or abiding with another. For individuals who are estranged from others, relationships are dead.

However, when one is merely separated from another, whether it be physically or geographically, the awareness of an abiding, caring presence can make relationships even more alive. This sense of "being with" is at the heart of intimacy. It represents the base from which any kind of separation is understood and accepted. This is especially true of celibacy for the clergy and members of religious congregations who might move from place to place more often than those who do not. While celibacy and separation can be considered partners, the same can never be said of celibacy and estrangement.

The more I have examined negative and positive interpretations of celibacy which stress what you can't do and what you must do, the notion of "separation" has become more significant to me. In this search, I have been helped very much by Christopher Kiesling's reflections on separation. He writes:

> Separation is another limitation to which celibate love between man and woman is subject. Celibate love means many wrenching good-byes that leave the spirit twisted and torn and wondering how often it can endure such torture. It means aching absences for long periods of time, perhaps with meager communication. Married people have to undergo separation from one another for various reasons, so this is not entirely the peculiar lot of celibates. Yet separation for long times at great distances can be assumed as an inevitable part of celibate love, while for the married such separation is exceptional. In any case, the celibate is usually not physically present with the beloved to the extent that a married person normally is.

> Separation is painful because it strikes at the very core of a love relationship.[5]

This notion brings us to the next part of fasting which moves celibacy from a preoccupation with what is given up to a priority related to the goal of celibacy itself.

Fasting *For*

Most men and women who have made some kind of public profession or vow regarding celibacy have been told that this is *for* something. Usually these statements include one or more of the following rationales: that celibacy is a way of being more available for ministry, that it signifies a commitment to some absolute, that it is a way to fulfill a ministry, or that it represents the only way people can be faithful to a sense of who they are called to be. Nuances of these rationales evidence motivations that might be called functional, conditional, instrumental, developmental, witness, *propter hic, ergo hoc*, and integrational. In this section I will attempt to show that, while having value, none of them are sufficient in themselves to represent why one would choose to be celibate. Yet each has been used, and continues to be used, as a rationale to justify what celibates are fasting *for*.

The functional argument has been used for years by defenders of a celibate priesthood. Building on elements of the Pauline rationale, the reasoning centers on the notion that one functions better as a minister when unmarried. If you are unmarried you are more free and available to serve others. Priesthood demands total availability. Therefore priests should remain unmarried. Yet, the argument is never extended to include doctors who must be "on call" at all times, or people in other professions demanding total availability.

In his inspiring article, "Living with Compulsory Celibacy," British priest James O'Keefe offers a nuanced critique of the traditional arguments about availability and celibacy in reference to the ability to function. He writes:

> The fundamental problem with this functional approach is that a person who is not free or becomes less available, through illness for example, still has to make sense of being celibate.

We cannot justify celibacy on the grounds of being "more available." At least, not if we presume that by available we mean free to get up and go at the drop of a hat, or be able to work all the hours that God sends. Availability is not about covering miles or not sleeping because there is a need somewhere. The danger is that the need is in the minister rather than the individual or the community. It is not the case that I am celibate in order to be more available, it is more the case that because I am celibate I may be more available. The availability flows from the fact of being celibate rather than being the cause of it.[6]

The more I have reflected on O'Keefe's argument, the more I find some faulty logic, at least for me. For example, what is the difference between being "celibate in order to be more available" and "because I am celibate I may be more available?" In both cases mentioned, a priest's "availability flows from the fact of being celibate." In neither case is availability the cause of celibacy. And, even if it would be recognized as a cause of the celibacy, we still would not know *why* someone is celibate. The apparent internal contradiction remains.

Expanding on O'Keefe's reflection on illness: what happens when a celibate gets sick and is not available? What happens when a celibate priest retires and isn't even available for supply or help-outs? Does his celibacy then have any purpose? Maybe the assumption made is that he's just too old now *not* to be celibate!

A second reason that has been proffered for celibacy represents the conditional argument. This was the rationale that prevailed when I entered religious life. I was "conditioned" to think celibacy represented a higher way of perfection, but this conditioning is not the conditional motivation I mean here. Rather, when celibacy becomes a condition required in order to do something else that one really desires, to embrace that goal does not mean that one embraces the condition, especially when mandated means to the end (celibacy) are not essential to achieving the end (ministry). The end does not justify the means; the consequence does not justify the conditions.

The conditional argument, despite all efforts to build it into a theology of "priestly celibacy," has proven quite futile. The old scriptural warrants have proved unacceptable and the new ones have proved to be embarrassing. The fact that priests in other churches affiliated with the Latin Rite are married makes it clear celibacy for priests is only a "man-made" condition (as Vatican II itself made clear). In fact, no other Christian denomination demands celibacy of its priests or ministers (although bishops in some churches must be celibate).

The instrumental rationale (as termed by Sandra Schneiders) is a related to the conditional rationale. Schneiders writes:

> [Another] collection of motivations for celibacy might be called instrumental in that celibacy is not chosen directly either as the symbolic expression of the most fundamental relationship in one's life or as the best or even necessary way of channeling one's spiritual energy. It is, in a sense, not chosen at all but accepted as the condition for something else which seems desirable enough to warrant paying the price of celibacy. Some people seek membership in a community which offers solidarity in relationships and mission. Others, often homosexually oriented, seek a same-sex environment free from the stigma and violence of a homophobic society. Some people, especially women whose feminist consciousness has been raised, need and want life companionship but have no attraction to patriarchally-defined marriage. An increasing number of men and women who have completed one career and/or outlived their marriage are looking at ministry as a "second career" and religious community offers a stable and organized context for that choice.[7]

In almost every one of the examples Schneiders uses, there is some kind of community-defined rationale for the celibacy. If this is so, the reasons for becoming a priest or religious are not related to celibacy, but to ministry and to being part of a ministerial community. Schneiders' explanation of the instrumental rationale represents my own motivation when I entered religious life. It was the way I would be able to do various things: respond to my sense of needing to be "perfect," to be a priest, to be radical in my life and ministry, and to have communal support.

This leads one to ask: what happens when the community, or even the ministry, that one first embraced no longer exists? Were celibates of the nineteenth century who entered congregations geared to minister to slaves free to marry when slavery was outlawed? Were those who joined communities of celibates in the years prior to World War II to work in orphanages able to be dispensed without any guilt when those orphanages went out of existence?

Or, what happens when the need for the ministry remains but the community no longer has the resources to support the ministry? What happens when one community, because of its decreasing numbers and unwillingness to join another, disbands? What happens when one group with one charism decides to join another group with another charism? What if you joined for the first charism and not the second? If celibacy is a charism, and the ministry no longer can continue if the charism is demanded, what is more important: the charism or the needs of the ministry? The questions are almost endless. The "instrumental" motivation for being celibate proves to be as illusory and filled with internal contradictions as the others. Yet it still is cited today as one of the primary motivators for people joining religious communities.

One time, following my pattern when giving a talk on celibacy, I asked a group of women religious: "How many of you entered religious life for the main reason of being celibate?" Nobody raised a hand. However, one sister raised a question I had never been asked. She said, "Why don't you ask: 'How many of you are now *remaining* in religious life for the main reason of celibacy?'" Her query reveals to me another motivation for celibacy that might be termed the "developmental" rationale. In other words, a person is able to ease into celibacy over a period of years. This understanding is reflected in the proverbial response of the monsignor celebrating his golden jubilee who was asked when he decided to be celibate. "Last year, it was, I think," he answered.

Sheila Murphy calls a developmental rationale "a process over product approach."[8] She notes that "vowed celibates who have been or are sexually active may report regret or guilt about their behaviors, but feel that their experiences have challenged them to greater depths of personal and spiritual growth and, therefore, report that they are better persons as a result."[9]

I think we all "grow into" our commitments, whether they be formally embraced as in chastity or celibacy or even less formally, as can be the case of people who just don't get married who may be single or widowed. However, while this approach might sound like it has its merits, especially upon hindsight, there often can be problems. The "growing into" celibacy rationale does not consider possible violations of vows and promises made *in the past*. It does not consider the effects of one's behavior on others who may be left behind. And it can beg the non-celibate ways we may have lived for years previously that were discussed, especially those in chapters five and six. Again while it may have some merit, the many internal contradictions do not make the developmental rationale viable as the reason *for* celibacy.

Next we have the witness-value rationale. A connection is made between the early church which witnessed to faith through martyrdom and the witness of celibacy as the next best thing. It is meant to articulate the kind of total gift of oneself that all must express in virtue of their baptism. David Knight describes this witness dimension well:

> Celibacy, then, like martyrdom or monastic exodus to the desert, is a sign that says something to the whole Christian community about the deepest identity of each individual member. What celibacy expresses is the reality of the Christian community's belief in the real presence of Christ, and of God through grace, to the mind and heart of every Christian. The celibate expresses it in a radical, unambiguous way, like the martyr who literally went to the cross with Christ, or like the monk who went out to the desert. But what the celibate expresses is a part of every Christian's life.[10]

When the witness rationale moves from being a sign for "every Christian's life" and is applied more specifically through the witness of diocesan priests, it is argued that their celibacy would enable them to more closely image the celibate Christ. When used to explain the purpose of religious life, celibacy-as-witness usually is explained as some counter-cultural manifestation of a rejection of the consumeristic and promiscuous elements of the prevailing culture. (Thus far, to my knowledge, church officials have placed no witness value on the celibacy demand for homosexuals who are neither priests nor religious.)

There may have been some value in the witness argument at one time, especially when it was lived less ambiguously. However, with more reports being made public about ways priests and religious have violated their vows and promises, the witness arguments often can seem hollow and even insincere. Because some celibates—cleric or religious—have become perpetrators who have violated their fiduciary relationship not only with their victims but with the broader public, including those in the church, the community's trust that priests and religious have been witnessing to celibacy has been eroded seriously. At this time, and for the foreseeable future, I think it's best we keep quiet about this "witness" rationale.

Once I lived in a city where a priest who hosted a weekly television show watched by thousands admitted having an ongoing affair with a woman after it became public in the media. This priest had offered retreats and conferences throughout our city. He coordinated a food and clothing center for the poor. He was adulated by more than a few. His celibate "witness" edified countless numbers of people. He was easily the most recognizable priest in our city. When the allegations of his sexual improprieties were made public, and he admitted the violation of his vow, many questioned not just him, but the rest of us as well. Who could believe that celibacy was a witness in such a case?

Other dynamics undermine, if not discredit altogether, the witness argument. Those include but are not limited to issues like abuse of power, insensitivity to issues related to women, and priests and religious dying of AIDS. Furthermore, there are other witness elements connected with vows—including those related to poverty and lifestyle—which many lay people have scoffed at for years saying, "If that's what poverty means, give me more of it." Given such weakening of the witness rationale, Sandra Schneiders concludes:

> Numerous factors in contemporary church culture and society have combined to obscure the once seemingly self-evident value and witness of consecrated celibacy. . . . The imposition of lifelong singleness on all Latin-rite Catholic clergy, many of whom are not called to or gifted for consecrated celibacy, has created a situation of nearly hopeless confusion and counter-witness not only among the laity and clergy themselves but even among some religious.[11]

When what is justified as a witness to a value becomes a counter-witness to it, we realize that the value needs another rationale if it is to offer any meaning. Furthermore, any institution that has linked the meaning-system of that value, in this case celibacy, with this "witness" needs to re-examine the value's purpose as well.

Another motivation for celibacy as fasting *for*, I call the *"propter hic, ergo hoc"* rationale or "because of this, therefore that." This argument applies especially to official church teaching related to homosexual people that states if one is homosexual, he or she must also be chaste, if not celibate. Because the top leaders in our institutional church have declared anything genital that is considered "natural" for a gay or lesbian person is really "unnatural" insofar as it is "intrinsically disordered"; the consequence is that non-genitality at the least, and celibacy at the most, must become normative. In this rationale, fasting *from* becomes the preoccupation rather than any fasting *for*.

I have already discussed the internal contradictions of this position in chapter three. Suffice it to say, the demand for homosexuals to be non-genital, especially when it is accompanied by homophobia in the institution which demands it, undermines any force of credibility the institutional representative may have in imposing it.

The previous pages noted problems connected to the conditional, functional, witness, developmental, and *propter hic, ergo hoc* rationales that have been used to make sense of celibacy, especially in situations where it has not been freely embraced. The next pages will offer a positive rationale for a life-giving celibacy termed the "integrational" rationale.

From what we've discussed thus far, it seems clear that the only celibacy that represents an authentic fasting must integrate the *from, for,* and *with* dimensions in a healthy way that nourishes one's life, one's relationships, and one's sense of meaningfulness. The integrational rationale does this only if it is anchored in the sense of what we are fasting for. This refers to the ultimate, transcendent goal or purpose that must sustain the way of celibacy. Jesus called this the reign of God (Mt 19:12); Paul referred to it in the sense of centering one's life on waiting for the divine presence (1 Cor 7:25-38).

In the passage about fasting from Luke 5:33-35 we considered earlier, Jesus seems to be saying that fasting was unnecessary as long as the object of the fast was realized as present. With the bridegroom experienced in one's midst, relations and intimacy could be expected to occur as a matter of course. With the bridegroom gone, fasting would be a kind of sacramental action to help the disciples remember that his presence could be sought in a more experiential way. Thus the implication in Luke is that fasting fosters the possibility of religious experience. Fasting in this sense becomes an act of religion. As such its purpose is to help us be mindful of our ultimate relationship with God.

The connection between celibacy and prayer will be discussed further in chapter ten. However, it is important to note here that the only rationale worthy of explanation or motivation for "celibacy" involves the One who alone is worthy of occupying the deepest parts of our lives. This is God. And the celibate, like a faithful person in a spousal relationship, is one who senses that, in one's depths, the hole in the heart can only be filled with God. The celibate is the one who freely accepts the gift of celibacy as from God and embraces it freely as for oneself. The sign of fidelity to the bridegroom will be determined by one's fidelity to prayer. This, I think, is what Fred Hickey meant when he said authentic celibacy demands that we find ways of being warm and intimate, but also that *we find a place in our hearts only for God.*

Prayer creates an expectant hope which helps us remember the bridegroom and "re-member" ourselves to the bridegroom. Without prayer there can be little remembrance of the bridegroom; without remembering God there is little hope of religious experience. Without prayer viewed as remembering (recollection) and as waiting (contemplation) to experience God-with-me (whether in the sense of absence or presence), I undermine the very basis that enables me to be in touch with the heart of celibate purposefulness—the reign, or presence, of God-with-me. Consequently, celibates who do not pray contemplatively in our age are like those who fast from food or drink, who die with another kind of gnawing within them: the doubt that their life and cause really might not have been worth such a radical commitment. Either form of death—in the body or in the spirit—would be tragic.

The celibate, as well as the person who is faithful to a spousal commitment, reveals the embrace of life that Jesus has manifested in the gospel. Warm, intimate, caring, and compassionate with and for others, Jesus had a place in his heart only for God. He could not explain himself except in God-terms. The same holds for anyone discipled to Jesus who would be an authentic celibate or live in chaste love. In this sense Donald Goergen writes of such a celibate:

> I am not defined by myself alone. I cannot be understood
> apart from God, who is part of my self-definition. Christian

celibacy is a response to the gift of the Spirit. Christian
celibacy places one's life in the history of that tradition of
following after Jesus. Christian celibacy is choosing to live
"for the sake of the gospel." One cannot understand celibacy apart from this call of the gospel, apart from a soul
thirsty for gospel, apart from this human yearning for self-
transcendence.[12]

As outlined above, I strongly suggest that we will have problems understanding authentic celibacy as long as we stress what
we are fasting *from* instead of what we are fasting *for*. But equally
we will have problems understanding celibacy as fasting *for* as
long as we tie it to any other purpose but to God alone and the person and message of Jesus revealed in the gospels. Unfortunately
that has not yet been done clearly enough.[13]

Fasting *With*

I do not want to end this chapter about fasting *from* and fasting
for, without some reflections on celibacy as fasting *with*.

Voluntary celibacy that finds one abstaining from something
good in favor of something we perceive to be better, at least in this
individualistic, consumeristic, and promiscuous culture, demands
participation in some kind of community. While this community
need not be limited to or composed of celibates and can be very
nourished among people committed to chastity, there is a value in
living in celibate relationships and even in communities characterized by this kind of mutuality.

Not expressing oneself genitally denies a natural inclination. Its
non-expression can affect us deeply. If we cannot share the effects of
fasting *for* something—when this affects an unnatural fasting
from—and if we cannot fast *with* others who have shared and who
continue to share the same experience, celibacy can often become
something solitary instead of something for solidarity. If we cannot
share our struggles to be celibate, we cannot share who we are. If
we cannot share in an atmosphere of confidence and trust, the
needs which arise from who we are as celibates, mistrust and alienation can easily occur. This demands an environment for sharing of
one's self, one's faith, and one's needs in a way that nourishes one's
celibate life rather than undermines one's celibate life.

Returning to the occasion of communal prayer which set the
context for this chapter, the more we Capuchins shared and

expanded on such ideas as many noted here vis-à-vis the Lukan notion of fasting, the clearer it became that life-giving relationships of intimacy are an essential element for celibacy. At the same time it became clearer to me that, given the unhealthy ways so many of us have lived as celibates, to expand on the thoughts of my candidate friend, I said that morning at prayer: "I will never again live in a community controlled by grouches." When one of the other friars challenged me, I explained that I find it difficult enough to sustain my own resources related to my celibacy; if the environment surrounding me becomes a countersign to my choice, my personal struggle will be all-the-more undermined.

An environment will either give life or take life from its members, even when they may not be aware of this. And while a community's environment might not purposely *take* life from its members, if it does not *give* life or nourish it, then it does indirectly take life by sapping the energy from them. Celibacy needs nourishment more than a life-support system.

Not only does a negative situation fail to nourish our growth; it can actually eat away our personal commitment. If people have a normal need for intimacy (which rightfully must be respected and nourished in some kind of community), and if this need is not met, it is not difficult to understand why some leave the diocesan priesthood and religious life saying it no longer gives them meaning. In the same way, groups like Dignity and Courage evidence the need of gays and lesbians for communities to support the difficulties they face in today's homophobic church and society. Because today's societal values and mores continually erode a choice for celibacy, we find more need for communities to create alternative environments that reinforce celibate commitments (as well as communities related to chastity itself). Thus fasting *from* and fasting *for* are quite impossible to live without fasting *with*.

Fasting with another or others does not just refer to one's community; it involves the way we relate to the one(s) with whom we are intimate. This involves mutual disclosure and sharing, nurture and correction, support and challenge. Mutual disclosure and sharing means involving other(s) in the deepest part of one's life stories, and with one's relationships. It doesn't just keep the mutual communication at a level of "what did you do?" but "how do you feel about that?" and "what do you think about it?" It moves people beyond the surface to deal with the feelings of anger, fear, losses, and disappointments. It celebrates each other's joys and hopes; their successes and dreams.

One of the greatest obstacles to the development of healthy relationships of intimacy happens when we fall into patterns that are not generative of growth and reformation. When routine takes the place of surprise and rituals replace wonder, a relationship once defined by intimacy can easily begin to wane. Rather than characterizing a relationship that has become routinized as normal, being taken-for-granted in a relationship actually evidences a slow dying in the dynamics of intimacy. The result is the "you don't send me flowers" and "you don't sing me love songs" refrain all over again.

I live with a brother, "Ray," with whom I have a personal relationship that reflects what I've termed "personal intimacy." While it may not be intimate at the second level of being sexual, we are intimate in the sense that we know we care deeply for and about each other. However Ray also has a very close and intimate relationship with a woman religious, "Dorothy." While he and I disclose and share many things with each other, their regular Sunday night phone call (that usually lasts at least an hour) tells me that Ray's and Dorothy's way of mutual disclosure and sharing is much deeper than his and mine. Our relationship is personally intimate. Theirs is that and more. And this is the way it should be with those you live with and care about, and those with whom you may not even live with but with whom you are sexually intimate, yet not genitally so.

Mutual support and challenge evidences a commitment that shows you are "there" psychologically, spiritually, and even physically when the other is in need. This kind of presence was very much in evidence when Ray heard the news that Dorothy was about to have a serious operation. He was in the middle of a two-month biking trip with another friar in the community. Instead of continuing, Ray left the trip, went to be with Dorothy during the operation, and used the rest of his sabbatical to stay with her. He supported her in her recovery and challenged her to keep hopeful. Such a commitment offered me a keen insight into what I've described as sexual intimacy.

In my mind Ray and Dorothy's way of relating reveals an environment where people nourish each other in their effort to be "warm and intimate" with others. In this case these others were not just Brother Ray and Sister Dorothy; their special relationship also involves those with whom they live. Presently there is too much suspicion among the confreres of celibates that many have to "sneak around" with their special friends instead of being able to share them with their community.

I continually discover this to be the case when I give workshops and retreats. Invariably this occurs among priests and men and women religious in their sixties and seventies. They have finally found someone with whom they can be warm and intimate in non-genital ways. In other words, they have experienced sexual intimacy, possibly for the first time. Yet they do not feel free to share their relationships with those among whom they live. When I ask if they are doing anything to violate their vows or promises, or if they are abusing the relationship in any way, they always say with some degree of surprise, "Well, no!" "Well why can't you share the good news of your relationship with your confreres?," I ask. "They wouldn't understand," is the response I continually hear.

Attitudes like this make me wonder how much longer it must take before we realize the absolute need to create communities of trust and intimacy, before it is too late to salvage the charism of celibacy.

9

Celibacy, Contemplation, and Compassion

In the last analysis I cannot be fulfilled as a person and be celibate unless I accept myself as a celibate person. I cannot find my rationale for celibacy in a custom that controlled my decisions in the past, in a system that sustains my ministry in the present, or in a fear of a God who will judge me in the future. I have to discover my rationale for being a celibate within myself. And I have to find my choice to embrace celibacy within my own freedom. In the last analysis, in "making" myself a celibate person, I have to be able to say: "This is who I am; this is where I can be my best self; this is where I can be the most free to be the image of God that 'I am.'"

Since I cannot find the rationale for celibacy in God's "command" or in the "opinion" of others, the ultimate rationale for my identity as a celibate cannot be found outside, but within my own self. I must decide that celibacy is the most authentic way I can say: "This represents the 'I am who I am.'" Only this kind of celibacy will reflect the embrace of a divinely offered gift inviting me to freely choose a life-commitment of abstention from genital intimacy. And this abstention from genital intimacy, from what is "natural," will not result in barrenness as long as I continue to develop alternate forms of intimacy with God and others. All this must be ultimately grounded in my own self-affirmation and sense of self-worth. In this sense I agree fully with Sandra Schneiders who writes of celibacy:

> It is a personal sense that one has found one's center, one's fulfillment in the relationship with God in some way that

181

makes an exclusive, sexually expressed lifelong commitment to another human being somehow incompatible with
who one most deeply is. Celibacy for such people is the
symbolic expression of this religious experience in the strong
sense of the word symbolic, i.e., it renders present, visible
and active something (in this case, a particular relationship
with God) which is imperceptible but very real.[1]

Until now many people, like me, viewed celibacy as a very
wide gate that many could pass through. In fact, even the Second
Vatican Council seemed to indicate as much. However, I don't
think asking for it will be enough to sustain celibacy in the future.
The gate will narrow. And the way to the gate will not be easy. To
paraphrase an image used by Jesus, for tomorrow's celibate: "The
gate is narrow and the road is hard that leads to life, and there are
few who find it" (Mt 7:14).

It has taken me years to find this "it" called celibacy. And, even
now, too often I still consider myself more a "eunuch that has been
made so by others" than a celibate made so by myself. Even
though I am on the way to celibacy, I often find the passage tight-
ening around me. Thus, to be faithful to this way is often very
hard. It has not always led me to life. Whether I will ever find "it"
and embrace it fully, I do not know. I do know the search to be both
celibate and intimate has not been easy. How to integrate the two
has represented a challenge that has had many ups and downs.
Only now am I beginning to discover some of its fruits.

Celibate Intimacy and the Need for Integration

"'You shall love [be intimate with] the Lord your God with all
your heart, and with all your soul, and with all your mind.' This is
the greatest and first commandment. And the second is like it: 'You
shall love [be intimate with] your neighbor as yourself.'" True love
is inseparable from intimacy.

Applying the notion of love in this great commandment (Mt
22:37-39) to the kind of love needed to be celibate "for the sake of
God's reign" involves three centers of intimacy: God, self, and others. While previous chapters have highlighted obstacles to loving
God, self, and others for those expected to be celibates,[2] my goal in
this chapter is to argue that these three objects of everyone's love
necessitate a high degree of intimacy, *especially* if one is to be an
authentic celibate.

Intimacy, for the celibate, involves three interrelated dynamics: de-centering one's self, centering on God as the "Other" through contemplation, and becoming centered on "others" through compassion. While I believe that though one need not be celibate to achieve this kind of intimacy, I will argue that celibates must integrate all three elements to create the only viable environment in which they can be healthy and holy.

The celibate must find celibacy's ultimate meaning and purpose within himself or herself. This demands that one discover where the "center" of his or her "self" might lie. Such a celibate approach is grounded in a kind of de-centering of the self for the Other. Here the conscious self is expanded beyond its ordinary "centeredness" in all the boundaries that limit it. These boundaries may have been self-imposed, or merely assumed by one's place in history, culture, religion, etc.

In this journey beyond the false self to the true self, from one's periphery to one's core, a person seeks that point of being centered in a greater reality. In this de-centering, one's self becomes centered in the self of the Other. The person moves from self to the Other, who now defines him or her. This represents *contemplation*—the loss of self in the Other. This is an invitation to find a place in one's heart "only for God," or "for God's reign."

I believe this de-centering of self in order to be centered in the Other necessitates some kind of self-transcendence. As such it fulfills the notion of mysticism described by Louis Dupre who sees in it "an expansion of the conscious self beyond its ordinary boundaries to a point where it achieves a union with a 'greater' reality."[3] In this mystical, contemplative experience we discover we have been touched by the Other.

The second element in authentic de-centering occurs in the way one goes beyond the ordinary boundaries which determine who will and who will not be allowed to be a part of one's life. When these barriers are broken and when the margins are extended to include those formerly excluded, I no longer find myself to be at the center of the universe. In fact, my center moves from the self outward. I become centered in concern and care for the universe and all it holds in its center. I call the de-centering through concern and care, that becomes increasingly universal, *compassion.*

All authentic de-centering demands a new kind of balance between the inner, contemplative, dimension and the external,

compassionate, expression. It involves an ebb and a flow in our life
(some say "a yin and a yang") that integrates within each person,
in mutually nourishing ways, the inner experiences of that which
transcends self and outer expressions that take one beyond oneself. This must be so if the healthy intimacy described above is to
be more than a dream for the celibate. Authentic celibacy thus
demands that one be radically de-centered from false self-centering at the same time one is radically centered in one's true self.
True de-centering, then, necessitates contemplation as well as compassion.

Since celibacy involves such a radical de-centering, any right-
centering for the celibate cannot be balanced without an equally
radical grounding in the Other through contemplation and in others through compassion. In the former we experience God's compassion; in the latter we offer a contemplative presence to others.
Contemplative intimacy involves a stance of care in which we
experience the embrace of God and then express that in an
embrace that extends to the universe itself. In contemplation, we
are touched by God's care. In compassion, the universe becomes
the focus of our care.

Contemplative Intimacy

I have tried for years to become contemplative—in my stance
toward life, in my environment, and in my prayer—but I feel I
have made little or no progress in this mystical dimension of my
life. Thus, knowing one cannot be an authentic celibate without
also being a contemplative, I felt considerable reluctance about
writing this chapter.

On January 11, 1995, I decided I had to begin writing this chapter, not because of any great insights, but because the deadline for
this book was at hand. I began my day on my little prayer-kneeler,
gazing at Andrew Rublev's beautiful icon of the Trinity. I tried to
allow the appropriate words to come to me that might become my
mantra for the prayer-time and for the rest of the day. Looking at
the image of the Trinity which appeared to invite me to their communion, words started to form from inside of me. Gradually they
got expressed in the phrase: "Gather me to your heart." I decided
this would be the phrase I would use to collect myself before my
God.

For my prayer that morning, then, I tried to repeat the phrase, mantra-like, as I visualized myself going through that narrow square in the table of Rublev's icon, into the trinitarian reign of God. But despite my attempt to pray and to recollect myself around the mantra "Gather me to your heart," I felt anything but gathered. In fact, I felt as if I were scattered all over the place. I was terribly distracted. My newly found mantra might have been charged with theological meaning, but it didn't get me very far into my spiritual center. I left the prayer area after an hour or so feeling quite empty.

I went to do my morning *physical* exercises, hoping I'd have more success. After doing some physical exercises, I joined the other brothers in the community for our hour of regular morning prayer. After singing a song that asked for God's word to be planted "deep inside," we listened as God's word came to us in the readings of the day. I took particular notice that morning of a passage from the first chapter of Mark. In the context of Jesus' healing and exorcising, the passage in the lectionary reported: "Rising early the next morning, he [Jesus] went off to a lonely place in the desert; there he was absorbed in prayer" (Mk 1:35). On hearing these words, I immediately began to wonder if Jesus' "absorption" in prayer might not have something to do with what we today call contemplation.

"Contemplation" is not a word used in the gospels at all. Thus, we need to find other clues to help us understand what Jesus' approach to prayer has to do with that characteristic we call mystical or contemplative. A characteristic of contemplative prayer, I discovered with my brothers that morning, was its capacity to absorb us just as Jesus was "absorbed in prayer."

Before sharing what absorbed "in prayer" might mean, we discussed what to be absorbed means in itself. The first image we thought of related to fabrics that soak up water. We thought of the old television commercial about "quicker picker-uppers"—those towels that just seemed to attract and slurp up water. This led us to think of those natural materials that absorb, sponges. In their natural environment, sponges are able to live only when they are filled with water absorbed from outside; also they are able to grow and give life to others in the process. Even when they are taken from their natural environment they still have a purpose insofar as they can keep absorbing liquids of every kind.

Another example from nature is the process of osmosis. When certain organisms absorb nutrients, their outer membranes are permeable enough to allow outside nutrients in. Photosynthesis is the process by which chlorophyll-containing cells in green plants absorb the energy found in light to synthesize carbohydrates from carbon dioxide and water.

Absorption has other connotations as well. People often use the word when speaking of being engrossed or immersed in something. Absorption might also refer to being consumed by someone or something. As we reflected on its meaning, we discovered that being absorbed in something seemed quite different from being obsessive or addictive; in fact, it seemed to be a healthy alternative to these destructive forces. "To be absorbed" involves full consciousness; to be obsessed or addicted implies having little control.

This part of our reflection gradually led us to discuss what "to be absorbed" might mean in relationship to prayer. We talked about how it involves being centered on something beyond oneself, to be caught up in something, to have single-mindedness, to have purity of heart, to be attentive in the same way deer become when they hear sounds in the woods. As we developed such images connected to prayer as being absorbed, one of the brothers said: "I would love to be able to be absorbed in God."

At that point in our scripture reflection, another brother surprised the rest of us by frankly admitting: "I'm afraid of being absorbed in anything. I don't want to be absorbed in anything or anyone, period. Including God." "Why not God?" somebody asked. "I don't really know," he responded. "Maybe it's got something to do with my need to control."

The more we reflected on his honest response, we came to understand that to be absorbed in God denies us the possibility of remaining in control. This led us to conclude that a major reason that keeps many of us from being absorbed in prayer, or being contemplatives, is our fear of giving up control. This applies even to our effort to control God in prayer itself! We also discovered that the fear of being absorbed in God can also keep us from experiencing intimacy with God, much less anyone else.

At other times, the more I probed the fear of giving up control in my own life, the more I found that this fear merely masks a deeper fear that is ultimately self-destructive. This is the fear of intimacy itself. In earlier chapters I related how my workaholism and perfectionism were institutionally-reinforced guises under which I operated. I did so, not just because I had to be in control, but even more so because I could not let go of that control. Only now do I realize that I feared letting go because I might then be touched by something that would make me see the futility of having to be in control. That touch would invite me to move to that energizing and passionate point of powerlessness within myself where I could discover intimacy itself. So, ultimately, the greatest fear that keeps us from becoming celibates revolves around intimacy.

When we fear giving up control and allowing room for God in our hearts and in our prayer, our approach to God becomes defined by the issue of control. We will constantly be conflicted about meeting God. God is not a God of control, but of intimacy. And when we can't give up control because of our fear of intimacy, we become self-centered rather than de-centered in a way that allows God to be God within us. Fear of intimacy ultimately alienates us from that God who is the essence of intimacy itself. In this context, David J. Hassel writes:

> Despite our fear of intimacy, we have been created by intimacy, we continue to be fostered through intimacy, and we are destined for the fullest possible intimacy after death. Because intimacy is, therefore, the source of our very being and of growth into full womanhood and manhood, it is the taproot of all prayer.[4]

The Greek word our scriptures used to describe Jesus as being "absorbed in prayer" is *proseuchomai* or *proseuchesthai*. While often translated simply as "prayer," it seems to imply an approach to prayer that finds one centered in God alone. It has a sense of worshipfulness about it. It includes the sense of being caught up in God's presence, of being aware of the awesomeness of the experience of being touched somehow by that presence. When I think of being "absorbed" in prayer and intimacy in prayer, my mind conjures up images such as being with someone whom I love deeply and passionately. I think of how I can just be in my beloved's presence without needing to say anything. In fact, in such a setting, words become redundant if not violent.

Sometimes, at airports, I watch people who seem very much in love, trying to say good-bye. They are totally absorbed in each other. They are silent in their embrace. They seem oblivious to the eyes of others. Their final kiss seems as though it has to be made in such a way that it will never be forgotten. Such is the form of intimacy that can be compared with being "absorbed" in the other.

Brought to prayer, the idea of being caught up in the embrace or kiss of the other most intimately invites us to find parallels in what it means to be God-absorbed. In many ways it reflects the way we fulfill the first part of the great command to love God with our whole heart, mind, and soul. Grounded in the sense of being held in the heart of God, it invites us to surrender our need to be in control in order to be embraced by God: our heart in God's heart, our self de-centered and centered in God, our self in the Other. This invitation to be absorbed more wholly in God's love seems to reflect what the *Song of Songs* (attributed to the male, Solomon) describes as the longing to be "kissed with the kisses" of God's mouth (Sg 1:2). In this context one might get a better grasp of the way this desire for intimacy with God might have affected the way the Jewish Jesus could have been "absorbed in prayer." (Parenthetically, in this effort I have found some help by examining how rabbinic legal and midrashic sources have tried to understand what it meant to receive the "kiss of God.")[5]

The experience of being embraced by God, of being touched on the mouth not only with God's word but with God's kiss, is of such forceful yet gentle impact that it becomes the context for the way we can begin to look at life itself. Traditionally this has been called the contemplative stance: a loving, caring, non-controlling embrace of all of life. In this sense Sandra Schneiders has written so eloquently:

> The unitive love which consecrated celibacy symbolizes is what the great religious figures of our tradition have called contemplation. . . . As a charism, celibacy is the public face of contemplative experience making visible in this world the absolute freedom, the captivating beauty, the supreme generosity, and the ultimate fidelity of that divine "love that moves the sun and the other stars." Its life-breath is prayer. Its ultimate explanation lies somewhere in the depths of Holy Mystery. And it is carried in fragile vessels of clay in order that it might be clear to all that the "transcendent power is from God and not from us" (2 Cor 4:7).[6]

There are three dimensions of contemplative prayer which I believe are critically necessary for the celibate if one is to grasp more fully the notion of intimacy with God that might be defined as "absorption."

The first dimension of the prayer of absorption involves indifference. By this I do not mean the kind of indifference that undermines intimacy. If the prayer of intimacy is to find us absorbed in God, the authenticity of this prayer will be characterized by care. Since care represents the opposite of control and since control is the antithesis of anything related to contemplative prayer, we can see how the only way to be free of control (to become absorbed in God) will be through a kind of holy indifference. At this point we come to understand a bit more clearly the wisdom in the phrase that opens Teresa of Avila's prayer: "Let nothing disturb you. . . ."

One of my favorite prayers comes from Paul's Letter to the Philippians where he prays that the community's experience of God might make them truly indifferent on the one hand and willing to make a difference on the other. My paraphrase of Philippians 1:9 says: "And this is my prayer: that your love may overflow more and more with knowledge and full insight to help you to determine what is best [what really can make a difference], so that in the day of Christ you may be pure and blameless, having produced the harvest of justice that comes through Jesus Christ for the glory and praise of God." Indifferent to all but God, God becomes the differentiating focus for everything else.

The second dimension of absorbing prayer needed to sustain a celibate choice involves the prayer of presence. However, especially for male celibates, this kind of prayer can often prove to be quite problematic, despite any goodwill. This point seems clear to me reading Joseph Guido's Harvard dissertation on seminarians and their experiences of God. What Guido discovered was: "first, that the presence of God is obtained in the absence of sexuality, and second, that the presence of God takes the place of sexuality."[7] In other words, for these men expected to be celibate, God's presence was sought through avoidance of that which constitutes the core of being human.

Guido relates an interview he had with a seminarian called "Ed." Somehow Ed's decision to be a priest was linked to a sense of loss of sexual innocence on the one hand, and a sense that celibacy would enable him to recapture the sense of God's presence. Before having sex, Ed had a keen sense of the divine presence. So desirous was he of recapturing his now-absent absorption in God, Ed came consciously to believe that it might be recaptured by repressing his natural sexual drive and his parallel need for intimacy. Unconsciously, however, Ed was seeking the presence of God in an absent god: the god of control. Until someone like Ed is free of this god grounded in his fears and guilt, he (or she) will never be open to meet the truly personal God.

Ed's case study reveals a discovery by Guido that seems to be reflected in tendencies found in the majority of the other seminarians interviewed as well. According to Guido, these men tend

> to regard sexuality as an impediment to God's presence. If the presence of God derives from a maternal matrix and is put at risk by the onset of sexuality—fathers forbid sons from sexual possession of their mothers—then it is understandable that these men would find in abstention from sexual expression the retrieval of the presence of God. That is, their abstention from sexual relations allows these men to sustain the presence of God and with it, maintain a special and exclusive relationship with their mothers that they would otherwise have to forfeit.[8]

Besides relating numerous stories such as Ed's futile search for God, Guido also has shown how the seminarians' notions of God's own being is quite conflictual vis-à-vis the notion of God that is at the heart of contemplation. On the one hand he shows that these men, despite being in a patriarchal institution that insists on calling God "father," actually have implicit spiritualities in which their notion of God is predominantly maternal in its associations. In fact, in two instances when fathers and sons are identified and when the seminarians associate father-dynamics with God, "the effect in both instances is painful and inhibiting."[9]

This idea of limiting God to male or female notions belies the reality of the third dimension of absorbing prayer that characterizes contemplation: the idea of God as transcendent. People have intuited for eons that to "name" a god was to control that god; to limit a god to any human form would be tantamount to making that god only as big as the idol that had been made. Once we name our God, it is only that: our god. It will be a god made in our image, after our likeness. Thus the Elohists' reluctance ever to name God. Thus the need to smash all false idols. Thus the demand that no "false gods" be placed *before* God. To make the God who transcends all categories, defined by any of them, is to control God through those categories and to limit God to those human definitions. It is to abdicate the search for God beyond what is merely present by our limited minds. To insist on God, therefore, in male terms or in other-culturally conditioned images not only reveals the failure of one's imagination; to our peril, it marks the futility of our mystical journey.

I read once in *USA Today* an extended article entitled "Seeing God through Spiritual Experts' Eyes." To my surprise, one of the "experts" sharing ideas about God-encounters was the singer and songwriter Kenny Loggins. His experience of God enabled him to express it in a way that transcended the traditional male categories that often have been used of God. "God speaks to me through love," he said. "God sings to me, through me. God holds me in her arms at night, and my heart opens again and again. I receive the gift of the love in her eyes. God is the grace of insight, the courage to let go."[10] The God Kenny Loggins experienced is the God of spiritual intimacy in feminine form.

A consequence of absorption in prayer will be the witness of one's life. The prayer of indifference might find us dealing with anger and resentment in entirely new or, at least, less unhealthy ways. The prayer of presence may enable us to find ways of welcoming the stranger in our midst or making a home for others through various forms of hospitality. The prayer of transcendence might enable us to begin reflecting that kind of wisdom that comes through suffering and pain to a sense of peace and hope. Noting the consequences of moving from anger to joy as another gift of contemplation, the 1994 "Contemporary Reflection on Apostolic Religious Life" for the Archdiocese of Milwaukee states:

> Contemplation is for all of us a means of attaining a quiet, deep-running joy that rescues us from grim determination or destructive anger as we become more acutely conscious of the problems that beset church and society. Contemplation strengthens us for the task of bringing imaginative and constructive solutions to these problems and for fashioning structures that nurture and sustain rather than oppress.[11]

While these dynamics seem to outline what it might mean for us to be "absorbed in prayer" in a way that deepens and nourishes our intimacy with God as contemplatives, contemplation is but one of the poles in the process of our healthy integration.

Compassion for the Crowd

Along with contemplation, compassion is the other pole necessary for the celibate's integration. And both must be centered in a life of care. If care reveals the core of contemplation, so care is also at the heart of compassion. And if care is the opposite of control, both contemplation and compassion reveal a life free of the need to control—God or others. In a similar vein, if celibacy demands contemplation, so we can say it is empty without compassion. And if contemplation enables us to be de-centered insofar as we become absorbed or centered on the Other, compassion reflects the way we become absorbed or centered on others. This connection between celibacy and compassion is well expressed by M. Basil Pennington:

> When we sense our oneness with others, when we are filled with compassion, how can we not be . . . chaste too? As we sense our own beauty and goodness, we are impelled to have reverence and respect for our own bodies and thus for the bodies of others, the exquisite works of God's constantly present creative love.[12]

For years I defined compassion based on a simple etymology the two concepts *com* and *passio* contain: to feel with another. But the more I have come to understand how Jesus seemed absorbed in compassion, it seems we need to nuance the *way* we feel with others if the definition is to reflect authentic evangelical compassion. Compassion represents the way we identify with and feel with others in their pain, their suffering, their shame, their embarrassment, and whatever else that seems to make them sense they are alienated from others. It means entering into their hurt and understanding it from their experience. Compassion means entering into the experience of the other with care and understanding, free of the need to control.

Matthew's gospel, which offers some sensible scriptural grounding for celibacy, also introduces a notion of compassion that I have found more helpful than any other. It occurs when that attitude of a heart that is moved with compassion and is extended beyond those we know to "the crowd." Matthew uses the word *splagchnizomai* to denote Jesus' heart as moved with compassion (in 9:36, 14:14, 15:32, and 20:34). In the first three instances the object of his compassion is "the crowds"; in 20:34 it refers to two blind men who were alienated from the crowd itself. A different use of the term is found in Matthew 18:27 where it is used to describe a characteristic of the very reign of God.

As I have attempted to understand the dynamics of developing "a heart moved with compassion" that reflects Jesus' motives and actions, I have discovered that, on the one hand *splagchnizomai* is initiated by a certain need. For example, in Matthew 9:36, Jesus saw the crowds who were harassed and helpless, like sheep without a shepherd; in Matthew 14:14, he witnessed a great crowd that seemed to contain many who were sick; and in Matthew 15:32, his compassion was triggered because the crowd "has been with me now for three days and has nothing to eat." In Matthew 18:26-27, a servant's large indebtedness ultimately triggers the master's compassion. In the incident including the two blind men (Mt 20:34), Jesus' compassion is triggered by their cry for help. In all these cases splagchnizomai was initiated by some need. However, this act of compassion was predicated on the act of seeing what the need was and what it would involve.

The process of having a heart moved with compassion thus begins with *seeing*. I find this a perfect link with contemplation, for contemplation represents a certain way of seeing. Might it be that one cannot be an authentic contemplative without being deeply compassionate? Might it also be that contemplative seeing becomes a total distraction and eventually blindness if it is not accompanied by a compassionate vision and action? Just reflecting on the ways the great mystics (e.g., Therese of Lisieux) were also the great missionaries attests to the connection.

The common thing that is seen or recognized and triggers *splagchnizomai* in each of the five gospel incidents is some kind of need: evangelization, suffering, hunger, debt, and blindness. Embracing this attitude of compassion not only seems to be contingent on recognizing some need, it also seems to reveal a kind of co-vision in the way God "sees" as well. Thus, Moses' first experience of God was the "burning bush" wherein God said to him: "I have observed [seen] the misery of my people who are in Egypt; I have heard their cry on account of their taskmasters. Indeed, I know their sufferings" (Ex 3:7).

If the sufferings and pains of others are the trigger that elicits a heart to be moved with compassion, then we can ask: what happens next? What does one do in face of these sufferings and pains? How does one respond? In the first example, when Jesus recognized the need for evangelization, he sent the Twelve to teach and to heal (Mt 10:1-8). In Matthew 14:14 he cures the sick. In Matthew 15:36, he provides food for the hungry crowd. The chapter eighteen story reveals how the debtor experiences the master's compassion by the forgiveness of his debt. In Matthew 20:34 the two blind men experience Jesus' compassion in the return of their sight. The pericope ends with the men following Jesus after they have regained their sight.

I don't think any celibate can be absorbed in Christ without following his example. This means following not only his prayer-dimension which describes his conscious contact with God, but also his compassion for others as represented by his conscious contact with the crowd, with people in their needs. In the last two decades, the most famous celibate has been Mother Teresa. "God absorbed" could more than adequately describe her. Yet, her whole life could also be summarized around her expression of compassion for people in need. In response to a question about what triggered her concerns she stated:

> To me, God and compassion are one and the same. . . . Just a smile, or carrying a bucket of water, or showing some simple kindness. These are the small things that make up compassion. Compassion means trying to share and understand the suffering of people. . . .When we ultimately go home to God, we are going to be judged on what we were to each other, what we did for each other, and, especially, how much love we put in that. It's not how much we give, but how much love we put in the doing—that's compassion in action.[13]

If seeing a need initiates one's compassion and if authentic compassion expresses itself in doing something about that need, then we might ask why so many of us fail in this regard. A possible answer is found in the story of the unmerciful debtor (18:21-35). Why didn't the debtor, after seeing and experiencing the results of compassion, act similarly when the occasion arose? Why did he fail to see his fellow servant's need? Why did he fail to respond to further reveal his share in the reign of God? An answer to these questions brings us back to an image very dear to me: the circle of care:[14]

The left side of the circle of care reveals how we *experience* the reign of God's care. The Hebrew scriptures tell us that, in the original religious experience of Israel in the desert, God "saw" the people's need, showed "care" by listening to the people's plight and was "called" to do something about that need. Contemplation represents its apogee. However, now that Jesus Christ has become the incarnation of God's care, we who are called to be celibate for the sake of God's reign, must *express* our experience (the right side of the circle) in the way we "respond" to others in need. We do so with our care. In the process we come to see God. Thus, in describing how we will be blessed with the gift of God's reign when our last day comes, whether or not we see God will be contingent on how we responded to those in need. (See: Mt 25:31-46). Compassion represents the apogee of the second half of the circle.

If the plight of the people and the cry of the crowd are those needs that elicited the care of God and the compassion of Jesus, we celibates might ask ourselves, as Pope Paul VI did: "How then will the cry of the poor find an echo in your hearts?" I find it fascinating how Pope Paul VI, in his letter outlining the meaning of celibacy in religious life, declared that this need of the people and the cry of the poor should elicit two actions on behalf of justice (for the crowd) by celibates. He stated: "That cry must first of all bar you from whatever would be a compromise with any form of social injustice. It obliges you also to awaken consciences to the drama of misery and to the demands of social justice made by the Gospel and the church."[15] The fact that the pope outlined the first two demands of justice as compassion-in-action are instructive for celibates today.

In examining the ways the great mystics also were radically concerned about justice, we find concrete examples of people—often celibates themselves—who experienced God's care in their contemplation. But they also were the ones who could see the needs that demanded a re-ordering through structural change in the church and in society. These celibates were people who have manifested both the mystical (contemplative) and prophetic (compassionate) dimensions of the reign of God. Thus we have Francis and Clare of Assisi, Catherine and Bernadine of Siena, Brigid of Sweden, Thomas Merton, and the two great Carmelites Teresa of Avila and John of the Cross.

Maybe it is only because they were such contemplatives that they were able to be compassionate. Maybe it's because they recognized their own needs and emptiness that they could have compassion for the needs and longings of others. A deep connection exists between the experience of one's inner loneliness and the expression of one's outer compassion. In experiencing the reign of God's care for us in contemplation we are able to be in solidarity, in care, with others who are in need. Our response in care thus echoes the care we have experienced in our own need. I think this sentiment may be what lies behind the beautiful words of Patrick J. Connolly. He writes: "My loneliness has a 'voice.' There is a Presence within the void. Deep friendships have brought me to this, and the inevitable good-byes. I meet my loneliness. And I learn that nothing else remains to be discovered except compassion."[16]

If seeing others' needs, caring about them, and trying to do something to alleviate them represents our response to the care God has first shown us, why are we not more absorbed in this dimension of God's reign? Why does it seem there can be such a chasm between people who indicate their commitment to the interior journey, but do their traveling apart from other human beings, especially the stranger along the way? Examining the obstacles to our "seeing"—the things that keep our hearts from being moved with compassion—may help to provide an answer.

The most obvious obstacle revolves around self-centeredness and various forms of narcissism. When our thoughts and emotions, ideas and feelings, are preoccupied with our own interests, the needs of others will not be factored in very easily. When our world is centered on ourselves, it can be quite a small world. When we do not allow ourselves to "see" the many worlds beyond us, we end up living in a very constricted environment that cannot echo the cries of people beyond ourselves. This is why it is so important to allow ourselves to be touched by the worlds of others beyond our own.

Delusion is a consequence of not being touched by the experiences of other people. We can live in denial about reality or be deluded into thinking ours is the only legitimate experience, ours the only truth. When this happens, we become blinded to outside forces and limit truth to our own experience. This can also lead to various forms of bias and prejudice, the exact opposite of compassion.

Probably the greatest obstacle to seeing is fear. I've known times in my life when my fears and anxieties have actually blinded me to what is right in front of me. If the greatest obstacle to seeing is fear, the greatest fear is giving up the need to control. Increasingly I am discovering that fear of letting go, of de-centering myself, of allowing others to be who they are, represents the main obstacle to true compassion. If control is the opposite of care, then fear of giving up control undermines the possibility of authentic compassion in our lives. When we are so self-centered that we must be in control, we are not able to identify with the pains and problems of others in a way that would define us as compassionate people.

There are also obstacles to the second point in our circle, to compassion, to caring itself. Recall that not caring is putting oneself outside the reign of God, for God's presence has been revealed in care. Therefore, "not caring" has two main partners: apathy and indifference. Both of these are concrete obstacles to compassion.

Apathy comes from the words *a* which means "without" and *pathos* which means sympathy, empathy, or compassion. In his classic book, *The Prophets*, Abraham Heschel has pointed out how mercy and care reveal God's pathos. He wrote that God can never be neutral or uncaring in the face of the pains of people or the injustice done them:

> God is always partial to justice. The divine pathos is the unity of the eternal and the temporal, of meaning and mystery, of the metaphysical and the historical. It is the real basis of the relation between God and humankind, of the correlation of the Creator and creation, of the dialogue between the Holy One of Israel and his people.[17]

Another obstacle to compassion is found in our indifference. In a culture such as ours where material values have come to override spiritual ones and where consumerism has taken hold of people's psyches, indifference to God and the needs of others cannot be far behind. Unlike the prayer of indifference noted above, this form of indifference is defined by the fact that nothing is important to us except those self-defined needs and wants that control our lives. We become indifferent to the needs of others; again we just don't care.

Returning to the "circle of care" chart can help us probe possible obstacles not only to our "seeing" and "caring," but to the *call* of the needs of others. Probably the greatest obstacle arises from the attitude that abdicates responsibility itself. "It's not my problem; I'm not responsible," is the general sense that gets conveyed. Many times this attitude develops in direct proportion to our distance from the problem.

The dynamics that often keep us from being responsible stem from two related factors: Though we become aware of the cultural dimensions and structural causes for many pains people must endure, at the same time we are overwhelmed with a sense of our own powerlessness and inability to make a difference.

Another factor that keeps us from becoming "response-able" comes from a kind of "blame-the-victim" mentality. Here we stress issues of personal responsibility while overlooking deeper structural dynamics that make the problem even more a systemic factor than an individual matter. When this occurs we blame migrant workers for welfare problems rather than criticize corporate entitlement programs; we are appalled by teens who kill others for tennis shoes or leather jackets, without challenging the advertisers of such corporate products that make millions for themselves and their sponsors by promoting their products as signs of success.

If we do not allow the cultural barriers and personal fears to become obstacles to our seeing and our caring, we can begin to bring the circle of God's care to completion. Having been seen, cared for, and called in our need, we experience contemplation. This enables us to respond with care ourselves. And when we respond by showing this care to others in their need, we see God (see Mt 25:37ff). When we manifest this compassion again, we are led to contemplation. Here our care and compassion will bring us back to the very core of contemplation: we will see God.

10

Celibacy and the Need for Communities of Trust

Some time ago, I was asked to address an all-province assembly of women religious, well-known for its progressive stances in the health care field, as well as in other social concerns. The planning committee asked me to discuss an issue they saw as critical for the future of their institute: *trust*.

From my experience with this group and other mainline congregations of vowed celibate women and men, including my own province, I have concluded that the future of celibacy will remain very tentative unless it is accompanied by a communal environment which engenders trust. Despite all the mission statements and provincial plans, all the visioning and pastoral programs, until we grapple with the fundamental issue of community and the erosion of trust among our members we will be skirting a key issue. Without trust-defined relationships, celibacy cannot be sustained, whether it be among religious communities or within members of the diocesan priesthood.

The Interplay Between Trust and Distrust

Though the group of women religious who invited me to speak could be characterized officially as a community of faith, its members had several problems with their faith in one another. At the same time, while it might also be characterized as a community of trust, its members had difficulties trusting each other.

To help those assembled, the planning committee had placed two large charts in the assembly hall. On each chart a large circle contained a smaller circle. On the inside circles the words "trust" and "distrust" were written. The sisters were asked to write within the large circles words describe how trust and distrust might look and feel for them personally. By the end of the day each circle was filled with powerful images:

DISTRUST	TRUST
Angry + Frustrated + Devastated	Affirmed + Self-possessed + Whole
Passive Aggressive + Rebellious	Empowered + Belonging + Respected
Half-hearted + Anxious + Hurt	Integrated + Warm + Giving Birth
Incapable + Outsider + Isolated	Responsible + Accepted + Generous
Powerless + Decimated + Pained	Powerful + Energized + Illumined
Humiliated + Defensive + Shamed	Loved + Oneness + Radiance + Safe
Disintegrated + Not Understood	Plenty good seeds + Free + Eager
A pit of powerlessness + Alone	Groovy + Solid-grounded + Loving
Withdrawn + Fearful + Inhibited	Explosion of creative expression
Misunderstood + Sad + Diminished	Understood + Happy + Expansive

While these descriptors can add much to our understanding of the dynamics of trust and distrust, the participants also discovered how difficult it is to limit our human relationships just to these two dynamics. People's lives and relationships are much more nuanced. Most of us can't say we *really* trust, yet distrust is also too strong to describe our stance. Consequently, it is usually more helpful to consider "distrust" and "trust" as two forces at the ends of a long continuum with many other forms in between. Some of these other forms can be labeled as "no trust," "don't trust," or "can't trust." Others get interpreted as "won't trust," "distrust," or "mistrust." Most of us cannot be placed at either end of our continuum; we fall somewhere between its two poles and align ourselves more closely to one of these other forms.

For example, some people exhibit a "no-trust" approach to life. These are people who have been violated so deeply that it is virtually impossible for them to develop even the smallest amount of trust with anyone. Others "don't trust," not because they distrust, but simply because they have never experienced trust. Some "won't trust" because they fear giving up their need to control or being vulnerable in the presence of another. Others will exhibit forms of "mistrust" due to past hurts and humiliations.

Trust in Self

God created all of us, males and females, as "good (enough)." Yet, we learn at an early age that others think there is something wrong with us. Distrusting our self, we try to cover up our nakedness, defending our self from further invasions by others (including God). We do this by each courting a self we hope will be acceptable to *them*. Thus our identity, our self, begins to be identified by *their* assumptions and expectations, *their* rules and regulations. These "others" can be our parents or any other force or authority that influences or controls our lives.

The resulting sense of biblical nakedness, which leaves us with the sense of not being good enough in our own eyes and the eyes of others, represents shame. Shame (self-rejection based on fear of others' rejection) is grounded in distrust of self. When shame-based images dominate our thoughts, feelings, and behavior, our freedom is constrained; we become preoccupied with meeting the standards imposed from outside persons, groups, or institutions. In traditional Catholicism, this sense of shame has undermined many people's sense of self; its consequences have been particularly painful for women and homosexual persons.

A residual problem facing religious from the pre-Vatican Council II era is that we entered into systems and structures that so completely defined our lives that we still find it hard to trust ourselves. We don't trust ourselves because, for years, we have given to others—our superiors, priests, bishops, popes, rules and regulations, canon law, or whatever—the power to define our reality. Consequently, many of our older members have little or no identity outside of these definitions.

To trust in oneself instead of in others and their definitions of us is a formidable task. It begins with self-awareness or self-knowledge. In the face of other voices saying something is wrong with us—which should make us ashamed of ourselves—the inner voice of self-awareness enables us to believe in ourselves as good, as precious in the eyes of God.

The title of one of Jesuit author John Powell's books asks: *Why Am I Afraid to Tell You Who I Am?* So often we can't be honest with each other about our thoughts, our feelings, or what we've done because we can't trust. However, this is a "Catch-22" dilemma. We can be bound by fear and not disclose ourselves, or we can risk disclosing ourselves and being rejected, abused, or humiliated. I have found that only increasing levels of mutuality enable us to move to self-disclosure, the second level of being centered rightly in oneself.

The third level is self-entrustment. People reach the level of self-entrustment when they have strong enough experiences of mutuality in relationships. Within this safe environment, they do not merely disclose their self; the "self" that is disclosed is so vulnerable and honest that it is disclosed only because an environment has been created wherein the other can be trusted not to violate the disclosure. It is at this level that someone says to the one who has made the self-entrustment: "Thank you for trusting me." The sense of gratitude and awe at being thus honored with the trust of another often testifies to the fact that an underlying environment already had been created that allowed the self-entrustment to take place.

Finally, the self—to be authentic—must be de-centered from the false self if one's identity is to be realized. This de-centering can only come through self-giving or self-donation. While we've seen how de-centering relates to contemplation and compassion, there is a communal dimension as well. De-centering does not come without trust. Without trust we return to our need to control; with it, we can risk our self for the sake of the other. This notion will lead us to the next part of our discussion about the need for celibates to find ways to trust each other in some communal way.

However, before moving to the next section, I think it is better to summarize what we have said thus far. The process of growth toward being centered rightly in oneself to the point of being able to trust ourselves involves four levels: self-awareness, self-disclosure, self-entrustment, and self-donation. Building from the chart describing the three levels of intimacy outlined in chapter seven, I find parallel movements involving these four levels of authentic self-centering:

LEVELS OF INTIMACY	LEVELS OF SELF-CENTERING
Personal	Self-Awareness
	Self-Disclosure
Sexual	Self-Entrustment
Spousal/Celibate	Self-Donation

We can also understand this process of trusting ourselves and authentic self-centering as a process of discovering what the goals of our search may be. In this context, the effort to become self-aware represents the search for authenticity. It reveals the desire of the self to discover an identity, to be someone who is self-defined. As shown in chapter nine, this represents that archetypal urge within each of us that longs to declare ourselves images of God to the degree that we too can declare: "I am who I am." In the very act of defining ourselves as our unique "I am," we move to self-disclosure; I cannot say "I am" except by disclosing this in relationship to another. This self-disclosure reveals the risk I take to be who I am in mutuality with the "I am" represented in the other. In effect, then, self-disclosure really represents our search for mutuality.

In the developing bonds that are nourished by mutuality we move from a fear of others because they might violate our "I am" to initial levels of trust. In the resulting entrustment to the other of the deeper self of who "I am," I reveal my need to fulfill another step in my personal search for meaning: the search to find friendship. Building on the kind of mutuality that leads to friendship and which enables me to maintain my own authenticity, I now can be open to the possibility of giving myself to the other. This self-donation, however, will only be sustained if there is a reality shared by both of us (or the group of us who live at this level), that is bigger than our combined selves. This represents every person's search for a cause. This personal search for a cause reflects Jesus' words in John's gospel about persons willing to lay down their life for their friends. The commitment represented in this self-donation represents the peak of faith. One cannot live a truly celibate life without having faith in someone or something bigger than the self. We will see how this someone or something bigger than self is what is meant by "the reign of God."

At this point, we can schematize the parallels between these two processes as follows:

LEVELS OF SELF-CENTERING	GOALS OF THE SEARCH
Self-Awareness	Search for Authenticity
Self-Disclosure	Search for Mutuality
Self-Entrustment	Search for a Friend
Self-Donation	Search for a Cause

How well the interaction occurs between trusting ourselves and self-centering, will determine what level of trust in others we will experience and express.

Trust in Others (from Persons to Institutions)

While trust of self may be a problem for many of us, I detect a deeper problem related to trust/distrust in the institutional church as well as in religious communities to which we belong. This gets expressed in our relationships. Recalling the group of celibate women that asked me to address issues of trust and distrust, the chapter planners also asked me to show their link to issues of individualism and community, power and powerlessness, empowerment and control, and the acceptance of differences.

If one's relationship with others in an institution depends on a definition of self made outside oneself, we need not be surprised when some of us mistrust those who have defined us, as well as the processes they have used. One need only review many women's responses to the U.S. Bishops' final draft of the pastoral letter on women. The document which attempted to define women virtually excluded women's input.

Chapters five and six covered other implications connected to the double crisis of meaning facing males who are expected to be celibate in the church today. I noted that every crisis in meaning involves some crisis of faith. At the same time, we can add, every crisis in faith (in each other, our leaders, our communities, or our church leaders) ultimately involves a crisis of trust. Trust, our dictionaries remind us, means implicit faith. When we experience a crisis of meaning and faith it affects our capacity for trust. And, the crisis of trust undermines the possibility of community.

Every crisis of trust invites us to (re)examine our faith. Building on James Fowler's notions related to faith,[1] I believe all kinds of faith (interpersonal, religious, or secular) involve a personal relationship of trust and loyalty (to someone, some values, etc.) that leads to commitment. This statement can be unpacked to reveal four levels of faith. Viewed schematically, they look like this:

Personal

Relational

Trust and Loyalty

Commitment

In the pericope of the healing of a centurion's servant in Matthew 8:5-13, there is evidence of all four levels of faith at work:

> When he entered Capernaum, a centurion came to him, appealing to him and saying, "Lord, my servant is lying at home paralyzed, in terrible distress." And he said to him, "I will come and cure him." The centurion answered, "Lord, I am not worthy to have you come under my roof; but only speak the word, and my servant will be healed. For I also am a man under authority, with soldiers under me; and I say to one, 'Go,' and he goes, and to another, 'Come,' and he comes, and to my slave, 'Do this,' and the slave does it." When Jesus heard him, he was amazed and said to those who followed him, "Truly I tell you, in no one in Israel have I found such faith. I tell you, many will come from east and west and will eat with Abraham and Isaac and Jacob in the kingdom of heaven, while the heirs of the kingdom will be thrown into the outer darkness, where there will be weeping and gnashing of teeth." And to the centurion Jesus said, "Go; let it be done for you according to your faith."

In this passage, Jesus clearly distinguishes between two kinds of faith *(pistis)*. Israel's "faith" represents what we recognize under rubrics, rites, rituals, and regulations. The centurion's faith, however, represents something much deeper than Israel's religiosity: his is the step-by-step process of coming to faith outlined on the chart. The centurion was a person; Jesus was a person. He encountered Jesus in a relationship. While this personal relationship between the centurion and Jesus was the grounding of what would become faith, it was not faith yet. Something about the relationship this person had with Jesus (we do not know the duration of it) enabled him to place his trust in Jesus as a person. The way he indicated his trust also revealed how he had come to place his loyalty in Jesus as well.

As a soldier, the centurion knew what constituted loyalty. His job demanded that his loyalty be to Caesar, but this did not mean he had faith in the emperor. He had soldiers under him on whose loyalty he depended, but this did not mean they had faith in him either. Indicating this kind of loyalty, the centurion had said to Jesus: "For I also am a man under authority, with soldiers under me; and I say to one, 'Go,' and he goes, and to another, 'Come,' and he comes, and to my slave, 'Do this,' and the slave does it" (Mt 8:9).

It is evident that these "secular" forms of loyalty were merely preludes to the kind of loyalty the centurion revealed in his personal relationship with Jesus that would be called a manifestation of his faith.

At this point we might wonder what there was about the personal relationship this man developed with Jesus that would lead Jesus to say in the very next verse: "Truly I tell you, in no one in Israel have I found such faith" (Mt 8:10). This same query was posed by our community at morning prayer some time ago as we reflected on this passage. As we prayed over it, an answer became clearer.

It is important to realize that this person had a very significant job. A centurion held a prestigious position in occupied Israel. He was a man in authority in a chain of command. Power, rank, and authority defined his relationships. However, what made his approach to Jesus so laudable was that in their personal relationship, the centurion had come to trust Jesus and Jesus' "authority" (*exousia*) as greater than his own. He was willing to put himself and his authority on the line to this Higher Power. This, we discovered, was what made the centurion's faith different from Israel's. It involved having the kind of trust that would make one submit in loyalty to another.

However, something else enabled Jesus to interpret the centurion's encounter with him as one of faith. This is found in the centurion's reply to Jesus' statement about coming to cure his sick servant: "Lord, I am not worthy to have you come under my roof; but only speak the word, and my servant will be healed" (Mt 8:8). The very fact that this Roman centurion would give to Jesus the title limited to his secular authorities reveals the final element of faith: commitment. Such a commitment could not be limited to mere words; it was grounded in a transfer of loyalty based on trust that he developed from their personal relationship.

This brings to the forefront the connections between trust and commitment. If my understanding of Fowler is correct, we don't make commitments (step 4) to persons or institutions we mistrust (step 3), unless we are unhealthy ourselves. We can't trust persons or institutions that have abused our relationships or continually test them. Where there is testing there is little trusting. Margaret Farley notes, "If our trust has been abused or we have lost our own selves in our commitment to another or to a cause or institution, then we can be afraid to put ourselves at risk again [through trusting relationships]."[2] As there can be no relationship (step 2) that is not personal (step 1), trust exists only when personal relationships reflect an integrity born of trust.

While the progression described above moves from personal relationships (level 2) to trust and loyalty (level 3) to commitment (level 4), movement in the opposite direction can also be possible: commitments also can nourish trust and loyalty and support personal relationships. Farley explains: "Commitment is destructive if it aims to provide the only remedy for distrust in a loving relationship. But it can be a ground for trust if its aim is honesty about intention, communication of how great are the stakes if intention fails."[3] Commitment nourishes trusting relationships among persons who can count on each other's loyalty.

At this point we may be able to see how these levels of faith relate to the other levels discussed in the book and this chapter thus far. Each of these four levels of faith builds on the former; without the former, the latter cannot take place. We can also see parallels between these levels of faith and the levels of intimacy as well as movement toward a healthy self-centering and a search for our goals that we have already examined. We can now chart the four groups we have discussed and show their relationships as follows:

Levels Of Intimacy	Self-Centering	Goals For The Search	Levels Of Faith
Personal	Self-Awareness	Search for Authenticity	Personal
	Self-Disclosure	Search for Mutuality	Relational
Sexual	Self-Entrustment	Search for a Friend	Trust/Loyalty
Celibate	Self-Donation	Search for a Cause	Commitment

As we examine the crisis of trust among communities and institutions, we find a crisis in our personal relationships also. There is also a crisis of intimacy. Consider the dynamics that often occur at gatherings of many celibates I know. When celibate men arrive at one another's houses, or meet each other at meetings, we give great hugs. But what happens then? What do we do, what do we say, how do we relate after the hug? What, really, do many of us share in common? Where is the intimacy, the self-disclosure, the self-entrustment? I began to ask these questions after an experience I had in my province, a community of professed celibates.

One of our communities celebrated the birthday of one of our brothers. Because so many of us have such full schedules, the planners decided the only way to ensure any kind of a crowd would be to have the celebration on a Saturday morning at 7:30. And they were right!

A good number came for the morning prayer and Mass (both finished in a half-hour). Then we gathered for breakfast. Greetings were made and more hugs were extended to new arrivals. The many repetitions of the question "How are you?" seemed more a social convention than a question inviting honest self-disclosure. In reply, we heard varieties of the words, "I'm just fine." The food was served before we had to make much more small talk. Breakfast also forestalled the possibility of any silence becoming too embarrassing.

This was not a group that should have needed to make small talk. Almost all of us were involved in work among the poor or in social justice. In practice we shared a common vision. So why couldn't more of us feel at home with each other? This could not be attributed to any lack of vision. Neither did the members have any ill will. What's more, we probably could say honestly we even cared about each other. Rather than look for an answer around these possibilities, it seems we needed to look elsewhere. We needed to examine the context for the vision and what may have stymied the goodwill or the care that each man there certainly had for the others.

Given all that has been written on the subject, it should not be a surprise if I'd say that I think individualism dominated us. That morning we had a great opportunity to celebrate one another's efforts, to listen to each other's problems, and to support our common vision of being in solidarity with the poor. But few did or could. We didn't talk about our vision or how we were striving to implement it. Again we might ask: "Why not"?

Perhaps we couldn't share genuine trust because we feared being genuinely truthful with each other. Possibly the reason could be another obstacle that may have undermined any goodwill, namely jealousy or competitiveness. What Lillian Rubin says of competition and jealousy among some women also might have applied to the men around the breakfast table who were not ready to have self-disclosure: The fact that people can't be honest with one another "create[s] a breach even if only a small one". . . . [It raises] "fears of envy, questions of trust. But even when such behaviors are not at issue, women's inability to deal directly with competitive feelings is a source of difficulty in their relations with each other."[4] Maybe we just were too busy the morning of the birthday party. Whatever the case, we finished breakfast and dishes in forty minutes. Everyone went his own way.

I left pondering the quality of our personal relationships and the level of our trust and loyalty, and, to a degree, not only my own willingness for self-donation to this group but my very commitment to these men as well. While this particular crisis of meaning in my own institution may have only been a small one, it pointed out one more erosion of faith in those to whom I am to be committed.

Given such experiences, we should not be surprised when people ask why there is so little self-donation to the group, why we would want to remain committed to such a group, especially when similar cases seem to confront us on a regular basis. If commitments are questioned, I believe, it's because something has failed at one of the first three levels determining the level of our intimacy and self-centering as well as our goals and faith. In my experience, a good part of the failure usually can be found between levels two and three of Fowler's schemes, between our personal relationships and the trust/distrust involved in those relationships.

Linking the occasion of that breakfast with similar incidents has led me to wonder whether the present institutionalized form of religious life, and the parallel insistence on celibacy for overworked diocesan priests, can generate enough trust among members of these groups to ensure lasting commitments.

If we question people's commitments regarding celibacy, I think we need first to examine the level of trust, both among us (community members and diocesan priests) and toward our institutional leaders. While we may have crises related to trust among us, I don't think it can be said, for instance, of us religious, that we actually distrust one another, either. Our dissolution has not yet reached that stage. Rather than the extreme experience of distrust, most of us find ourselves elsewhere on that continuum between trust and distrust. Consequently some of us don't trust, others won't trust, and still others can't trust.

The communities that are necessary to sustain celibacy will not be able to generate trust, much less loyalty, to say nothing about commitment, unless we can entrust ourselves to specific others in personal relationships of intimacy. Yet how can we share ourselves, our shame as well as our dreams, our fears and our phobias, our questions and our commitments, if we don't know if we can trust one another, if we fear self-disclosure?

For instance, what if one of our members said publicly that he or she no longer participates in liturgies presided over by male clerics in a church that denies women the possibility of doing the same? What would the reaction be? While some might be supportive, others might immediately question that person's commitment to the community or loyalty to the Holy Father. Still others would experience an erosion of confidence (or faith) in the person. At the least, the trust level with this person might be seriously jeopardized. So, fearing that our own confreres may consider us disloyal, many of us don't say what we think, what we feel, or what we do.

When community members lack the trust to voice their opinions and differences, silence and passive-aggressive behavior often result. This "don't talk, don't feel, don't trust" dynamic characterizes a dysfunctional system. Unless checked, it often results in hostility and systems breakdown. The way this disintegration occurs might be charted as follows:

poor intercommunication —> unwillingness to cooperate —>
increasing distrust —> hostility —> breakdown

On one occasion I witnessed this process take over a group of celibates as it developed first a vision statement, next a provincial plan, and finally a pastoral plan. The first step of developing the vision statement went smoothly and enthusiastically. The final version of the statement even mentioned the group's willingness to take risks. The work on the provincial plan, linking its communal goals and ministerial goals, easily sailed through the group's chapter. It seemed like a common cause now would engender deeper trust and commitment from the members of this group.

Things changed, however, when work began on the pastoral plan which was meant to determine the dwindling group's allocation of human resources through the year 2000. Soon it became clear that the proposed pastoral plan would allow every individual to continue doing what he was already doing. There would be no structured processes to invite real openness to any wider environment that might demand personnel changes. There was no examination of needs outside the group that might invite reallocation of the group's financial and personal resources. No sacrifice would be asked of the members.

While interest groups (teachers, poverty ministries, individualized ministries, white parishes, preachers, etc.) did share their opinions mutually with each other, all participants seemed dominated by one preoccupation: not to jeopardize their individual ministries. Despite earlier talk about "reading the signs of the times," self-interest and self-preservation defined the final process. As I read the reports from each group, I couldn't help but think of people on a sinking ship changing the location of their deck chairs.

In my mind, the consequence of this lack of openness to a wider church and environment, this lack of genuine intercommunication, this lack of cooperation, reveals basic dynamics related to forms of distrust at the worst and lack of trust at the best. This was evident when the provincial leaders called an assembly of the province to describe in detail the signs that indicated to them a crisis faced the province. The leaders clearly outlined the breakdown in the three critical areas of spirituality around which the celibate religious life traditionally has functioned, namely prayer, community, and ministry. They asked the membership to respond, to offer challenges, to give alternatives.

However, rather than hearing rebuttals, other opinions, or even support for their analysis, silence virtually reigned in the assembly of all the members of the province. But once outside the session, plenty of very animated conversations ensued. Some men gathered in informal groups and complained about being "manipulated" and "railroaded." Others used less-flattering images to indicate their distrust of the leadership. Still others left the meeting and went home to their work. The search for a cause got stymied at the second level: there was little or no mutuality, thus there would be no trust or commitment.

A consequence of distrust among religious becomes more critical when we consider it in light of Erik Erikson's developmental theory. If Erik Erikson is correct, people will not develop to another stage unless they complete the tasks assigned to the previous stage. Furthermore, he noted, the most primitive stage is that of survival. The task of this stage is to address the basic conflict between trust and distrust. Unless the child finds ways of resolving the tension between trust and distrust, there will be no healthy life synthesis. Erikson shows that, at this first stage of survival, the synthesis of the trust/distrust tensions results in hope.

If we can project Erikson's notions about the individual development to the corporate development of a community, a few conclusions can be drawn. First, if we now experience critical problems related to the basic issue of trust/distrust, this may indicate that, at its organizational level, religious life has reverted to the survival stage, the most primitive stage of life for an organism. Second, because we lack ways to address the tension by entrusting ourselves (including our self-disclosure) to each other, scant hope remains for us at the level of our organizations. Without this hope our present, institutional, organizational form of religious life will move ever more rapidly into diminishment, dysfunctionality, and dissolution. This brings us to the third conclusion: death cannot be far beyond.

As celibates, we will have little or no hope in our future until we search for ways of sharing with one another in personal relationships, until we can really entrust ourselves confidently to one another, until we can experience some level of personal intimacy with some of our compatriots. If Erikson's theory is correct, and if we analogously can apply it to the organizations of which some of us are a part, we cannot avoid this issue in our effort to move our organizations beyond survival into hope.

Trust in the Divine

In preparing my talk on trust to the women religious, the final area they asked me to address contained notions related to faith and freedom, contemplation and risk-taking, and paradigm shifts and shifts in our metaphors of God. In regard to this latter point, two significant experiences came to mind.

In 1991, while in Rome, I met the eighty-two-year-old revered expert on Franciscan spirituality, Optatus van Ossledink. We participated in a meeting at our Capuchin generalate. One day during a break, he said, "Mike, do you know about the work of Sallie McFague?"[5] When I said I used her material in my dissertation, his eyes lit up. He said, "She makes so much sense about our need to change and grow from one image of God to another. And isn't her notion of God as Friend wonderful?" That day, for all new reasons, I discovered why so many think Optatus embodies the Franciscan wisdom about which he has written so eloquently.

Returning to Milwaukee, I had another wisdom experience with an older Dominican sister who worships at our parish. She was preparing to celebrate her golden jubilee. In contrast to someone like Optatus, many, especially males, consider her to be a bone of contention rather than a figure of wisdom. The reason? To her, the Divine One certainly is not a Father, nor even "Friend," but Goddess. And Goddess is the One she makes regular efforts to name for others, especially at Mass when sexist words and images might be communicated in the people's response! Having had numerous experiences of her approach, my own feelings of mistrust toward her were in place. My lack of trust may have been heightened because one never knew when she publicly would challenge ministers at liturgies about sexist words or concepts in the rituals, songs, and homilies.

One day, after Sunday liturgy, I invited her to lunch. My first reaction was defensive. In the beginning of our conversation I felt I had to defend God, as if God needed to be defended by me! Yet, the more she talked, I found it wasn't God I needed to defend; it was *my idea* of God (and this somehow involved a defense of *myself*).

Then I asked her to tell me what was happening in her life. The more I listened to her, the more I understood her. And the more she self-disclosed, the more I respected her. The combination of self-disclosure and listening, understanding and respect led me to trust her experience—though vastly different from mine—as authentic. Her self-entrustment led me to trust her.

I also came to better understand her Goddess. I wondered if this image of the divine—who seemed much more inclusive and whole—was any less authentic than my tribal "God" who legitimated exclusivity and male control. I learned that her notion of Goddess not only was authentic; it also represented the best in our tradition by which we have come to experience the One revealed originally by the name "I am." She helped me realize that unless each of us is able to define the Divine as "I am," we will not drink very deeply of the divine reality revealed within. Again, we will be dependent on the definitions others form of God. Her "Goddess" reflected her own unique "I am"; to have integrity, her own femaleness had to be imaged in a female deity.

We belong to an institution that seems preoccupied with defining God as male. But once we limit God to this human characteristic, God becomes only as big as the definitions with which we hem "him" in. However, when God becomes Goddess and Goddess becomes "I am" for some of us made in the image of that Goddess, we show how we have begun to trust ourselves, our God, and one another. I believe that when we begin to trust one another enough with our God/Goddess, with the divine image of our "I am," we can begin to know a deeper level of community. We can sacrifice all our idols and images of God to celebrate the God/Goddess of others as well.

I find it fascinating to listen to different images of the Higher Power shared at Twelve-Step meetings. There, people have come to trust their own experience, their own selves. They sit in safe, nonjudgmental environments which invite all to entrust themselves to others. Consequently, in their sharing of their experiences of the Higher Power—their God, their Goddess—they find deeper community. Why is it that many of them have no problem in the way others define their experience of this "High Power," yet will not trust each other's experience in institutionalized religion when it is translated in ways different?

Moving Through the Trust/Distrust Conflict into Communities of Hope

If so much distrust exists at the three levels of self, others, and the divine, where can celibates dare to find hope? I personally discover this hope when I find members within my community choosing life. They do so by deciding to become a new kind of organism within the old, a living body in the midst of one surrounded by buzzards, a dynamic community in the midst of decay. This community cannot be envisioned in the same way we experienced community in the past because so much of what passed for "community" in former days was organizationally defined rather than organically driven.

Many of us involved in reflecting on the future of religious life as well as the institutional expression of Roman Catholicism have concluded that our hope, if not the only viable model for our church, will be the creation and/or recovery of small, intentional communities. These will be constituted of like-minded people who can entrust themselves to one another on basic issues and share basic values. Their gatherings will invite the members to intimacy, to a more contemplative approach to prayer, and to a compassionate approach to the world.

In Twelve-Step language we call this necessary context for recovery "the meeting." In Latin America this context for liberation is the basic ecclesial community. Every celibate—whether recovering addict or liberation seeker—needs such "communities of entrustment," which provide three key functions free of control: care, correction, and commitment. Robert Kegan, and his feminist corrective Mary Baird Carlsen, call this kind of community "the holding environment." Mary Baird Carlsen explains:

> In using this terminology Kegan cites Winnicott (1965) who writes of "the envelope of care—the holding environment" which provides three very significant functions:
>
> 1) *Confirmation*—a supportive (not restrictive) "holding on" of the person as the individual is given acknowledgment and recognition. For, as Kegan says, we each need to be able to excite someone—"to turn the lights on in their eyes."
>
> 2) *Contradiction*—a "letting go" as the individual is encouraged within the framework of the holding environment to reach out beyond the current embeddedness to new steps in personal differentiation. And with the knowledge that the holding environment remains as a supportive backdrop for new experience the person is enabled to grow and change.
>
> 3) *Continuity*—a kind of "sticking around" as the individual keeps a sense of ongoing support and personal consistency within new forays into life.[6]

At Harvard, people like Kegan, Carlsen, and Sharon Parks have pioneered new approaches to therapeutic processes and adult development. Originally therapists concentrated primarily on the truth of the biblical adage that people—whether individuals or groups—perish for want of vision. So vision was seen to be essential for life. But then, given the work of people like Victor Frankl and Rollo May, many therapists came to recognize meaning—individual as well as communal—as another essential for quality life. Now, therapists have concluded that neither strong vision nor deep meaning can be sustained without a third force: some kind of support system. Traditionally, this support system has been called community.

I believe commitment to community in the form of "holding environments" is essential to sustain the celibate commitment. Unless we celibates link our quest for meaning and vision with a viable support system, I believe we will teeter and eventually collapse. That support system of community must be strong enough to invite us to make a self-donation of our individualism for the only cause worth sacrificing for: the reign of God.

Robert Bellah and company show in *Habits of the Heart*[7] and *The Good Society*[8] that the language of individualism is taught by culture. This cultural pattern undermines bonds of community that once contributed to a sense of meaning, supported our personal relationships, and nourished our vision and commitments. But when, because of our individualism, meaning becomes vacuous, and visions remain on paper rather than in each other's hearts, it's hard to fathom how we will fashion community. I am not talking about community in the old sense of living together lockstep, or even the new sense of voluntary associations with a life expectancy of a generation, much less those relationships that make a community merely equal to the sum of its parts. Rather, I envision new kinds of "holding environments" or synergistic gatherings of people. Here people's shared meanings and visions will empower them into communities wherein the community, the whole, will be greater than the sum of its individual parts. These will be faith communities of entrustment.

Even though individualism overly defines North American life, increasingly, people are finding community. However, very often this is experienced outside those to whom we initially bonded (in my case, outside the Capuchins). What primary communities have many of us developed? Look at how we spend our free time. For some of us the primary community is our family or friends. For others, it is our coworkers or peers. For still others, it is an exclusive group of our significant others, male or female, depending on our sexual orientation. This leads me to ask if the personal relationships and the trust and loyalty that have traditionally supported our past forms of community with one another are presently strong enough in face of these new commitments we have made.

Today, candidates come to religious communities and diocesan priesthood seeking meaning and vision in prayer and ministry; yet they also want a third pillar, a support system. The three legs of meaning, vision, and support system constitute this triad. Although our behaviors have made the support system quite shaky, few of us acknowledge this weakness. Even fewer seem willing to forego some of our individualism to create non-suffocating and liberating relationships of trust which might secure this leg and rebuild the triad. We find little or no reason for self-donation or commitment to make these traditional communities work.

Here, I fear, we may enter various forms of denial lest our individualism give way to a new emphasis on community. But until we do make at least a modicum of sacrifices of our self-interest for a vision bigger than ourselves—that is, some cause that invites self-donation—we will continue in our present form of corporate self-destruction. Even a biologically oriented approach to organizations tells us that unless members exhibit some form of self-sacrifice, those organizations will quickly move into decay and decomposition, dissolution and death.

Building Communities of "Entrustment"

How might we work to develop the dynamics to create such communities? First of all, we need to create safe environments within which authentic faith can be nourished and expressed. Recalling our chart, this means relationships among persons cannot be perfunctory; they must nurture mutuality. Within this environment we can share ourselves, including our shame and fears, our dreams and hopes, our gifts and our gaffes, with one other in a context that ensures each other's trust. We need confidence in each other in order to reveal each of our "I ams" in faith-sharing. Perhaps an example might make this clearer.

In 1991 I joined four other Capuchins in creating a new kind of community, inserted among the poor. We really had no operating norms to guide our future, only a commitment to be faithful to an hour of daily faith-sharing. As the months went on, our sharing of our lives, personal fears, cares, and concerns grew. And because of this our personal relationships developed. Thus, without knowing it, we were entering into the first two levels of faith. Gradually the third level of entrustment began to take shape. One day, one of the brothers felt safe enough to risk sharing himself to the others.

The sharing occurred in the context of Romans 13:8-9 scriptures of the particular day:

> Owe no debt to anyone except the debt that binds us to love another. Those who love their neighbor have fulfilled the law. The commandments, "You shall not commit adultery; you shall not murder; you shall not steal; you shall not covet," and any other commandment there may be are all summed up in this, "You shall love your neighbor as yourself."

In our dialogue, it became clear that problems related to loving our neighbor connect with problems in loving ourselves. This led us to discuss issues related to self-love, especially the dynamics of shame. One of the friars went to his room and returned to read a passage from Bradshaw's *Healing the Shame that Binds You:*

> When shame has been completely internalized, nothing about you is okay. You feel flawed and inferior; you have the sense of being a failure. There is no way you can share your inner self because you are an object of contempt to yourself. When you are contemptible to yourself, you are no longer in you. To feel shame is to feel seen in an exposed and diminished way.[9]

This brother then shared his efforts at recovery from the paralysis of shame that had bound him. Having moved from initial questions of trust to sharing such intimate thoughts took him months; however, gradually an entrustment community had made this self-disclosure possible. Now he felt safe to entrust to the members of his community this deeper part of himself. His sharing invited further disclosure on the part of others. His self-disclosure became an invitation to the others to share more of themselves, to entrust their fears and doubts as well as their dreams and visions.

The next morning at prayer, we continued reading from Romans 14:7-8: "None of us lives as our own master and none of us dies as our own master." Then one of the brothers said, "You know, I think I have been living too much as my own master. I haven't really been too responsible to you. And I don't want to continue living so individually. I'd like you to challenge me when you see me unaccountable to you for what I do and how I do it." Such a statement could never have occurred without trust and a sense of loyalty to a group of people whose trust he had felt. He had experienced personal relationships strong enough to make him sense a kind of communal trust and loyalty. Now he could make a commitment to us and we could make our commitments to him—and to each other.

What happened that day, I believe, could only have happened because we had created an entrustment community. Given this trust, we were now open to make a commitment to each other.

Commitments in (and to) community, I believe, will be short-lived unless they can be grounded in some form of entrustment among the members. In this sense, I envision celibates coming together in such communities of entrustment.

They will develop personal relations wherein:

1. All can be themselves without being judged defective.

2. All can show their true opinions and feelings, which will be honored, even if not always agreed with.

3. Strong relationships among the parties exist; they are firm and lasting.

4. The parties wish each other well; no one consciously hurts the others.

5. The parties have a personal investment in the relationship.

6. There is consistency; no "here today and gone tomorrow."

7. The members can confide in each other without fear that confidences will be violated.

8. The parties can rely on each other, as well as their word.

As I conclude this chapter, I think of the founder of the community of celibates of which I am a part, Francis of Assisi. In his *Rule*, he offers us a beautiful vision of what I've called a community of entrustment:

> And wherever the members of the community may be together or meet each other, let them give witness that they are members of one family. And let them, in trust and loyalty, make known to each other their needs. For if a mother loves and cares for her child according to the flesh, how much more would we not love and care for each other who are brothers (and sisters) in the Spirit?[10]

Conclusion

I was in my late twenties and very frustrated with my ministry and life at St. Elizabeth's parish in Milwaukee. We had lost a thousand families in my first three years there as "white flight" took over. I wondered what was happening to my church, my order, and my life. Already I seemed to have lost my enthusiasm and spontaneity. Gradually I decided I was ready to leave everything. However, I knew I would only "leave everything" if it would be with Mary.

I dated Mary in my senior year of school at St. Mary's Springs Academy in Fond du Lac, Wisconsin. She also was dating someone else, but somehow that didn't matter to me. I told myself she couldn't really love him; how could she when I loved her so much? Denial can help at times like that!

Although I had dated ever since my freshman year, I also had carried in my heart a deep nagging that never seemed far away. This was the notion that, somehow, God wanted me to be a priest. Thus, after high school, because I believed it was "God's will," I had entered the seminary. Unwillingly, as I noted in chapter one. As I entered the seminary for my first year of college, Mary went to Rosary College in River Forest, Illinois for hers.

At Thanksgiving time we all gathered for the first party with the group we hung around with in high school. Mary was there. I knew my feelings for her had not changed just by going to the seminary. She told a funny joke using an accent that was hilarious. But somehow, after having a good laugh, a sadness came over me. Already I felt different, as though I didn't belong. So I walked outside by myself and stood near the road. Within a few minutes, Mary was standing there. She had something she wanted to tell me. "Mike," she said, "I've decided I'm going to enter the convent." I couldn't believe what I was hearing.

Here I was going to be a priest and she was going to be a nun. I wanted to hold and embrace her like I did before. But now I had been given another code. It had taken me just three months—from September to November 1958—to learn its rules. So I just stood there, feeling stupid, trying to find something to say. Apart from her.

The party ended. We went our separate ways, Mary to the Dominicans and I to the Capuchins. We lost contact. Then in 1963, I received a Christmas card from Sr. Mary. She was working in Omaha. She had read an article I wrote in *America* magazine that noted that I was living in Indiana. So now she could make contact. Over the next couple of years we wrote to each other sporadically as our schedules would allow. After ordination in 1966, in the summer of 1967, I worked at a prison outside of Fond du Lac, our hometown. One day I got a call. It was from Mary. She asked if she could come to visit me at the prison. Hearing her voice the first time since 1959, I realized from my reaction that, although all my feelings had been dormant for many years, nothing had changed. I felt the same rush inside of me that I did as a high-school senior when I'd drive to her house waiting in anticipation for her to arrive at the door. My feelings had not changed one bit.

However, as I noted in the Introduction, I had become like Newland Archer in *The Age of Innocence*, bound by my promises and institutional conventions. And although I didn't realize it then, my feelings toward her were somewhat different than hers toward me. When she arrived, we exchanged a proper kiss. Our conversation never turned to our relationship. She was happy in her work. I enjoyed my work as well. Life was good for both of us. Our futures looked bright.

Once finished with my "pastoral year" I was assigned to St. Elizabeth's. I would visit Mary at her family's house each Christmas so we could spend some quality time together. It was shortly before one of these annual visits that I had decided to "leave everything," the order and the priesthood. However this was conditioned on whether Mary would also leave and we would get married.

I had received some Christmas money for ties. Under the guise of getting Mary out of the house, I asked her if she would go downtown to help me select some ties at one of the men's stores. As we drove there, not knowing how to broach the subject, I began my probe by asking her, "How happy are you in your life?" "Oh Mike," she responded, "I'm as happy as I could be. I can see myself a Dominican for the rest of my life."

Immediately I had the feeling of a door being closed. I had tried to open the door to invite her into my life, but she had closed the door. The subject was changed. We went on with the business of buying the ties.

This is why, at the conclusion of *The Age of Innocence*, when the maid closed the shutters in Ellen Olenska's apartment overlooking the place where Newland Archer sat, I just knew what he would do. I had been at that fountain too. When the shutters were closed to him, Newland Archer would get up and go on.

For Newland Archer it was as though the final period had been placed at the end of a series of chapters in his life. In getting up from the fountain and walking away, he opened the possibility of another chapter which would no longer be defined by the same story line which came before. When I, who had believed it was God's will that I be celibate in responding to the call to be a priest, discovered in the Dubuque Airport that no "command" of the Lord was involved at all, a new chapter opened for me as well.

I didn't walk away from celibacy, but the path I have walked since that day has taken me in directions I did not have open to me before. In the process I have learned one thing that helps me understand the uniqueness of Jesus' articulation of the "celibate" way as found in Matthew's gospel: in the last analysis anyone who is going to be an authentic celibate *must make himself or herself so.* Newland Archer did not close the window, but he had to make his own future after someone else did. To keep sitting at the fountain or to grieve over a spent past would only do more damage to him and his heart.

Like him, I had to decide my future. When I realized that God could care less whether I was celibate or not and that, even if I were one of those "anyones" who did not "accept this," it would not matter that much to God what I did. The ball was in my court. Any further choice about being celibate had to come from *within* me. To have it depend on anyone or anything *outside* of me would make me personally irresponsible. The psychologist Mary Anne Coate refers to this call from within to be celibate as what happens when *"the 'inner world' of a person demands it."*[1]

We have discussed, especially in the first chapters of this book, the detrimental and dysfunctional things that can happen when the "outer world" demands that we be celibate. The result of living with such contradictory messages is often expressed in very unhealthy patterns of behavior for celibates and greater dysfunctionality in a system of patriarchal clericalism that somehow needs celibacy among its clergy to survive. However, the only free and responsible way that one can be celibate now and the only way to be celibate in a future which will offer few props to sustain it, will be when we freely choose it.

When Jesus said that "there are eunuchs who have made themselves eunuchs," and that "anyone" who could "accept this" could do so, he was talking about choice. Who really chooses celibacy? Only those to whom it is "given." And this "given" does not come from an institution that imposes it; it is not for the sake of ministry or relationships; it cannot be because there is no other choice. It only occurs when it is recognized as a gift; and that gift must be freely accepted.

It seems to me, circumstances make people realize this is what they must choose if they are to be fulfilled, if they are to be happy, if their life is to have real meaning. So, who chooses celibacy, especially when the *natural choice as put in our very being* is for us to choose marriage?

This demands a rigorous examination of the various motives that might be at play in making the choice to be celibate. I am convinced that the vast majority of those in the consecrated life and the priesthood who have taken on a celibate life have done so for reasons that were instrumental, to use Sandra Schneiders' image. People who made *instrumental* choices represent the whole story behind *The Age of Innocence*. In a culture still controlled by the image of celibacy such people may break society's codes only at their own peril. Too many people have been broken by those codes.

Too many people have had to live unfreely. We have come to the end of that gilded age that was New York of the 1870s. We have likewise come to the end of that paradigm which has imposed celibacy in the Roman Catholic church. In the future, celibacy will have to be embraced for its own sake. And when it is, people will be able to shut windows and doors themselves. Or, if they are shut by others, they will know they are still free. These will be celibate individuals who gather in community for the sake of the reign of God. To do anything less would only continue to do violence not only to the vision of Matthew's Jesus, but to whoever so "chooses." In the wise words of Mary Anne Coate:

> The more we are aware of what is going into our choice the more stable and fruitful that choice is likely to be. Deeply unconscious material may not apparently cause us as much disturbance or distress as that which is more accessible to consciousness, but if it stays unconscious it may inhibit and stunt both human and spiritual development. On the other hand, if what has been deeply unconscious erupts into consciousness—perhaps through a sudden and overwhelming sexual attraction and arousal—and to the degree that this is at variance with the previous conscious awareness of the person, the more likely there is at that point to be a crisis of vocation.
>
> Then there is need for another choice, perhaps a more informed one, and this time it may go either way. The inner world demands again; the result may be an acceptance of the loss and sacrifice involved in celibacy with a truer awareness of just what this means emotionally. Acceptance of the loss and pain makes possible the mature defense of sublimation—namely the discovery of alternatives to, not substitutes for, sexual fulfillment. Or the inner need for intimate relationship and expression of sexuality may become such that denying it results in stunted growth or a suffering that the person's emotional being cannot easily bear. This is not to remove the responsibility of choice or to claim a spurious complete freedom for this second choice, but rather to ask that this choice be allowed to be made.[2]

When one makes the choice for celibacy, for the sake of the reign of God, all one can simply say, in resignation as well as gratitude, is *this is who I am.* Celibacy represents my best self. I am a celibate; I am celibate. To be otherwise would be to violate my best self. This is the best kind of human being whom *I can be.* The final choice for celibacy must represent a choice to make oneself so for the sake of God's reign in oneself, one's relationships, and one's world. The free celibate says: "Not only is this who I am; this is how I am going to be; this is the way I will relate."

The celibate way of relating is at heart a way free of the need to control, manipulate, dominate, exploit, or abuse. For the celibate, the other is viewed as a person to be cared for with commitment rather than someone or something that can be used for my plea-sure. And when the situations arise in a relationship of intimacy that move one to be tempted to be genital, celibate intimacy demands of oneself a free response that closes the door to that gen-ital way of thinking about the other, desiring the other, or acting out with the other. When those situations arise, the celibate—who has freely chosen to be so—cannot find sufficiency or an escape from it by saying such things as: "I can't; my vow doesn't allow it," or, "I mustn't; it wouldn't be right," or, "this shouldn't be what I do here; it's against my promises." Rather the celibate who is truly free will say: "No, this is not who I am. And I'd be misleading myself or you if I did anything but what I know I must to remain who I am and to respect who you are."

In the last analysis, even allowing for outside forces or dynamics that close doors or shutter windows for us, tomorrow's celibates will be the ones who don't try to open them again. These celibates will be able to live with that part of their house—and their heart—closed. Following John of the Cross, these celi-bates will be the ones whose house can be at rest. And why? Because they have found ways to be warm and intimate with oth-ers. They will be the ones who have found a place in their heart only for God.

Definitions

Celibacy: the embrace of a divinely-offered gift inviting one to freely choose a life-commitment of abstention from genital intimacy which expresses itself in an alternate intimacy with God and others. The celibate is a person who freely embraces the divine offer to refrain from genital intercourse, who finds ways to be warm and intimate with others and who has a place in his or her heart only for God.

Intimacy: the characteristic of a relationship of loving closeness, familiarity, and friendship that is marked by mutual disclosure, struggle with differences, and trust. By definition, all intimacy is personal intimacy. Thus, this definition of intimacy implies "personal" intimacy.

Sexual Intimacy: the characteristic of a non-exploitative and non-genital relationship of loving closeness, familiarity, and friendship that is marked by mutual disclosure, struggles with differences, which is expressed in affection, gestures, and physical manifestations of care.

Celibate intimacy: the characteristic of a relationship among people who have committed themselves to be non-genital in response to a divine gift, a relationship of loving closeness, familiarity, and friendship that is marked by mutual disclosure, struggles with differences, and trust which is expressed in affection, gestures, and physical manifestations of care.

Spousal Intimacy: the characteristic of a relationship of loving closeness, familiarity, and friendship that is marked by mutual disclosure, struggles with differences, and trust, and is expressed in affection, gestures, and physical manifestations of care between people who accept the responsibility involved in expressing their communion through genital intercourse in a permanent commitment.

Spiritual Intimacy: a relationship of loving closeness and personal familiarity with God that is expressed in compassion for others. At its core it is love-making (God in us) and making-love (compassion for the world).

Notes

Introduction

1. "Celibate," *Webster's Ninth New Collegiate Dictionary*, (Springfield, MA: G. & C. Merriam Company, 1991), 219.

2. Women as doctors in the church came later.

3. "Virgin," *Webster's, Ibid.* (Springfield, MA: G. & C. Merriam Company, 1991), 1317.

4. "Virginity," Charles Earle Funk, ed., *Funk & Wagnalls New Practical Standard Dictionary of the English Language* (New York: Funk & Wagnalls Company, 1955), 1459.

5. I have discovered, in the intervening years, that "John's" attitude, which support the possibility of genital sex for homosexual celibates, is quite widespread. This also seems to be the experience of Sandra Schneiders. See her "Celibacy as Charism," in *The Way Supplement 77* (1993), 20-21.

6. This section is heavily dependent on these reviews. Of all the reviews I read, I was most helped by Richard Grenier, "Society and Edith Wharton," *Commentary*, 96 (1993), 48-52. This study has helped shape my comments here. I quote from it extensively, especially in the parts where dialogue takes place. I am deeply indebted to Mr. Grenier's review for providing me this help.

7. Michelle Pfeiffer, quoted in *Newsweek*, September 20, 1993, 64.

8. Anthony Lake, "Gilded Pleasures," *The New Yorker*, September 13, 1993, 122.

9. Martin Scorsese, quoted in *Newsweek, op.cit.*

10. Martin Scorsese, quoted in Francine Prose, "In 'Age of Innocence,'" *The New York Times*, September 12, 1993, 29.

11. Richard N. Ostling, "The Secrets of St. Lawrence," *Time*, June 7, 1993, 44.

12. This statement of Pope John XXIII in a private talk with Etienne Gilson seems to have been printed first in *La France Catholique*, n. 862, (7-6,1963). It is cited as well in Ruud J. Bunnik, "The Question of Married Priests," *Cross Currents*, 15 (1965), 108-109. The exact statement has the Pope saying: "Ecclesiastical celibacy is not a dogma. Scripture does not impose it. It is even easy. . . . I need only take a pen and sign an act, and tomorrow the priests who want to do so will be able to marry. But I cannot do it. Celibacy is a sacrifice which the church has taken upon itself freely, magnanimously, heroically. Recently I told the Cardinals, "Can we allow it to pass that before long people will not be able to speak any more of the 'one, holy, and chaste church?' I cannot do it. No, I cannot do that."

13. Andrew M. Greeley, "A Sea of Paradoxes: Two Surveys of Priests," *America*, July 16, 1994, 7 and "In Defense of Celibacy?" *America*, September 10, 1994, 11.

14. Richard A. Schoenherr, "The Catholic Priests in the US: Demographic Investigations," quoted in Mary Beth Murphy, "Forty Percent Loss of Priests Foreseen," *Milwaukee Sentinel*, July 14, 1990. I find it interesting that Andrew Greeley considers the author of this study, Richard A. Schoenherr, "the acknowledged expert in this area," yet challenges data others reach that support Schoenherr's conclusions. See Greeley, "In Defense of Celibacy?" *Op. Cit.*, 11. See also Schoenherr, *Full Pews and Empty Altars: Demographics of the Priest Shortage in U.S. Catholic Dioceses* (University of Wisconsin Press, 1993) and *Goodbye, Father: Celibacy and Patriarchy in the Catholic Church* (New York: Oxford, 1995).

15. The very rise in numbers of lay people involved in apostolic volunteer programs and an increase in affiliations of people with associate membership in religious communities belies any so-called arguments that people are selfish or don't want to sacrifice. A 1985 study revealed that, among Catholic college students, the interest in lay ministry is about fifty times higher than interest in religious vocations. Congregations with apostolic volunteer programs have little difficulty in attracting recruits who, in some congregations, outnumber candidates for vowed membership by about ten to one. See: "Called Anew by the Spirit: A Contemporary Reflection on Apostolic Religious Life" (Milwaukee: Archdiocese of Milwaukee, 1994), 18.

16. While I was writing this book, a popular book discussing male and female differences in relationships remained on the *The New York Times* bestseller list: John Gray's *Men Are from Mars, Women Are From Venus: A Practical Guide for Improving Communication and Getting What You Want for Improving Communication and Getting What You Want in Relationships* (New York: HarperCollins, 1992).

Chapter 1

1. Xavier Leon Dufour, *Dictionary of Biblical Theology*, rev. ed. (New York: Seabury/Crossroad, 1973), 635.

2. Tony W. Cartledge, "Vows in the Hebrew Bible and the Ancient Near East." *Journal for the Study of the Old Testament Supplement Series*, 147 (Sheffield, England: JSOT Press, 1992).

3. Harvey McArthur. "Celibacy in Judaism at the Time of Christian Beginnings," *Andrews University Seminary Studies* 25 (1987), 163. Where McArthur discusses various individual rabbis who seem to have been celibate, he invariably finds a link with ritual purity that was temporary.

4. Wayne A. Meeks, *The First Urban Christians: The Social World of the Apostle Paul* (New Haven and London: Yale University Press, 1983), 102.

5. Jerome Murphy-O'Connor, *1 Corinthians* (Wilmington, DE: Michael Glazier, 1982), 75.

6. *Anagke*, or "distress," seems to have been a technical word which described the sufferings characteristic of the last days (see: 1 Thess 3:7; 2 Cor 6:4; 12:10).

7. Whether the "thorn in the side" of Paul referred to something sexual has been discussed at great length. As early as 1926 Joachim Jeremias surmised that Paul might be a widower. See his *War Paulus Witwer?*, *Zeitschrift NW*, 25 (1926), 310-312 and *Nochmals: War Paulus Witwer? Zeitschrift NW*, 28 (1929), 321-323. Against his view see Erich Fascher, *Zur Witwerschaft des Paulus und der Auslegung von 1 Cor 7*, 28 (1929), 62-69.

8. Murphy-O'Connor, 59.

9. Peter F. Ellis, *Seven Pauline Letters* (Collegeville, MN: The Liturgical Press, 1984), 74.

10. Much of the problem regarding "this teaching" depends on verse 11. Does Jesus' teaching in Matthew refer to the way someone must remain who is divorced (19:4-9) or does it refer to the following text about the third kind of eunuchs (19:12). Most Catholic scholars have chosen the latter. For instance, John P. Meier of the The Catholic University of America writes: "Traditionally, this total continence has been understood in terms of unmarried persons, who freely choose to remain so (cf. 1 Cor 7:25-30)." He does say it is possible that Matthew understands it in the sense I hold: that it refers "to an innocent husband

in a broken marriage, who must now remain alone." See *The Vision of Matthew: Christ, Church and Morality in the First Gospel* (New York/Ramsey/Toronto: Paulist Press, 1978), 138.

11. I believe much of the discussion about this passage parallels the notion of *dikaiosyne* (justice or righteousness) that has accompanied the translation and interpretation of Martin Luther. His influence on the notion was so great it is virtually impossible to be free of this overlay. The same follows for the overlay of celibacy in the tradition of the church after the third century and the need to find some scriptural basis for it. I follow the interpretation of Dom Jacques Dupont, *Mariage de Divorce dans l'évangile: Matthieu 19, 3-12 et parallèles* (Bruges, Belgium: Desclee de Brower, 1959). See also Quentin Quesnell, "Made Themselves Eunuchs for the Kingdom of Heaven (Mt 19:12)," *Catholic Biblical Quarterly*, 30 (1968), 335-358 and Donald Senior, C.P., "Living in the Meantime: Biblical Foundations for Religious Life," in Paul J. Philibert, O.P., ed., *Living in the Meantime: Concerning the Transformation of Religious Life.* (New York/Mahwah, NJ: Paulist, 1994), 65-66.

12. Dupont, 192-193. I am indebted to my Capuchin confrere, Michael Fountain, for translating the entire third part of this classic work on eunuchs. Without his help this section would be sorely missing the good scholarship that he has provided for me.

13. Dupont, 195.

14. Dupont, 161-174.

15. Jerome Murphy-O'Connor, O.P., *What Is Religious Life?: A Critical Reappraisal* (Wilmington, DE: Michael Glazier, 1977), 54.

16. *Ibid.*

17. Dupont, 198.

18. John P. Meier, *Matthew* (Wilmington, DE: Michael Glazier, 1980), 216.

19. Dupont develops a whole chapter on "Those Who Understand" (175-190). However he seems to assume that Matthew's oft-used word for understanding, *syniénai* (13:13, 14, 15, 19, 23, 51; 15:10m 16; 16:12; 17:13) is used here. It is not. The Greek word is *chorein*: "make room for" or "hold." I find it fascinating that the three main Greek words for understanding used by the synoptics (*syniénai, noein,* and *chorein*) are all used in one passage in Matthew and, in this sense, help *our* understanding: "Then he said, 'Are you also still without understanding (*syniénai*)? Do you not see (*noein*) that whatever goes into the mouth enters (*chorein*) the stomach, and goes out into the sewer?'" (Mt 15:16-17).

20. Daniel J. Harrington, S.J., "Matthew," in Dianne Bergant, C.S.A., and Robert J. Karris, eds., *The Collegeville Bible Commentary* (Collegeville, MN: The Liturgical Press, 1988), 889-890.

21. Paul J. Beaudette, *Ritual Purity in Roman Catholic Priesthood: Using the Work of Mary Douglas to Understand Clerical Celibacy* (Berkeley, CA: Graduate Theological Union, 1994), 96. Beaudette refers to Leonard M. Weber, "Celibacy," in Karl Rahner, ed., *Sacramentum Mundi* , 1, 276.

22. Pope John Paul II, "Church Committed to Priestly Celibacy," *L'Osservatore Romano*, July 21, 1993.

23. *Ibid.*

24. *Ibid.* Edward Schillebeeckx seems to have argued the same way in his 1968 book, *Celibacy* (New York: Sheed and Ward, 23-24). However while Schillebeeckx sees celibacy as something embraced by some disciples in the "group of Jesus," Pope John Paul II's wording seems to have applied the passages to all.

25. The first effort to link priestly celibacy with the apostles seems to have come in 1878 with Gustav Bickell (*Der Zölibat eine apostolische Anordnung, Zeitschrift für Katholische Theologie* 2 (1878), 22-64, and *Der Zölibat dennoch eine apostolische Anordnung, Zeitschrift für Katholische Theolgie* 3 (1879), 792-799. In more recent years the argument has been reintroduced by others. See Roman Cholij, *Clerical Celibacy in East and West* (Herefordshire, England: Fowler Wright, 1989), Christian Cochini, *The Apostolic Origins of Priestly Celibacy* (San Francisco: Ignatius Press, 1990), Henri Deen, *Le Celibat des Prêtres dans les Premiers Siècles de l'Eglise* (Paris, 1969), and A.M. Stickler, *Tratti salienti nella storia del celibato, Sacra Doctrina* 15, (1970), 585-620.

26. "Celibacy Rule Is Reaffirmed by Pope," *The Catholic Herald*, August 4, 1993, 9.

27. National Conference of Catholic Bishops , "When I Call for Help: Domestic Violence against Women," *Origins* 22 (1992), 355.

28. *Ibid.*, 356.

29. Jane Ursel, "The State and the Maintenance of Patriarchy: A Case Study of Family, Labour and Welfare Legislation in Canada," in J. Dickinson and B. Russell, eds., *Family, Economy and the State* (London and Sydney: Croom Helm, 1986), 59.

30. N.C.C.B., 357.

31. Sandra M. Schneiders, I.H.M. "Women in the Fourth Century and Women in the Contemporary Church," *Biblical Theology Bulletin* 12 (1982), 35.

32. N.C.C.B., 357.

33. *Ibid* , 357.

34. I used this image before I read its use in another context. Writing in *The Florida Catholic*, Bishop W. Thomas Larkin, the retired bishop of Tampa-St. Petersburg, challenged a column entitled "The Pope Is Wrong to Ban Women Priests." The opinion piece by Anna Quindlen appeared in *The New York Times* after Pope John Paul II made his statement regarding the non-possibility of women being priests. The Bishop wrote: "I am not surprised that Ms. Quindlen quotes Father Richard McBrien, a theologian at the University of Notre Dame, and Daniel Maquire, a professor of moral theology at Marquette University. They have been the darlings of the liberal press for years, and are well-known for their antipathy toward Pope John's [sic] teachings on several issues including the ordination of women. Whenever a columnist or a TV anchor person wants to take a shot at the church, they drag out these two gentlemen as representatives of the church. It is the same as putting a fox in a hen house" (Bishop W. Thomas Larkin, "Ordination a Matter of Church Doctrine," *The Florida Catholic*, June 24, 1994, A8).

35. Sandra M. Schneiders, referring to *Gaudium et Spes, Ibid*, 37.

Chapter 2

1. Henry C. Lea has written the definitive history of clerical celibacy entitled *The History of Sacerdotal Celibacy in the Christian Church*. Although it was published in 1867 and reflects an anti-Catholic bias, it is one of the few full-length comprehensive historical surveys of the topic. For a more recent overview which is very comprehensive in itself, see Paul J. Beaudette, *Ritual Purity in Roman Catholic Priesthood: Using the Work of Mary Douglas to Understand Clerical Celibacy* (Berkeley, CA: Graduate Theological Union, 1994). Paul, a classmate of mine when I attended the GTU, sent me his dissertation as I wrote this chapter. I have rewritten various sections to include his very helpful insights and comments.

2. I outline the basic characteristics of patriarchal clericalism in my *The Dysfunctional Church: Addiction and Codependency in the Family of Catholicism* (Notre Dame, IN: Ave Maria Press, 1991), esp. 79-86.

3. Pope Paul VI, "On Priestly Celibacy," June 24, 1967, no. 1 (Washington, DC: United States Catholic Conference, 1967), 1.

4. Philip Sheldrake, "Celibacy and Clerical Culture," *The Way Supplement* 77 (1994), 32. Not long after this article was published, Sheldrake, *The Way's* general editor, took a leave of absence from the Jesuits and the priesthood to pursue marriage.

5. Beaudette, 141-142.

6. Peter Brown, "Late Antiquity," in P. Veyne (ed.), *From Rome to Byzantium* , vol. 1 of *A History of Private Life* (Harvard: Belknap, 1987), 263.

7. Canon 33, Council of Elvira, in Henricus Denzinger and Adolfus Schonmetzer, SJ., eds, *Enchiridion Symbolorum, Definitionum et Declarationum de Rebus Fidei et Morum*, 119 (Barcinone, Friburgi Gensgoviae, Romae: Herder, 1971), 51. The dating of Elvira recently has been debated. However a greater debate revolves around the text in question. Tradition had it that Canon 33 arose from the Council of Elvira. This is the position of Christian Cochini, S.J., *Apostolic Origins of Priestly Celibacy*, tr. Nelly Marans (San Francisco: Ignatius Press, 1990), 159. However others believe that it was inserted as a canon of the Elvira Council much later and actually arose in the late 4th century. See M. Meigne, "Concile ou Collection d'Elire?" in *Revue d'Histoire Ecclesiastique* 70 (1975), 361-87.

8. Samuel Laeuchli, *Power and Sexuality: The Emergence of Canon Law at the Synod of Elvira* (Philadelphia: Temple University Press, 1972), 88. See also Beaudette, 165ff.

9. This story is recounted by Mary Malone in her short study on the history of clerical celibacy in the Latin Church. See "The Unfinished Agenda of the Church: A Critical Look at the History of Celibacy," *The Way Supplement* 77 (1993), 71.

10. Crosby, 69-74. See also Charles A. Frazee, "The Origins of Clerical Celibacy in the Western Church," *Church History* 41 (1972), 156.

11. Pope Siricius, *Ad Himerium*, 185, in Denzinger-Schonmetzer, 74.

12. Cochini, 5.

13. Donald L. Gelpi, S.J., "Theological Reflections on the Priestly Character of Our Jesuit Vocation," *Studies in the Spirituality of the Jesuits*, 19/3 (1987), 57-59.

14. Noted in Edward Schillebeeckx, *Celibacy*, tr. C.A.L. Jarrott (New York: Sheed and Ward, 1968), 43.

15. Peter Brown, *Body and Society: Men, Women, and Sexual Renunciation in Early Christianity* (New York: Columbia, University Press, 1988), 142-144.

16. Beaudette, 190.

17. Peter Damian, *De Celbatu Sacerdotum*, PL 145.410ff, in Anne Llewellyn Barstow, "Married Priests and the Reforming Papacy: The Eleventh Century Debates," *Texts and Studies in Religion*, 12 (New York: Edwin Mellen, 1982), 61.

18. Ulric, quoted in Barstow, 119.

19. James A. Brundage, *Law, Sex, and Christian Society in Medieval Europe* (Chicago: University of Chicago Press, 1987), 215.

20. Barstow, 71.

21. Crosby, 71-76.

22. Thomas F. O'Meara, *Theology of Ministry* (New York/Ramsey: Paulist Press,

1983), 106.

23. Beaudette, 214.

24. Barstow, 98.

25. Bernard J. Cooke, *Ministry to Word and Sacraments: History and Theology* (Philadelphia: Fortress Press, 1976), 559. See also Beaudette, 264ff.

26. H. Daniel-Rops, *The Protestant Reformation*, trans. Audrey Butler (London: J. M. Dent & Son and New York: E. P. Dutton, 1961), 268.

27. Canons 9 and 10, Council of Trent, in *The Church Teaches: Documents of the Church in English Translation* (St. Louis/London: B. Herder, 1964), 338.

28. Canon 132 in John A. Abbo and Jerome J. Hannan, *The Sacred Canons: A Concise Presentation of the Current Disciplinary Norms of the Church* (St. Louis/London: B. Herder, 1952), 186.

29. J. D. Crichton, "Church and Ministry from the Council of Trent to the First Vatican Council," in Nicholas Lash and Joseph Rhymer, eds., *The Christian Priesthood* (Denville, NJ: Dimension Books, 1970), 124. Again, I am indebted to Paul Beaudette for directing me to this source.

30. Crichton, 124-125.

31. Beaudette, 316.

32. "Decree on the Training of Priests (Optatan Totius)," October 28, 1965, no. 10, in Austin Flannery, O.P, gen. ed., *Vatican Council II: The Conciliar and Post Conciliar Documents* (Collegeville, MN: The Liturgical Press, 1981), 715.

33. Pope Paul VI, "The Value of the Free and Sovereign Choice of Celibacy," *L'Osservatore Romano*, February 13, 1975, 2.

34. Heinz-J. Vogels, *Celibacy—Gift or Law? A Critical Investigation* (Kansas City, MO: Sheed & Ward, 1993), 63ff.

35. *Ibid.*, 19.

36. Malone, 66.

37. "Priestly Life and Ministry," no. 16 in Walter M. Abbott, S.J., gen. ed., *The Documents of Vatican II* (New York: Herder and Herder/Association Press, 1966), 565, 566.

38. F. Wulf, 217, in Vogels, *Ibid.* Wulf was a German commentator on #16 of the Second Vatican Council's document on priests, *Presbyterium Ordints*.

39. Vogels, *Ibid.* 62.

40. Canon 277, in James A. Coriden, Thomas J. Green, and Donald E. Heintschel, eds., *The Code of Canon Law: A Text and Commentary* (New York/Mahwah: Paulist Press, 1985), 209.

41. Gordon Thomas, *Desire and Denial: Celibacy and the Church* (Boston/Toronto: Little, Brown and Company, 1986), 5.

42. Sheldrake, 35.

43. Dean R. Hoge, *The Future of Catholic Leadership: Response to the Priest Shortage* (Kansas City: Sheed and Ward, 1987), 144-145.

44. Karl Rahner, "The Celibacy of the Secular Priest Today," *The Furrow* 19 (1988), 64.

Chapter 3

1. That this passage extends beyond the Jewish leaders of Jesus' time or even Matthew's time is clear from David Garland, who wrote in his classic study on Matthew 23 that it is "not just a denunciation of Jewish leaders or Judaism: it is a warning to the entire Christian community. It is a *didache*, a polemic against the abuse of authority" See David E. Garland, *The Intention of Matthew* 23 (Leiden: E. J. Brill, 1979), 62. See also my *The Dysfunctional Church: Addiction and Codependency in the Family of Catholicism* (Notre Dame, IN: Ave Maria Press, 1991), 119-146.

2. I have been asked by some why I am limiting my remarks about celibacy to religious, priests, and homosexual people and do not include single people in the church. The simple reason is that I have not had much experience with this group and, therefore, while I may have theoretical notions to share, I am void of concrete exemplifications. My approach to writing comes from a praxis that integrates experience and theory; this, unfortunately, has not been available for me as regards single people in the church. However, I believe the notions herein are apropos for single people and widow(er)s as well as those who make a more formal commitment to be celibate.

3. John Jay Hughes, "Married Priests: Solution or Sellout?," *Worship* 43 (1969), 145.

4. Eighth General Synod of Bishops, Working Document, *The Consecrated Life and Its Role in the Church and In the World* (Vatican City: Typis Vaticanis, 1994), no. 6, 9.

5. *Ibid.*, no. 5, 8.

6. *Ibid.*, no. 8, 11.

7. Edward Schillebeeckx, *Celibacy*, tr. C. A. L. Jarrott (New York: Sheed and Ward, 1968), 89.

8. Thus the 1994 "Called Anew by the Spirit: A Contemporary Reflection on Apostolic Religious Life" from the Archdiocese of Milwaukee which resulted from six months of "conversations" involving religious, former religious, and non-religious concluded: "If we look to younger religious, we get some insight into the future of religious life from the vantage point of 1994. What do candidates to religious life seek? Their most common answers include: authentic spirituality; mutual support in community and ministry; continuing service to the poor, oppressed, and exploited; and unity in the midst of diversity." Celibacy is not mentioned once. (Milwaukee: Archdiocese of Milwaukee, 1994), 17.

9. Sandra M. Schneiders, "Celibacy as Charism," *The Way Supplement* 77 (1994), 16.

10. Lucien Roy, "Shifting Paradigm: Lay Leadership in the Year 2000," *Listening* (1993), 7.

11. Stephen J. Rossetti, "Statistical Reflections on Priestly Celibacy," *America*, June 18, 1994, 22. I find it interesting that 42.8% of the priests surveyed supported mandatory celibacy. What this means in light of my thesis would be intriguing to investigate. Unfortunately the study did not delve into the rationale for the response by the priests.

12. For this and other data see Richard A. Schoenherr and Lawrence A. Young, *Full Pews and Empty Altars: Demographics of the Priest Shortage in United States Catholic Dioceses* (Madison, WI: University of Wisconsin Press, 1993). This study was originally sponsored by the United States Catholic Conference, the arm of the U.S. Bishops, and endowed by a grant from the Lilly Foundation. However, as its findings were gradually released through private interim reports to the U.S. Bishops, several became irate over the gloomy projections and reportedly sought to terminate the project. As the data became clearer about the severe crisis, the

USCC ceased its sponsorship. For its rationale as to why it would do so, its Director of Research explained that the data was already publicly known and the study had taken too long.

13. Pope John Paul II, General Audience, July 17, 1993, *L'Osservatore Romano* weekly edition, 21 July, 1993, 11.

14. Pope John Paul II, "Letter to the Nuns at Auschwitz," April 9, 1993, in *Origins* 22 (1993), 795.

15. Crosby, 49-52. See also my paper on the subject given at the Catholic Theological Society of America in 1993. For a report on my paper see Eileen P. Flynn, "Doing Moral Theology in Light of an Ecclesiology Reflective of Matthew 18 and Matthew 16," Seminar on Moral Theology, in *Proceedings of the Forty-Eighth Annual Convention*, The Catholic Theological Society of America (Santa Clara, CA: Santa Clara University Press, 1993), 156-157.

16. Rev. Robert J. Loftus, B.A., M.A., *The Differences between Priests Legally and Personally Committed to Celibacy* (Notre Dame, IN: Department of Graduate Studies in Education, 1992), 62.

17. *Ibid.*

18. *Ibid.,* ii-iii.

19. *Ibid.,* iii.

20. Richard Sipe, *A Secret World: Sexuality and the Search for Celibacy* (New York: Brunner/Mazel, 1990). See also, Richard Sipe, *Sex, Priests, and Power: Anatomy of a Crisis* (New York: Brunner/Mazel, 1990).

21. Christian Cochini, *The Apostolic Origins of Priestly Celibacy* (San Francisco: Ignatius Press, 1990).

22. Patrick Viscuso, Review of *The Apostolic Origins of Priestly Celibacy*, in *Religious Studies Review* 19 (1993), 77.

23. I, Morsdorff, in Heinz-J. Vogels *Celibacy—Gift or Law? A Critical Investigation* (Kansas City, MO: Sheed & Ward, 1993), 84.

24. Vogels, 66.

25. Paul E. Dinter, "Celibacy and Its Discontents," Op-Ed piece, *The New York Times*, May 6, 1993.

26. "Desire to Marry Seen as Key Factor in Priest Shortage, Survey Reveals," CNS item in *[Milwaukee] Catholic Herald*, April 4, 1990.

27. Most Reverend Rembert G. Weakland, O.S.B., "Facing the Future with Hope," First Draft, nos. 39 and 50, *[Milwaukee] Catholic Herald*, around January 7, 1991.

28. Archbishop Rembert G. Weakland, O.S.B., "Facing the Future with Hope: A Pastoral Letter on Parishes for the People of the Archdiocese of Milwaukee, 10, November 1, 1991 (Milwaukee: Archdiocese of Milwaukee, 1991), 4.

29. Bishop Denis Croteau, quoted in "Canadian Bishops Want Married Native Priests," *The Toronto Catholic Register*, October 2, 1993.

30. *Ibid.*

31. See John Gallagher, ed., *Homosexuality and the Magisterium: Documents from the Vatican and the U.S. Bishops 1975-1985* (Mt. Rainier, MD: New Ways Ministry, 1986).

32. Congregation for the Doctrine of the Faith, Letter to the Bishops of the Catholic Church, "The Pastoral Care of Homosexual Persons," *Origins* 16 (1986), 377, 379-382.

33. The Sacred Congregation for the Doctrine of the Faith, "The Vatican Declaration on Sexual Ethics," 8, *Origins* 5 (1976), 489.

34. National Conference of Catholic Bishops, "Pastoral Letter on Moral Values," *Origins* 6 (1976), 363.

35. Congregation for the Doctrine of Faith, "The Pastoral Care," *Ibid.*, no. 3, repeated in the July 23, 1992 Statement from the Congregation for the Doctrine of the Faith, "Observations on Legislative Proposals Concerning Discrimination against Homosexual Persons," in *Origins* 22 (1992), 175.

36. William H. Shannon, "A Response to Archbishop Quinn," in Jeannine Gramick and Pat Furey, *The Vatican and Homosexuality: Reactions to the 'Letter to the Bishops of the Catholic Church on the Pastoral Care of Homosexual Persons,'"* (New York: Crossroad, 1988), 26.

37. Congregation for the Doctrine of the Faith July 23, 1992 Statement, *Ibid.*, 7, 176. This is a reiteration of the 1986 Letter, *Ibid.* 10, 381.

38. Statement of the National Board of the Conference of Major Superiors of Men, August 29, 1992 (Silver Spring, MD: Conference of Major Superiors of Men).

39. Congregation for the Doctrine of the Faith, July 23, 1992 Statement, 2 *Ibid.*,175.

40. *Catechism of the Catholic Church*, 1832 (New York: Catholic Book Publishing Company, 1994), 451.

41. *Ibid.*, 915, 241.

42. *Ibid.*, 1579, 395.

43. *Ibid.*, 2359, 566.

44. Crosby, *Dysfunctional Church, Ibid.*

45. Kenneth R. Mitchell, "Priestly Celibacy from a Psychological Perspective," *The Journal of Pastoral Care* 24, 1970, 222.

46. *Ibid.*, 223.

47. *Ibid.*, 225.

Chapter 4

1. For more on the dynamics that reverted the original version using inclusive language, see Peter Hebblethwaite, "How U.S. Bishops' Inclusive Policy Got Sabotaged," *National Catholic Reporter*, November 11, 1994.

2. Some may vigorously challenge my contention, especially when discussing Pope Pius XII and his efforts. I have shown elsewhere that the good manifested in the various efforts he made does not compare with the overall harm inflicted elsewhere. See my *The Dysfunctional Church: Addiction and Codependency in the Family of Catholicism* (Notre Dame, IN: Ave Maria Press, 1991).

3. I am not saying that, with optional celibacy, sexual problems such as pedophilia will disappear altogether. However, I think we need to realize that the historical situation that has resulted in the ongoing allegations of celibate pedophilia may result in very different statistics when people will freely embrace the celibate gift in the future. It is my thesis that this group will be very small. It will be nourished by a deeply contemplative life and compassion. Finally, it will be supported by others who embrace freely the same values. Given such motivation and supportive environment, I would expect that the numbers of sexual abusers in this latter group will be smaller.

4. For a balanced discussion of the high incidence (psychologically speaking) of

ephebophilia versus pedophilia in the priesthood, see the responses to questions asked of Archbishop Rembert Weakland, O.S.B., of Milwaukee in Marie Rohde, "Damage to Church Is Far-Reaching: Archdiocese Tries to Help Victims, Priests," *The Milwaukee Journal*, November 13, 1994, A15. In the interview Archbishop Weakland noted that, in every case in the Archdiocese he knew about, all dealt with ephebophilia. "In fact," he stated, "I have never dealt with a pedophile." Legally, all acts of sexual abuse by an adult with a minor are called pedophilia. The archbishop was not discussing the legal dimensions, but the pastoral issue of how to minister to priests who may be legally pedophiles, but actually are psychologically ephebophiles, those attracted to post-pubescent minors.

5. Pope John Paul II, reported in Alan Cowell, "Pope Rules Out Debate on Women as Priests," *The New York Times*, May 31, 1994. For text see Apostolic Letter "Ordinatio Sacerdotalis," no. 4, May 30, 1994, in *Origins* 24 (1994), 51.

6. For more on the nature of the binding-degree of the statement, see Francis Sullivan, "New Claims for the Pope," *The Tablet* 248 (1994), 767-769.

7. "Pope John Paul's Pre-Emptive Strike," *The Tablet* 248, (1994), 691.

8. Pope John Paul II, quoting Pope Paul VI, Apostolic Letter, *Ibid.*,1, 49.

9. *Ibid.*, 2, 51.

10. Vatican statement, quoted in Cowell. The full statement can be found in "An Overview of the Apostolic Letter," *Origins* 24 (1994), 52.

11. Michael Crosby, "Power in the Church: Moving from Abuse to Mutuality," Call to Action National Conference (Elkridge, MD: Chesapeake Audio/Video Communications, 1993).

12. For a further discussion on the male and female approaches to "truth," see Lisa Sowle Cahill, "Accent on the Masculine," *The Tablet* 247, 11 December, 1993, 1618.

13. For more on this see my *The Dysfunctional Church*, 49-52. See also Eileen P. Flynn's report on my paper "Doing Moral Theology in Light of an Ecclesiology Reflective of Matthew 18 and Matthew 16," Seminar on Moral Theology, in *Proceedings of the Forty-Eighth Annual Convention*, The Catholic Theological Society of America (Santa Clara, CA: Santa Clara University Press, 1993), 156-157.

14. I found it interesting that the first part of this passage was highlighted, in its Matthean form (22:30) as a foundation for celibacy in the "Working Document" from the Vatican in preparation for the 1994 Synod on *The Consecrated Life and Its Role in the Church and in the World*. In this same vein, the document asked: "How can we teach today a commitment as demanding as that of celibacy?"

15. Crosby, *The Dysfunctional Church*, Ibid.

16. Jeff Hearn, *Men in the Public Eye: The Construction and Deconstruction of Public Men and Public Patriarchies* (London and New York: Routledge, 1992), 2.

17. Sebastian Moore, O.S.B., *The Inner Loneliness* (New York: Crossroad, 1982), 74-75.

18. *Ibid.*, 75.

19. National Conference of Catholic Bishops, "When I Call for Help: Domestic Violence against Women," in *Origins* 22 (1992), 355.

Chapter 5

1. Philip Sheldrake, "Celibacy and Clerical Culture," *The Way Supplement* (1994), 26. Sheldrake's conclusions seem reinforced in a 1993-1994 study of diocesan seminarians by the Dominican Joseph John Guido. He wrote: "In the first major study of seminarians after the close of the Council, the decision to withdraw from the seminary was most frequently associated with doubts about celibacy. While in more recent studies doubts about celibacy continue to be associated with a decision to withdraw from the seminary, the fact that such doubts are no longer of greatest importance and that doubts about a sense of call and felt religious experience suggests that more than demographics have changed since the close of the Council" See *Schooling the Soul: The Psychological Nature and Function of God Images among Roman Catholic Seminarians.* Thesis (Cambridge, MA: Harvard University School of Education, 1994), 14.

2. "New Study Puts Sunday Mass Attendance in U.S. at Twenty-Six Percent," *[Milwaukee] Catholic Herald,* January 5, 1995.

3. Recent studies of priests and religious which have discussed their level of satisfaction indicate a high degree of personal satisfaction with what they are doing and even indicate many would choose this way of life again. See Greeley and the *Los Angeles Times* studies. As indicated earlier, I am not going to discuss any studies in a way that would create a thesis, for I have discovered all can be interpreted in ways that really do not offer constructive directions to the crisis that is facing the *structure* and *environment* of celibacy in the Western Roman Church today.

4. Sharon Parks, *The Critical Years: The Young Adult Search for a Faith to Live By* (San Francisco: Harper & Row, 1986), 12, 13-14.

5. *Ibid.,* 14.

6. *Ibid.,* 177.

7. Donna Markham, O.P., Ph.D., "Data Prepared for the Quinn Commission on Attitudes Toward Religious Life," April, 1987, (Silver Spring, MD: Leadership Conference of Women Religious, 1987), 16.

8. Donna Markham, O.P., Ph.D., "Religious Life and the Decline of Vocations in the USA: Reflections from a Psychological Perspective," April, 1987 (Silver Spring, MD: Leadership Conference of Women Religious, 1987), 16.

9. Victor Frankl, *The Unheard Cry for Meaning* (New York: Simon and Schuster Touchstone Books, 1978), 20. Frankl's words rang true to my experience as I wrote the above quote for this book in its first draft. A lay brother in a religious order who attended a workshop I recently gave at a renewal program finished the program with a thirty-day retreat. The evening the retreat ended he took his life. He had just been accused of abusing a thirteen-year-old boy he picked up at a shopping mall near the retreat house.

10. Andrew Oldenquist, *The Non-Suicidal Society* (Bloomington, IN: Indiana University Press, 1986), 5.

11. Frankl, 26.

12. See the conclusions from two studies of priests in Andrew M. Greeley, "A Sea of Paradoxes: Two Surveys of Priests," *America,* July 16, 1994, 6-10.

13. Markham, "Religious Life and the Decline of Vocations . . .," *Ibid.,* 5.

14. For more on this theory see Carol Tavris, *Anger: The Misunderstood Emotion* (New York: Simon & Schuster Touchstone Books, 1989), 164.

15. Guido, 169-180.

16. Martin Pable, O.F.M. Cap., "Psychology and Asceticism of Celibacy," *Review for Religious*, 34 (1975).

17. Brenda Hermann, M.S.B.T., A.C.S.W., "Anger Revisited," *Human Development* 11 (1990), 15-16.

18. Janet Malone, "Exploring Human Anger," *Human Development* 15 (1994), 34.

19. Tavris, 14.

20. Malone, 34.

21. Carol Gilligan, *Joining the Resistance: Psychology, Politics, Girls and Women* (Harvard University: Unpublished Manuscript, 1990), 17.

22. Guido, 158.

23. Crosby, *The Dysfunctional Church*, 29.

24. Joseph H. Fichter, Ph.D., *The Rehabilitation of Clergy Alcoholics: Ardent Spirits Subdued* (New York/London: Human Sciences Press, 1982), 23.

25. Patrick Carnes, Ph.D., *Out of the Shadows: Understanding Sexual Addiction* (Minneapolis: CompCare, 1983), 10.

26. What Carnes calls "level one," I call "genital addictions."

27. Crosby, *The Dysfunctional Church*, 29.

28. Anne Wilson Schaef, *Escape from Intimacy: Untangling the 'Love' Addictions: Sex, Romance, Relationship* (San Francisco: Harper & Row, 1989), 39.

Chapter 6

1. In 1983 I wrote an article that included reasons why I thought I was "still celibate." Not having had the experience of being that close to a woman kept me from experiences that would have colored the way I wrote that article then. See Michael H. Crosby, "Celibacy as Fasting," *Spirituality Today* 35 (1983), esp. 236-237.

2. Michael H. Crosby, *The Dysfunctional Church: Addiction and Codependency in the Family of Catholicism* (Notre Dame, IN: Ave Maria Press, 1991), see especially 17-24 and 147-173.

3. Michael J. Doyle, *The Relationship of Cultural and Family Background to Dependency — Conflict and Need for Power Among Alcoholic Roman Catholic Priests.* (Berkeley, CA: California School of Professional Psychology, 1991).

4. Victor J. Seidler, *Rediscovering Masculinity: Reason, Language and Sexuality* (London: Routledge, 1989), 107-108.

5. Joseph John Guido followed the taxonomy of Kegan, Broderick, Guido, Popp and Portnow which studied people in their thirties. They discovered five orders of consciousness ("epistemologies") which characterized people at various stages of development in this age group. *Schooling the Soul: The Psychological Nature and Function of God Images Among Roman Catholic Seminarians.* Thesis (Cambridge, MA: Harvard University School of Education, 1994), 42-43, 80-81.

6. *Ibid.*, 78.

7. *Ibid.*, 79.

8. *Ibid.*, 44.

9. Private conversations between the author and Guido.

10. Jeff Hearn, *Men in the Public Eye: The Construction and Deconstruction of Public*

Men and Public Patriarchies (London and New York: Routledge, 1992), 59.

11. Carroll Juliano, S.H.C.J. and Loughlan Sofield, S.T., call such behavior "pseudoprofessionalism." See their "Ministry Demands Intimacy," *Human Development* 9 (1988), 33.

12. "Called Anew by the Spirit: A Contemporary Reflection on Apostolic Religious Life" (Milwaukee: Archdiocese of Milwaukee, 1994), 13.

13. Terry A. Kupers, *Revisioning Men's Lives: Gender, Intimacy, and Power* (New York/London: The Guilford Press, 1993), 30-31.

14. Benjamin K. Hunnicutt, *Work without End* (Philadelphia: Temple University Press, 1988).

15. Benjamin K. Hunnicutt, "No Time for God or Family," *The Wall Street Journal,* January 4, 1990.

16. Leonard Greenhalgh, quoted in Walter Kiechel III, "Workaholics Anonymous," *Fortune* (August 14, 1989), 117.

17. Wilkie Au, S.J., Ph.D., and Noreen Cannon, C.S.J., Ph.D., "The Plague of Perfectionism," *Human Development* 13 (Fall, 1992), 6.

18. William F. Kraft, "Celibate Genitality," *Review for Religious* 36 (1977), 604-605.

19. For corroboration, see the Introduction, note 12.

20. Kraft, *Ibid.,* 608.

21. Harry Stack Sullivan, "Conceptions of Modern Psychiatry," in *Collected Works I* (New York: W. W. Norton, 1955), 22-23.

22. Crosby, *The Dysfunctional Church,* 107-108. The percentage figure came from *The Report of the Commission of Enquiry into the Sexual Abuse of Children by Members of the Clergy* (Winter Commission Report, St. John's, Newfoundland: Archdiocese of St. John's, 1990), 35-36. See also James G. Wolf, *Gay Priests* (San Francisco: Harper & Row, 1989).

Chapter 7

1. Erik H. Erikson, *Childhood and Society* , 35th Anniversary Ed. (New York: W. W. Norton, 1985), 264.

2. As I wrote the first draft of this chapter, I read about Linda Wachner, CEO of Warnaco, the nation's third largest manufacturer of "intimate apparel." According to an article in *USAToday,* "She landed on a 1993 list of the Seven Toughest Bosses in America for calling her salesmen eunuchs. She made her mark on the lingerie business by suggesting that retailers display intimate apparel on hangers instead of stashing it discreetly in department store drawers. Before her innovation, almost all but the undies on the mannequins were out of sight". Ellen Neuborne, "Lingerie Firm's CEO Steers a Turnaround," *USAToday,* August 4, 1994, C2.

3. The "True Love Waits" campaign wherein teens take vows of chastity until they "enter a covenant marriage relationship" began in Nashville, Tennessee in a Southern Baptist Church. Within a year more than 100,000 had made the pledge.

4. Kenneth R. Mitchell, "Priestly Celibacy from a Psychological Perspective," *The Journal of Pastoral Care* 24 (1970), 220.

5. Victor J. Seidler, *Rediscovering Masculinity: Reason, Language and Sexuality* (London: Routledge, 1989), 162.

6. Mary Elizabeth Kenel, Ph.D., "A Celibate's Sexuality and Intimacy: Exploring a

Major Problem of Personality Integration for Religious and Priests," *Human Development* 7 (Spring, 1986), 14.

7. *Ibid.*, 15.

8. Sheila Murphy, *A Delicate Dance: Sexuality, Celibacy, and Relationships among Catholic Clergy and Religious* (New York: Crossroad, 1992), 43-44.

9. Seidler, 174.

10. Christopher Kiesling, O.P., *Celibacy, Prayer and Friendship: A Making-Sense-Out-of-Life Approach* (New York: Alba House, 1978), 205.

11. While at Berkeley, I found much help in understanding a feminine notion of friendship in Lillian Rubin's *Just Friends* (New York: Harper & Row, 1985). These characteristics can be found on page 18.

12. Kenel, *Ibid.*, 16.

13. Donald J. Goergen, O.P., "Introduction," in Sheila Murphy, *A Delicate Dance: Sexuality, Celibacy, and Relationships among Catholic Clergy and Religious* (New York: Crossroad, 1992), 9.

14. Kiesling, O.P., *Ibid.*, 47.

15. Goergen, *Ibid.*, 8.

Chapter 8

1. I originally developed the core reflections in this chapter in "Celibacy as Fasting," *Spirituality Today* 35 (1983), 230-240.

2. William F. Kraft, "Celibate Genitality," *Review for Religious* 36 (1977), 609-610.

3. Christopher Kiesling, O.P., *Celibacy, Prayer and Friendship* (Staten Island: Alba House, 1978), xvii.

4. George A. Aschenbrenner, S.J., "A Celibate's Relationship with God," *Human Development* 5 (1984), 42. While my understanding of loneliness agrees with Aschenbrenner's, I believe my notion of aloneness is not as relational as is his.

5. Kiesling, O.P., *Ibid.*, 199.

6. James O'Keefe, "Living with Compulsory Celibacy," *The Way Supplement* 77 (1993), 41.

7. Sandra M. Schneiders, "Celibacy as Charism," *The Way Supplement*, 16.

8. Sheila Murphy, *A Delicate Dance: Sexuality, Celibacy, and Relationships among Catholic Clergy and Religious* (New York: Crossroad, 1992), 51, 119f.

9. *Ibid.*, 51.

10. David M. Knight, "Will the New Church Need Celibates?," *New Catholic World,* 216 (193), 210-211.

11. Schneiders, 13.

12. Donald J. Goergen, O.P., "Introduction," Murphy, 12.

13. As noted earlier, even in such fine materials as the "Working Document" for the 1994 Synod of Bishops on The Consecrated Life and the "Contemporary Reflection on Apostolic Religious Life" from the Archdiocese of Milwaukee, I find images and concepts that still reflect a period that links celibacy almost exclusively with ministry and community. While these are manifest expressions, the core of celibacy represents something much deeper, as I have been trying to say throughout these last chapters.

Chapter 9

1. Sandra M. Schneiders, "Celibacy as Charism," *The Way Supplement* 77 (1933), 14.

2. In addition to what I have written in earlier chapters, I also have described some of the obstacles to "seeing God" specifically in two books: *Spirituality of the Beatitudes: Matthew's Challenge to First World Christians* (Maryknoll, NY: Orbis Books, 1981/1993), 161-166 and *The Dysfunctional Church: Addiction and Codependency in the Family of Catholicism* (Notre Dame, IN: Ave Maria Press, 1991), 200 - 207. I have discussed the obstacles to intimacy with self more in oral presentations than in anything written. See especially the set of my tapes from a day of reflection at the Call to Action National Conference, November 4, 1994: *Where Are Our Hearts: Developing a Spirituality in Violent Times* (Elkridge, MD: Chesapeake Audio/Video Communications, 1994).

3. Louis Dupre, *The Deeper Life: An Introduction to Christian Mysticism* (New York: Crossroad, 1981), 20.

4. David J. Hassel, S.J., *Dark Intimacy: Hope for Those in Difficult Prayer-Experiences* (New York/Mahwah: Paulist Press, 1986), 13.

5. A good source in this direction is Michael Fishbane, *The Kiss of God: Spiritual and Mystical Death in Judaism* (Seattle: University of Washington Press, 1994).

6. Schneiders, 24, quoting the last line of Dante's *Paradiso* (Canto XXXIII, 145).

7. Joseph John Guido, *Schooling the Soul: The Psychological Nature and Function of God Images among Roman Catholic Seminarians*. Thesis (Cambridge, MA: Harvard University School of Education, 1994), 148.

8. *Ibid.*, 152.

9. *Ibid.*, 134.

10. Kenny Loggins, quoted in Leslie Miller, "Seeing God through Spiritual Experts' Eyes," *USAToday*, January 10, 1995, 4D.

11. "Called Anew by the Spirit: A Contemporary Reflection on Apostolic Religious Life" (Milwaukee: Archdiocese of Milwaukee, 1994), 15.

12. M. Basil Pennington, O.C.S.O., *Centering Prayer: Renewing an Ancient Christian Prayer Form* (New York: Doubleday Image Books, 1982), 130.

13. Mother Teresa, quoted in Leslie Miller, *op.cit.*

14. I have gained much from this insight, originally presented by the late Richard Byrnne of Duquesne University. See my *Spirituality of the Beatitudes*, 20-21.

15. Pope Paul VI, "The Evangelical Witness of the Religious Life," 17, *The Pope Speaks* 16 (1971), 115.

16. Patrick J. Connolly, "A Priest's Thoughts on His Own Celibacy," in Mary Anne Huddleston, I.H.M., ed., *Celibate Loving: Encounter in Three Dimensions* (New York/Ramsey: Paulist Press, 1984), 138. The chapters in Huddleston's book proved to be very helpful to me in writing this book.

17. Abraham Heschel, *The Prophets* (New York: Harper & Row, 1962), 11.

Chapter 10

1. James W. Fowler, "Faith and the Structuring of Meaning," in *Faith Development and Meaning*, ed. Craig Dykstra and Sharon Parks (Birmingham, AL: Religious Education Press, 1986), pp. 15-42.

2. Margaret A. Farley, *Personal Commitments* (San Francisco: Harper & Row, 1986), 8.

3. *Ibid.*, 34-35.

4. Lillian B. Rubin, *Just Friends* (San Francisco: Harper & Row, 1985), 84.

5. Sallie McFague, *Metaphorical Theology: Models of God in Religious Language* (Philadelphia: Fortress Press, 1985).

6. Mary Baird Carlsen, *Meaning-Making: Therapeutic Processes in Adult Development* (New York and London: W. W. Norton, 1988), 51.

7. Robert N. Bellah, Richard Madsen, William M. Sullivan, Ann Swidler, and Steven M. Tipton, *Habits of the Heart: Individualism and Commitment in American Life* (Berkeley, Los Angeles, London: University of California Press, 1985).

8. Robert Bellah, Richard Madsen, William M. Sullivan, Ann Swidler, and Stephen M. Tipton, *The Good Society* (New York: Knopf, 1991).

9. John Bradshaw, *Healing the Shame that Binds You* (Deerfield Beach, FL: Health Communications), 13.

10. This is my paraphrase of *The Rule* of 1223 according to St. Francis of Assisi, VI, 7-8.

Conclusion

1. Mary Anne Coate, "Who Chooses Celibacy—And Why?" *The Way Supplement* 77 (1993), 101.

2. *Ibid.*, 104-105.